WHY DO BAD THINGS HAPPEN GOD IS GOOD?

RON RHODES

HARVEST HOUSE PUBLISHERS

EUGENE, OREGON

Cover by Terry Dugan Design, Minneapolis, Minnesota

WHY DO BAD THINGS HAPPEN IF GOD IS GOOD?
Copyright © 2004 by Ron Rhodes
Published by Harvest House Publishers
Eugene, Oregon 97402

Rhodes, Ron.
  Why do bad things happen if God is good? / Ron Rhodes.
    p. cm.
  Includes bibliographical references.
  ISBN 0-7369-1296-7 (pbk.)
  1. Theodicy. 2. Good and evil—Religious aspects—Christianity. I. Title
  BT160.R47 2004
  231'.8—dc22   2004002098

Printed in the United States of America

  04 05 06 07 08 09 10 11 / BP-MS / 10 9 8 7 6 5 4 3 2

This book is dedicated to Tusabe, a young sister in Christ in the West Congo.

For a number of years, our family has donated monthly support to a missionary organization that feeds and educates children around the world. The young girl we have sponsored is named Tusabe.

Not long ago, we were informed by the missionary organization that intensified tribal wars in the area left many people dead, including whole families. Some people had to flee for their lives to other parts of the country. The missionaries had no choice but to withdraw from the area.

Today we do not know whether Tusabe is still on earth or is in heaven. We have kept her pictures and the letters she has written us, and we continue to pray for her. She is in God's hands.

We look forward to meeting her one day in the eternal city of heaven, where senseless killing and other forms of evil will be a thing of the distant past.

Acknowledgments

Kerri, David, and Kylie—

You are a treasure and a blessing to me. It is a joy to serve in the kingdom alongside each of you. Without your love and undying support, this book simply would not have been written. *Blessed be the Lord for His goodness in giving me this wonderful family!*

Contents

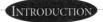

A HARD LOOK AT REALITY

Life can be cruel sometimes.

It was in early 1999 that tragedy struck our family. My younger brother Gary called to let me know that Greg, the oldest son of our older brother, Paul, was hit by a car and instantly killed. He had been trying to cross a highway and made it across one lane. After leaping over the median, he found himself face-to-face with a high-speed car that hit him head-on. He was thrown 100 feet and run over by two more cars. I cannot even begin to imagine what my brother Paul felt as he went to the morgue to identify his firstborn.

I called Paul immediately. How I wish I could have driven over to his house to be with him and his family—but I was in southern California, he in Corpus Christi, Texas. On the phone, he wept, but he managed to get out the words that all this had happened just a little while ago. Greg had been alive and well—conscious and enjoying life—just a short time earlier, but now he was gone forever from this earthly life. Paul was numb from the suddenness of it all.

I caught the next flight from California to Texas. When I arrived at Paul's house, we hugged for a long time. I remember wishing I had words to say that would make his pain go away, but of course, no such words exist. We just hugged, and for the moment, that said everything that needed to be said.

7

One of the hardest things I have ever done in my life was to speak at Greg's funeral. What could I possibly say to make all this any easier for anybody? My main message was that when we do not understand why certain things happen in life, we need to anchor ourselves on the things we do understand. And we *do* understand that God loves all of us, that God certainly loved Greg, that God would help us all through this horrible tragedy, and that all Christians will one day be reunited, never again to be separated. Death will one day be a thing of the past.

After the funeral service, the question that seemed to linger on the minds of those present was, Why did something like this have to happen? It is the same question people through the ages have asked whenever tragedy strikes. *Why do bad things happen to good people?* And what are we to think about God when such things occur?

The Big Question

Pollster George Barna was commissioned not long ago to inquire of people what one question they would ask of God if they had the opportunity. By an overwhelming margin, the most urgent question was this: Why is there so much suffering in the world?[1] I am quite sure that most readers of this book have asked this question at one time or another.

Most people tend to grapple with this issue in terms of their own individual sufferings. I know this has been true of me at times. It's not that we're necessarily blind to the sufferings of others, but because we are so acutely aware of *our own* pain and suffering, our worlds tend to have a very narrow focus.

When I began research for this book, however, my perspective broadened considerably. In my day-to-day reading, I came across one example after another of how horribly many human beings have suffered—Christians included. I came to see that as bad as the situation had been for my family, others had suffered even worse catastrophes.

Do you remember what you were doing on 9–11? I suspect you do. I was in my bedroom in southern California with my wife, not long after 7 A.M., when our phone rang. That's never a good sign because people rarely call us that early. I picked up the phone, and a friend asked, "Have you turned on your television this morning?" I said, "No—what's going on?" She told me what happened, and I immediately turned on the television, only to watch in horror an event that ended up taking 2749 lives. I would later ponder to myself the terrible grief that must be felt by the spouses, children, relatives, and friends of loved ones crushed as the Twin Towers collapsed. I've *been* in those buildings. What an unimaginable horror it must have been. Many have since wondered where God was on 9–11.

I think back to the 14 teenagers (most of them Christians) and one teacher who were heartlessly killed at Columbine High School in April, 1999, in Littleton, Colorado. Our finite thinking cannot grasp how a loving and caring God could allow such a thing to happen. But such things *do* happen—and good people are not exempt from tragedies.

This week I watched Barbara Walters interview Christopher Reeve on the news program *20/20*. He talked about how being paralyzed has affected virtually everything in his body—even simple matters we take for granted like going to the bathroom. Ms. Walters noted how Reeve's entire life was changed in an instant. At one moment, he was perfectly healthy, riding his horse as he had done a hundred times before. The instant after his horse suddenly stopped and threw Reeve off, he was paralyzed, never again to be the same. As far as I know, Reeve is a good man, yet he has suffered immensely.

During the writing of this book, I came across an Associated Press report about a group of high school cross-country runners—wholesome kids—who had gathered by the side of a highway to pray. A car struck the group, killing one and injuring a number of others.[2] I grieve when I think about the parents whose son was run down and killed while praying to the living God. *Why did God let it happen?*

Of course, this was an accident. But history has plenty of examples of *purposeful* human evil. John Wenham, in his book *The Enigma of Evil,* laments that every age contains examples of man's inhumanity to man: "Spain had its Inquisition, Britain its Atlantic slave trade, Germany its gas chambers, Russia its Siberian labor camps."[3] William Lane Craig suggests that a forceful way of proving man's inhumanity to man is to read a book like Robert P. Mannix's *History of Torture* or to pay a visit to a medieval castle and inspect some of the dreadful devices used to mete out pain on prisoners.[4]

One of the most disturbing books I have read relating to human suffering is *This Way for the Gas, Ladies and Gentlemen,* by Tadeusz Borowski. This book details some of the horrific events associated with the Holocaust. We read that Nazi leaders tore families apart, remained indifferent to massive disease, and even injected people with typhoid and malaria germs. They forced women into immoral sex and denied privacy at the latrine. They gassed millions of Jews to death and packed their bodies in trains that stunk of sweat and excrement. Guards murdered people by breaking their necks, shooting little girls, and assigning prisoners a double role—executioner and victim. The Nazis extracted gold teeth from the dead and made lampshades of human skin, jewelry of bones, and soap out of other remains.[5] Such acts clearly reveal the utter and pervasive depravity of the human heart.

In our day the hydrogen bomb casts a long shadow over the people of this tiny planet. And people today are increasingly thinking about the unthinkable—terrorists getting their hands on such superbombs. *Is God watching over us, controlling and guiding human history?*

In addition to all the suffering generated by man's inhumanity against man is the massive amount of natural evil that occurs in our world. Natural disasters such as earthquakes, typhoons, tornadoes, and floods kill innumerable people and wreck whole communities. Horrible diseases such as cancer, leukemia, polio, and smallpox claim millions of lives each year—not to mention the AIDS epidemic presently ravaging Africa. Congenital defects such as muscular dystrophy and cerebral palsy cripple untold numbers of people. Little children drown. People perish in forest fires. Disasters strike without warning. Inconsolable grief may descend on us in an instant.[6] No wonder H.G. Wells once commented that God seems to be "an ever-absent help in time of trouble."[7]

Man Is Born to Trouble

Human suffering is nothing new. It is a seemingly ever-present reality for the human race. Job 5:7 tells us, "Man is born to trouble as surely as sparks fly upward." Job 14:1 asserts, "Man born of woman is of few days and full of trouble."

Bad things have been happening to good people for a long time—even among God's people in biblical days. Who can forget the horrible suffering of Job (he lost his family *and* his belongings)? David, who was to become king of Israel, was chased and persecuted by the jealous and wrathful Saul for years (1 Samuel 20:33; 21:10; 23:8). Hosea's wife was unfaithful (Hosea 1:2; 2:2,4). Joseph was cruelly mistreated by his brothers and sold into slavery (Genesis 37:27-28). John the Baptist was beheaded at the request of Herod's stepdaughter (Matthew 14:6-10). Paul was tossed into jail a number of times, suffered shipwreck, was beaten and left for dead, and much more (2 Corinthians 11:25).

Sometimes Christians think that whoever obeys God and seeks to be a good Christian will not experience horrible suffering. But if bad things can happen to such people as Job, John the Baptist, and the apostle Paul, they can certainly happen to good Christians today. I read of a Christian leader who was sledding and ran into a barbed wire fence he hadn't seen. He was instantly beheaded. I read of a pastor who got into his car and backed out of the driveway—right over his infant son, killing him on the spot. I read of a Christian woman who witnessed her husband and child get hit by a car and killed. *Christians are not exempt from horrible tragedies.* [8]

Nor are children exempt from suffering. Peter Kreeft tells the touching story of a little boy who had a rare disease and had to live his entire life inside a sterile plastic bubble:

> Any touch, a single germ, could kill him. All communication, recreation, education, everything was through the bubble. Finally, he was dying. Since he was doomed anyway, he asked to touch his father's hand—his father, who had loved him and stayed with him all his life. What unspeakable love and pain was in that one touch! [9]

And what about all the innocent victims of various crimes in our country? The FBI museum in Washington D.C. features "The Crime Clock," which displays frequency statistics on various crimes. According to this clock:

> In the United States, someone is murdered every 33.9 minutes; forcibly raped every 5.8 minutes; the victim of aggravated assault every 34.6 seconds; the victim of a violent crime every 22.1 seconds; the victim of a robbery every 1.3 minutes; the victim of a burglary every 15.4 seconds; a larceny every 4.5 seconds, and a property crime every 3.1 seconds. [10]

Still further, innumerable good people in our world are experiencing what we might call existential pain in their hearts. Christian philosopher Cornelius Plantinga, Jr. explains:

> Thoughtful human beings suffer pangs from aging. They gain an acute sense of the one-way flow of time that carries with it treasures and opportunities and youthful agilities that seemingly will not come again....Though we walk through the valley of death just once, we spend our whole lives in the valley of the shadow of death. [11]

Physical pain, emotional pain, existential pain—all of these are ever-present thorns in our lives. Just wait long enough, and everyone gets pricked in one way or another.

Understanding the Problem

Christian thinker Paul W. Powell once said that "trouble is not a gatecrasher in the arena of our lives; it has a reserved seat there." [12] Based on many years of personal experience, I think Powell is right!

I have purposefully started this book out with a hard look at reality. I know it's been a little hard to swallow. But we need to realistically understand why so many people believe the problem of evil poses a serious challenge to the Christian faith. Christian theologian Ronald Nash is quite candid in affirming that

> every philosopher I know believes that the most serious challenge to theism [belief in a personal God] was, is, and will continue to be the problem of evil. I share the view that the most serious intellectual obstacle that stands between many people and faith is uncertainty about the existence of evil.[13]

The problem of evil, simply put, is this:

> Either God wants to abolish evil, and cannot; or he can, but does not want to; or he cannot and does not want to. If he wants to, but cannot, he is impotent. If he can, and does not want to, he is wicked. But, if God both *can* and *wants* to abolish evil, then how comes evil in the world?[14]

In attempting to deal with this problem, people have come up with a wide variety of solutions, most of them unsatisfactory in one way or another. For example, some modify the idea that God is all-powerful. They argue that God is indeed good but that He is simply not strong enough to stand against the evil that is in our world. This viewpoint is known as finite godism and was popularized by Rabbi Kushner's book, *When Bad Things Happen to Good People.*

Other people modify the idea that God is entirely good. They argue that God does indeed do some good things, but He is not *fully* good. He does things that, from our vantage point, seem evil—including such things as allowing little children to be run over by cars or abused by parents. If a chain-saw murderer kills a family in Texas, it is argued, then God willed this tragedy to occur, and that can only mean God is not entirely good.

Others modify the idea of evil itself. For example, people associated with the (cultic) mind sciences conclude that evil is just an illusion. It doesn't really exist. It is simply an erroneous perception of the finite mind.

Others interpret the problem of evil through the grid of reincarnation and karma. In this viewpoint, if a person does good things in this life, he will be born in a better condition in the next life. If a person does bad things in this life, he will be born in a worse (evil) condition in the next life. This viewpoint is common among Hindus and New Agers. Ideally, through multitudes of lifetimes, a person's suffering gets less and less with each progressive life.

Still others, particularly in New Age circles, believe we create our own realities by the power of our minds. By using techniques such as visualization and positive affirmations, we can create our own realities. If we have a negative (evil) reality, it is only because our own minds have created this condition. To do away with such a condition, we must use our minds to create a more positive reality. So, for example, the people who died in the Twin Towers somehow collectively created their evil reality. By contrast, the financial success of Bill Gates exists because he created that reality.

As this book unfolds, I will address these and other errant explanations for the problem of evil. I will also offer what I believe to be a biblical perspective on the issue.

Can We *Really* Know Answers?

I realize I am treading on dangerous ground in even suggesting that one can make sense of the problem of evil from a Christian viewpoint. A professor at Dallas Theological Seminary (where I attended from 1980 to 1986) used to say, "One of your problems as young theologians is trying to unscrew the inscrutable."[15] The fact is that much of what God does in our world *is* and *will continue to be* inscrutable to our finite minds. We will never know why certain bad things happen in this universe. Some of God's ways will remain a mystery to us.

In Isaiah 55:8-9 God affirmed:

> "For my thoughts are not your thoughts,
>   neither are your ways my ways," declares the LORD.
> "As the heavens are higher than the earth,
>   so are my ways higher than your ways
>   and my thoughts than your thoughts."

In the same vein, the apostle Paul pondered in Romans 11:33-34: "Oh, the depth of the riches of the wisdom and knowledge of God! How unsearchable his judgments, and his paths beyond tracing out! 'Who has known the mind of the Lord? Or who has been his counselor?'"

This is one of the main lessons we derive from the book of Job. In this book, God never does explain to Job why He permits bad things to happen in the world. The main lesson Job learns from God is that regardless of what happens—even if one can't make sense of the human pain and suffering—we are to trust God in everything (Job 13:15). Job learned that God's ways are inscrutable, but he also learned to trust God entirely, and God blessed him for this faith.

One day, when we get to heaven, things will be clearer for us. Jay Kesler agrees: "The first sound we will hear from every throat when we get to heaven is 'Ahhhh...Now I see it! Now I realize why. Now it all makes sense before my eyes, this great once-mysterious panorama of events.' "[16] Chuck Swindoll, whose church is just down the road from where I live in Frisco, Texas, reflects:

> It all will have worked together for good, including the tragedies and the calamities and the heartaches, the illnesses and diseases and what we call premature deaths, the terrible deformities and birth defects and congenital illnesses. All will unfold, and we will see that God's plan was right.[17]

As it is now, we do not see the entire tapestry of life. From our limited vantage point, we only see one thread in the tapestry at a time. And we do not comprehend how all the different threads fit together. I, like Job, must learn to trust God with things I do not fully comprehend.

Yet, while I cannot "unscrew the inscrutable," I do believe God wants us to be fully aware of all the insights the Bible provides on this issue. We may feel the Bible does not reveal enough on this issue, but what the Bible does reveal is significant and gives us good reason to trust in God and His purposes. The more we understand what Scripture reveals on this subject, the more our faith will be bolstered so that we can trust God with all that we do not understand.

My Goal in this Book

After an extensive tour across the United States, the famous German pastor and theologian Helmut Thielicke was asked what he saw as the greatest defect among American Christians. He replied quite candidly, "They have an inadequate view of suffering."[18]

My goal in this book is to examine some of the tough questions about evil and suffering from a Christian vantage point. I want to provide an adequate view of suffering that is faithful to the biblical testimony.

I approach this subject with some trepidation, knowing that a proper treatment of it would probably require a 12-volume tome, not just a medium-sized book. Abbreviated treatments always run the risk of superficiality. But I don't have the time or resources to write a 12-volume tome, and even if I did, I strongly doubt you would want to take the time to read it. (And who can easily afford to buy 12-volume tomes these days anyway?)

The book you are holding in your hands contains a summary of the wisdom I have gleaned from Scripture on this issue. My prayer is that the book will help provide an anchor for you so that when you face pain and suffering, your faith in God will not be shaken.

You will notice, as this book unfolds, that I am approaching the subject from several different angles. At times I write as a theologian, summarizing and evaluating positions from a theological and biblical perspective. At other times I write as a philosopher, pointing out philosophical strengths and weaknesses of various opinions about the problem of evil. Yet at other times I write as a pastor or perhaps as a friend, sharing heartfelt counsel to help you get through the pains and toils that all of us inevitably face in day-to-day living. (Most chapters have a section at the end entitled "Healing Hearts," in which I provide comforting insights from Scripture.) Actually, these three angles—the theological, the philosophical, and the pastoral—are closely related, for the most beneficial pastoral counsel must be built on the solid foundation of good theology and sound philosophy.

You will also notice that this book has 15 chapters. An examination of the problem of evil is not like looking through a telescope at a single item. It is more like looking into a kaleidoscope, for there are many facets to this problem, many different aspects of reality that relate in some way to this complex issue. By the time we are done, I think you will be able to see how all these relate to the big picture of the problem of evil. Some of these chapters may overlap, but only to the extent necessary to preserve a logical flow of thought within each chapter.

Having said that, let us begin our journey. First stop—Have bad things ever caused you to wonder if God really exists?

DOES EVIL PROVE GOD DOESN'T EXIST?

This past year I saw the movie *A Walk to Remember*. In the movie, Jamie Sullivan (the main Christian character, played by Mandy Moore) is portrayed as dialoguing with Landon Carter (a hooligan played by Shane West). She is very open about her faith and asks him if he believes in God. Using profane language, he says something to the effect, "No, there's too much bad stuff happening in the world!"

Many people see the seemingly pointless and unnecessary evils in the world and conclude that there is no God. Or perhaps there *was* a God at one time, but He has now died. As Alvin Plantinga put it, "Many believe that the existence of evil (or at least the amount and kinds of evil we actually find) makes belief in God unreasonable or rationally unacceptable."[1] Theologians William Hamilton and Thomas Altizer have flat out concluded that God is dead. Others believe that if there is a God, He certainly has no morally sufficient reasons for allowing such horrible evils to occur.

We have seen that the problem of evil is a conflict between three realities: *God's power*, *God's goodness*, and *the presence of evil in the world*. Common sense seems to tell us that all three cannot be true at the same time.[2] Solutions to the problem of evil typically involve modifying one or more of these three options: *Limit*

God's power, limit God's goodness, or *modify the existence of evil* (such as calling it an illusion).[3]

Certainly if God made no claims to being good, the existence of evil would be easier to explain. But God *does* claim to be good. If God were limited in power and unable to withstand evil, the existence of evil would be easier to explain. But God *does* claim to be all-powerful. If evil were just an illusion that had no reality, the problem does not really exist in the first place. But evil *is not* an illusion. It is painfully real.[4]

Today we face the reality of both *moral evil* (evil committed by free moral agents, including such things as war, crime, cruelty, class struggles, discrimination, slavery, ethnic cleansing, suicide bombings, and other injustices) and *natural evil* (including hurricanes, floods, earthquakes, and the like). God is good, God is all-powerful, and yet evil exists. Because evil exists, and because this evil seemingly cannot be reconciled with a good and all-powerful God, many have chosen to simply reject belief in God altogether.

This includes such prominent thinkers as David Hume, H.G. Wells, and Bertrand Russell.[5] Hume put it succinctly when he wrote this of God: "Is he willing to prevent evil, but not able? Then he is impotent. Is he able, but not willing? Then he is malevolent. Is he both able and willing: whence then is evil?"[6] If there *is* a God—and He is all-good and all-powerful—then, it is argued, such atrocities as Hitler's murder of six million Jews should never have happened.

Certainly Christians agree that what Hitler did to the Jews was a horrendous, unconscionable crime. But categorizing Hitler's actions as evil raises an important philosophical point. As many thinkers have noted, if one is going to claim there is evil in the world, one must ask *by what criteria* something is judged to be evil in the first place?[7] How does one judge some things to be evil and other things not to be evil? What is the moral measuring stick by which people and events are morally appraised? Christian apologist Robert Morey put it this way:

> How do you know evil when you see it? By what process do you identify evil?...My point is that, as Socrates demonstrated a long time ago, to make a distinction between particulars in which one is good and one is evil, you must have a universal or absolute [standard] to do it. Once you see this, then the ultimate result is that without an infinite reference point for "good," no one can identify what is good or evil. God alone can exhaust the meaning of an infinite good. Thus without the existence of God, there is no "evil" or "good" in an absolute sense but everything is relative. The problem of evil does not negate the existence of God. It actually requires it.[8]

The point is, then, that it is impossible to distinguish evil from good unless one has an infinite reference point that is absolutely good.[9] Otherwise one would be like a person on a boat at sea on a cloudy night without a compass—that is, there would be no way to distinguish north from south. God is our reference point for determining good and evil.

Consider *All* the Evidence

While Christians recognize that the problem of evil is viewed by some as a rational argument against the existence of God, they suggest that the arguments *for* God's existence far outweigh arguments *against* His existence.[10] And the reality of evil, while obviously problematic, is nevertheless viewed as compatible with a Christian worldview (as this book will demonstrate).

Christians thus argue that one should not focus sole attention on one narrow aspect of evidence (such as the existence of evil) but should consider all the evidence together, including the various arguments that have been suggested in favor of the existence of God through the centuries.[11]

1. *The Cosmological Argument.* This argument says that every effect must have an adequate cause. The universe is an "effect." Reason demands that whatever caused the universe must be greater than the universe. That cause is God (who Himself is the uncaused First Cause). As Hebrews 3:4 puts it, "Every house is built by someone, but God is the builder of everything."

2. *The Teleological Argument.* This argument highlights the obvious purposeful and intricate design of the world. If we found a watch in the sand, we would assume that someone created the watch because the parts obviously didn't just jump together. Similarly, the perfect design of the universe argues for a Designer, and that Designer is God.

3. *The Ontological Argument.* This argument says that most human beings have an innate idea of a most perfect being. Where did this idea come from? Not from man, for man is an imperfect being. Some perfect being (God) must have planted the idea there. God can't be conceived of as not existing, for then, one could conceive of an even greater being that did exist. Thus God must in fact exist.

4. *The Moral Argument.* This argument says that every human being has an innate sense of "oughtness" or moral obligation. Where did this come from? It must come from God. The existence of a moral law in our hearts demands the existence of a moral Lawgiver (see Romans 1:19-32).

5. *The Anthropological Argument.* This argument says that man has a personality (mind, emotions, and will). Since that which is *personal* cannot derive from the *impersonal*, there must be a personal cause—and that personal cause is God (see Genesis 1:26-27).

Of course, some people, even when aware of some of these arguments, still reject belief in God. Perhaps Reformer John Calvin was right when he said that the unregenerate person sees these evidences for God in the universe with blurred vision. It is only when one puts on the "eyeglasses" of faith and belief in the Bible that these evidences for God's existence come into clear focus and become convincing.

If Calvin is right, then Christians do well to offer not only evidences for God's existence but also evidences that demonstrate the reliability of the Bible. I am convinced that if we add to the above philosophical arguments the overwhelming historical and archaeological support for the reliability of the Bible, the historical support for Jesus Christ (including the resurrection), the pinpoint accuracy of biblical prophecies, and the testimony of innumerable Christians down through the centuries, we can make a very strong case for the existence of God to any reasonable person.[12]

Termites and the Architect

The universe designed by God is like a house designed by an architect. Just as the presence of termites in a house does not disprove the existence of the architect, so the existence of sin and evil in the universe does not disprove the existence of the *divine* architect. Before we pursue this line of thinking, however, we need to take a brief detour to address the question, What is evil? Once we have properly answered this question, the architect analogy becomes a helpful way of understanding God and His relation-ship to a fallen universe.

What is evil? From a philosophical perspective, evil is not some-thing that has an existence all its own; rather, it is a corruption of that which already exists. Evil is the absence or privation of something good. Rot, for example, can only exist as long as the tree exists. Tooth decay can only exist as long as the tooth exists. Rust on a car, a decaying carcass, blind eyes, and deaf ears illus-trate the same point. Evil exists as a corruption of something good; it is a privation and does not have essence *by itself.*[13] Norman Geisler tells us, "Evil is like a wound in an arm or moth-holes in a garment. It exists only in another but not in itself."[14] Intelligent design theorist William Dembski puts it this way:

> Evil always parasitizes good. Indeed all our words for evil presuppose a good that has been perverted. Impurities pre-suppose purity, unrighteousness presupposes righteousness, deviation presupposes a way (i.e., a *via*) from which we've departed, sin…presupposes a target that was missed, and so on.[15]

Actually, we can be a little more precise. Evil involves the absence of something good that *ought* to be there. When good that should be in something is not in that something, that is evil. For example, health ought to be in a human body, but sometimes people get cancer. That is evil. Hearing ought to be in an ear, but sometimes people go deaf. That is evil. Sight ought to be in an eye, but sometimes people go blind. That is evil. Notice, by contrast, that the tree in my front lawn cannot see, but that is *not* evil because my tree was never supposed to see. Likewise, if my nose is missing a wart, that is not evil, because a wart was never supposed to be on my nose to begin with. So evil involves the absence of something good that ought to be there, like sight in an eye, or hearing in an ear, or health in a body.[16]

I could illustrate this meaning of evil with many real-life people and events. For example, when former president Ronald Reagan can no longer remember certain things due to Alzheimer's disease, that is evil because something good that ought to be there (memory) is missing. When a man succumbs to looking at pornography, that is evil because something good that ought to be true of him (personal purity) is missing. When a Southern California mountain biker is attacked and killed by a mountain lion, that is evil because something good that ought to be in the biker (life) is missing. On a larger scale, when terrorists fly airplanes into the Twin Towers, that is evil because something good that ought to be there (life in humans, buildings with structural integrity) is missing. *Evil is a corruption or privation of something good that ought to be there.*

This brings me to the primary point I want to make. When God originally created the universe as the divine Architect, it was perfectly good in every way. Indeed, as Genesis 1:31 tells us, "God saw all that he had made, and it was very good." Nothing was wrong. There was no evil. There was no situation in the universe of which it could be said that something good ought to have been there but was missing. Everything was good.

Today, however, everything is not good. In fact, a great deal of evil now exists in the universe that was once entirely good. That can mean only one thing. Something dreadful has happened between then and now to cause the change. A colossal perversion of the good has occurred. As a house may suffer a massive termite invasion, the universe has suffered a massive invasion of sin.

Jimmy H. Davis and Harry L. Poe, in their book *Designer Universe: Intelligent Design and the Existence of God*, suggest that the existence of evil in our universe does not disprove the existence of God any more than termites in a house disprove the existence of an architect:

> The fact that ugliness, thorns, death, pain, suffering, and chaos are present in the world does not disprove design. Infestation by termites does not prove the house did not have an architect. Vandalism does not prove the house did not have an architect. Arson does not prove the house did not have an architect. Sloppy homeowners who do not paint or carry out the garbage do not prove the house did not have an architect. These matters simply raise questions about the situation of the house *since it was built.*[17]

Theologically, the Bible is clear that God exists and that He created the universe in a perfectly good state. The Bible is also clear that things have changed dramatically since God created the world. I will talk more about man's fall and his sin problem later in the book. At this juncture, it is enough to note that because of sin, things are not now as they were created to be. God's original design has been corrupted by an intruder—the intruder of sin. God's good universe is no longer good.

God Is Not Dead

In view of the above, it seems like sheer folly to suggest that God is dead merely because of the presence of certain forms of evil in the world. Ever since man's fall, God has been alive and active in this fallen world. Theologians Gordon R. Lewis and Bruce A. Demarest make a keen observation in this regard:

Had Altizer and Hamilton [the two theologians who say God is dead] lived at the time of the Flood, they might have concluded that God had died in their time. But God was there in righteous judgment on the incorrigibly wicked and in matchless grace for Noah and his family. Had they been pursued by King Saul as was David, the Lord's anointed, they might well have concluded that God was dead. But God was there, and at the appointed time David became king. If any of us had been present when Israel and then Judah were taken into captivity, we might have concluded that God was dead. But God was there in just judgment on evil without respect of persons and he was there in grace, sending prophet after prophet to call his people back to significant fellowship and service.[18]

While we may be tempted to think that God is not in control or that He is not involved in our lives, the reality is that He is actually *still* with us, working behind the scenes to bring about His sovereign purposes, all the while remaining perfectly good, just, righteous, and holy. At the end of human history, when we are with God in heaven, we will all no doubt revel in God's brilliance in bringing about His purposes on a fallen planet without compromising a single of His perfect attributes. While some of His actions may seem incomprehensible to us in the present, it is really no different from a young child might not comprehend why his parents would allow something so dreadful as a visit to the dentist. Just as human parents operate according to a higher wisdom than children do, so God operates according to an infinitely higher wisdom than we do.

God Is Among Us

Contrary to the idea that God is either dead or inactive among His people, the Bible often refers to God as "the living God"

(Deuteronomy 5:26; 1 Samuel 17:26,36; Psalm 84:2). The living God is truly among His people (Joshua 3:10). This is illustrated in one of my favorite Old Testament passages: Daniel 6, which records Daniel being thrown into the lions' den.

The backdrop is that even though King Darius personally liked Daniel, other governmental leaders despised him. These unscrupulous men tricked the king into signing an irrevocable edict that decreed that no one could pray to any god or man besides Darius for the next 30 days. Undaunted, Daniel continued his practice of praying three times a day to the true God. Upon being discovered by the scheming governmental leaders, Daniel was thrown into the lions' den overnight. Due to the irrevocable nature of the edict, Darius could not intervene, but the king admonished Daniel, "May your God, whom you serve continually, rescue you!" (Daniel 6:16).

The next morning, the king ran to the den and shouted, "Daniel, servant of the living God, has your God, whom you serve continually, been able to rescue you from the lions?" Daniel affirmed that yes indeed, the living God had rescued him. The king quickly had Daniel removed from the den and issued a decree that all the people in his kingdom must fear and reverence the God of Daniel, for He is "the living God" who endures forever and who performs signs and wonders (Daniel 6:19-27).

In his wonderful little book *The Living God*, Bible scholar R.T. France explains how the ancients viewed God:

> Watch the hand of this living God intervening, in answer to His people's prayers, working miracles, converting thousands, opening prison doors, and raising the dead, guiding His messengers to people and places they had never thought of, supervising the whole operation and every figure in it

so as to work out His purpose in the end. Is it any wonder they prayed, constantly, not in vague generalities, but in daring specific requests? To them, God was real; to them He was the living God.[19]

But who is this living God among us? Because the existence of evil in the world often compels unbelievers to level false charges against God, we do well to remember what God is really like.

God Is Loving

God isn't just characterized by love. He is the very personification of love (1 John 4:8). Love permeates His being. And God's love is not dependent upon the lovability of the objects (human beings). God loves us despite the fact that we are fallen in sin (John 3:16). (God loves the sinner, though He hates the sin.)

This is important for us to remember, especially during those times when we're acutely aware of our own failures. Sometimes we feel guilty and unworthy of God's love. In fact, we might feel like worms before God because of our personal evil. But this feeling is not rooted in God's feelings toward us. He loves us even when we are unlovable.

God Is Everywhere-Present

The Scriptures tell us that God is everywhere-present (Psalm 139:7-8; see also 1 Kings 8:27; 2 Chronicles 2:6; Jeremiah 23:23-24; Acts 17:27-28). How comforting to know that no matter where we go, we will never escape the presence of our beloved God. Like a good shepherd never leaves his sheep, so God never leaves His children alone (Psalm 23). We will always know the blessing of walking with Him in every trial and circumstance of life.

God Is Holy, Righteous, and Just

God's holiness means not just that He is entirely separate from all evil but also that He is absolutely righteous (Leviticus 19:2). He is pure in every way. God is separate from all that is morally imperfect. The Scriptures lay great stress upon this attribute of God:

- ✑ Who is like you—majestic in holiness? (Exodus 15:11).

- ✑ There is no one holy like the LORD (1 Samuel 2:2).

- ✑ The LORD our God is holy (Psalm 99:9).

- ✑ Holy and awesome is his name (Psalm 111:9).

- ✑ Holy, holy, holy is the LORD Almighty (Isaiah 6:3).

- ✑ You alone are holy (Revelation 15:4).

A key ramification of such verses is that if we want to fellowship with God, we have to take personal holiness seriously. Walking in daily fellowship with God necessarily involves living in a way that is pleasing to Him. God can't fellowship with those openly involved in evil.

God is also *singularly* righteous, with no hint of unrighteousness (unlike the concept of God in some other world religions). We read, "LORD, God of Israel, you are righteous!" (Ezra 9:15). "You are always righteous, O LORD" (Jeremiah 12:1). "For the LORD is righteous, he loves justice" (Psalm 11:7). "The LORD loves righteousness and justice" (Psalm 33:5). "Righteousness and justice are the foundation of your throne" (Psalm 89:14).

That God is just means He carries out His righteous standards justly and with equity. There is never any partiality or unfairness in God's dealings with people (Zephaniah 3:5; Romans 3:26). His justness is proclaimed emphatically in both the Old and New

Testaments (see, for example, Genesis 18:25; John 17:25; Hebrews 6:10). The fact that God is just is both a comfort and a warning. It is a comfort for those who have suffered abuse. They can rest assured that God will right all wrongs in the end. But it is a warning for those who think they have been getting away with evil. Justice will prevail in the end! (See the Appendix.)

God Is Compassionate

God has tender compassion for His people. In Psalm 103:13 we read, "As a father has compassion on his children, so the LORD has compassion on those who fear him." Psalm 135:14 affirms, "the LORD will vindicate his people and have compassion on his servants." Psalm 34:18 tells us, "The LORD is close to the broken-hearted and saves those who are crushed in spirit." In Isaiah 49:15 God proclaims, "Can a mother forget the baby at her breast and have no compassion on the child she has borne? Though she may forget, I will not forget you!"

When God must discipline His disobedient children, He is always compassionate after the discipline has taken place. God affirms, "After I uproot them, I will again have compassion and will bring each of them back to his own inheritance and his own country" (Jeremiah 12:15; see also Isaiah 54:7-8). Note that God's discipline itself is a sign of His love and compassion, for God loves His children too much to let them harm themselves by remaining in sin (Hebrews 12:6).

We can get a firsthand glimpse of the compassion of God by observing the life of Christ. When we witness Jesus, we witness the very heart of God. (Jesus Himself said that when we see Jesus, we see the Father—John 14:9.) Examples of Jesus' compassion abound in the New Testament. Recall that after spending some time alone in a boat, Jesus went ashore and saw a great multitude and "had compassion on them and healed their sick" (Matthew 14:14). Later, a crowd of 4000 people became hungry as they listened to Jesus teach. Jesus called His disciples and said to them, "I have compassion for these people; they have already been with me three days and have nothing to eat. I do not want to send them away hungry, or they may collapse on the way" (Matthew 15:32). So Jesus multiplied seven loaves of bread and a few small fish so that everyone had plenty to eat (verses 35-39).

Still later, when two blind men pleaded for mercy from Jesus, He did not need to be coerced to help them. "Jesus had compassion on them and touched their eyes. Immediately they received their sight and followed him" (Matthew 20:34).

The wonderful mercy and compassion of Jesus prompted this exhortation from the writer of Hebrews:

> For we do not have a high priest who is unable to sympathize with our weaknesses, but we have one who has been tempted in every way, just as we are—yet was without sin. Let us then approach the throne of grace with confidence, so that we may receive mercy and find grace to help us in our time of need (Hebrews 4:15-16).

Whenever you are tempted to wonder about God's goodness or His compassion, reflect on the Jesus of the gospels, for this will give you an accurate picture of God's heart. By observing Jesus' compassion in the gospels, we can see God's compassion in action.

Does this compassion of God mean that you will never suffer in life? No, it does not. Obviously, the pages of the Bible are filled with examples of suffering. The apostle Paul is a good example. Here is a man who served God full-time, and was acutely aware of the compassion of the God he served. Yet, we read this in 2 Corinthians 11:24-27:

> Five times I received from the Jews the forty lashes minus one. Three times I was beaten with rods, once I was stoned, three times I was shipwrecked, I spent a night and a day in the open sea, I have been constantly on the move. I have been in danger from rivers, in danger from bandits, in danger from my own countrymen, in danger from Gentiles; in danger in the city, in danger in the country, in danger at sea; and in danger from false brothers. I have labored and toiled and have often gone without sleep; I have known hunger and thirst and have often gone without food; I have been cold and naked.

Bad things *do* happen to good people. Yet, all the while, God is with us, walking with us side by side as we limp our way toward heaven. God does not exempt us *from* suffering, but He is always with us *in* our suffering just as He was in the fiery furnace (Daniel 3) and the lions' den (Daniel 6).

God Is Sovereign

Divine sovereignty means that God is the absolute Ruler of the universe. He may utilize various means to accomplish His ends, but He is always in control.[20] Nothing can happen in this universe that is beyond His reach. All forms of existence are within the scope of His absolute dominion.

Psalm 50:1 makes reference to God as the Mighty One who "speaks and summons the earth from the rising of the sun to the place where it sets." Psalm 66:7 affirms that "He rules forever by his power." We are assured in Psalm 93:1 that "the LORD reigns" and "is armed with strength." Job affirmed to God, "I know that you can do all things; no plan of yours can be thwarted" (Job 42:2). Isaiah 40:15 tells us that by comparison, "surely the nations are like a drop in a bucket; they are regarded as dust on the scales; he weighs the islands as though they were fine dust." Indeed, "Before him all the nations are as nothing" (Isaiah 40:17). God asserts, "My purpose will stand, and I will do all that I please" (Isaiah 46:10). God assures us, "Surely, as I have planned, so it will be, and as I have purposed, so it will stand" (Isaiah 14:24). God is said to be "the blessed and only Ruler, the King of kings and Lord of lords" (1 Timothy 6:15). Proverbs 16:9 tells us, "In his heart a man plans his course, but the LORD determines his steps." Proverbs 19:21 says, "Many are the plans in a man's heart, but it is the LORD's purpose that prevails." In Proverbs 21:30 we read, "There is no wisdom, no insight, no plan that can succeed against the LORD." Ecclesiastes 7:13 instructs, "Consider what God has done: Who can straighten what he has made crooked?" Lamentations 3:37 affirms, "Who can speak and have it happen if the Lord has not decreed it?"

James Montgomery Boice, in his excellent book *The Sovereign God*, speaks of the many ways God showed His sovereign control in biblical times:

> God showed his sovereignty over nature in dividing the Red Sea so the children of Israel could pass over from Egypt into the wilderness and then by returning the waters to destroy the pursuing Egyptian soldiers. He showed his sovereignty in sending manna to feed the people while they were in the wilderness. On another occasion he sent quails into the camp for meat. God divided the waters of the Jordan River so the people could pass over into Canaan. He caused the walls of Jericho to fall. He stopped the sun in the days of Joshua at Gibeon so that Israel might gain a full victory over her fleeing

enemies. In the days of Jesus, God's sovereignty was seen in the feeding of the four and five thousand from a few small loaves and fish, in acts of healing the sick and raising the dead. Eventually, it was seen in the events connected with the crucifixion of Christ and the resurrection.[21]

What does God's sovereignty mean to you and me and our struggle with "bad things"? We can rest assured that all such things are subject to God, and nothing can touch us unless God in His wisdom allows it. When He allows it, we can be sure that He does so for our own good.[22] Anyone who doubts that God has the ability to sovereignly weave events in daily life for our utmost good should read the book of Esther in the Bible. In this book, we find God sovereignly, providentially, and *relentlessly* working behind the scenes on behalf of His people. He does the same for us. Often, though, we do not recognize that God is at work. Jerry Bridges agrees:

> From our limited vantage point, our lives are marked by an endless series of contingencies. We frequently find ourselves, instead of acting as we planned, reacting to an unexpected turn of events. We make plans but are often forced to change those plans. But there are no contingencies with God. Our unexpected, forced change of plans is a part of His plan. God is never surprised; never caught off guard; never frustrated by unexpected developments. God does as He pleases and that which pleases Him is always for His glory and our good.[23]

The hard thing for us is that God does not sit us down and say, "Okay, listen, I'm going to allow some bad stuff to happen this next week, but I'm in control, and I'm using this event to bring about a great good. So don't worry about it. Everything's fine."

Certainly God did not sit down and explain to Job why he suffered so terribly. Judy Salisbury offers this explanation:

> It was as if God was saying to Job, "Job, this is huge, this is bigger than you. It has to do with My eternal plan. You're temporal, Job, and you think that way. I am infinite, you are finite—and if I even began to explain it to you, you couldn't handle it, Job. I am not going to give you every answer, but know this—not a sparrow falls to the ground that I don't know about. So how much more do you think I am concerned about those who bear My image?"[24]

You and I are given the privilege of going behind the scenes in Job's life by reading the book of Job. But we are *not* able to go behind the scenes and discern the mysterious ways that God works in *our* lives. That's why we have to trust Him. We usually are not aware of why God engineers our circumstances the way He does. But we may always rest assured that He continually has our best interests at heart.

I think Chuck Swindoll is right when he says, "The sovereignty of God relieves me from anxiety. It doesn't take away my questions. It takes away my anxiety. When I rest in it, I am relieved of the worry."[25] Indeed, he says, "The sovereignty of God frees me from explanation. I don't have to have all the answers. I find ease in saying to certain individuals at critical times, 'You know, I don't know. I can't unravel His full plan in this.'"[26]

Healing Hearts

I know that some of my readers may have endured significant suffering and been tempted to conclude that God does not exist, or that perhaps He does not care. I hope I've convinced you otherwise in this chapter.

Please allow me to offer a nugget of truth that has always helped me when life throws me a punch: *When you do not understand why certain things have happened in your life, that is the time to anchor yourself on the things you do understand.* I mentioned this principle earlier when I spoke of delivering a eulogy at my nephew Greg's funeral. It is a powerfully helpful principle.

Here are a few of the truths from this chapter you may want to anchor yourself to:

- ✺ The arguments in favor of God's existence are far more pervasive and convincing than those against His existence. Even a house with termites has an architect.

- ✺ God is a living God who walks with you through every circumstance you encounter (see Daniel 6:19-27).

- ✺ God loves the unlovable—including you and me (1 John 4:8). In your mind's eye, try to picture yourself resting in the loving arms of God.

- ✺ God is everywhere-present. He is with you every moment whether you're consciously aware of Him or not (Psalm 139:7-8).

- ✺ God is just. If someone has treated you unfairly, count on the fact that God will right all wrongs in the end (Genesis 18:25).

- ✺ God is compassionate and has tender feelings for you. When you are tempted to doubt God's compassion, reflect on the Jesus of the gospels, for this will give you an accurate picture of God's heart for you.

≈ God is sovereign. Nothing can touch you unless God in His infinite wisdom allows it. Even when you can't understand why certain things happen, you can rest in the assurance that God is in control.

DOES EVIL PROVE
GOD ISN'T GOOD?

Blaise Pascal once said God's fate is to be everlastingly mis-understood.[1] This is certainly true when it comes to the problem of evil. Some people have so misunderstood God that they have concluded He is not entirely good, at least as traditionally understood. As one person put it, "How can evil be compatible with the concept of a good God who is actively ruling this world? There are natural disasters: fires, earthquakes, floods. In the past these have been called 'acts of God.'"[2]

Is God entirely good? Consider these two case studies of those who do not hold to the traditional understanding of God's goodness. Then see what the Bible says about the issue.

Case Study 1: Christian Theologian Gordon Clark

One prominent Christian theologian, Gordon Clark, has dealt with the problem of evil in such a way that, at least by implication, God's goodness is redefined.[3] Clark is well known in theological circles as being a fervent Calvinist[4] who believes that God acts in a deterministic way to cause all things in the universe, including the individual acts of human beings. Because God causes all things, human beings do not truly have a free will.[5] Clark writes, "Free will is not only futile, but false. Certainly, if the Bible is the

Word of God, free will is false, for the Bible consistently denies free will."[6] God's will is in absolute sovereign control over all things—including humans.

While maintaining that all that God causes is good, Clark nevertheless states, "I wish very frankly and pointedly to assert that if a man gets drunk and shoots his family, it was the will of God that he should do it." This is so every bit as much as it was the Father's will that Jesus be crucified on a criminal's cross.[7] At the very least, then, Clark understands God's goodness quite differently than most Christians.

Theologian Millard Erickson summarizes Clark's position this way:

> Whatever happens is caused by God.
> What is caused by God is good.
> Whatever happens is good.[8]

Clark draws a distinction between God's *preceptive will* and His *decretive will.* God's preceptive will, Clark says, relates to what God commands in the Bible, such as the Ten Commandments. God's decretive will relates to God decreeing or causing all events in the universe. "It may seem strange at first that God would decree an immoral act, but the Bible shows that he did."[9] For example, Clark notes that the Bible records that God caused prophets to lie (see 2 Chronicles 18:20-21). This ultimately means that God is the cause of sin:

> Let it be unequivocally said that this view certainly makes God the cause of sin. God is the sole ultimate cause of everything. There is absolutely nothing independent of him. He alone is the eternal being. He alone is omnipotent. He alone is sovereign.[10]

By this, Clark means not that God Himself *commits* personal sin, but that God decrees that *humans* sin, thereby making it a sure thing that humans will indeed sin. Yet, Clark says, God is not responsible for human sin. The responsibility lies squarely on the shoulders of human beings.[11] Sin involves a transgression of God's law, but God Himself is said to be above law altogether. "There is no law, superior to God, which forbids him to decree sinful acts. Sin presupposes a law, for sin is lawlessness."[12] God is thus the divine Creator, and He has unlimited rights. No one is above Him, no one can punish Him, and no one can hold Him accountable.[13]

> Man is responsible because God calls him to account; man is responsible because the supreme power can punish him for disobedience. God, on the contrary, cannot be responsible for the plain reason that there is no power superior to him; no greater being can hold him accountable; no one can punish him; there is no one to whom God is responsible; there are no laws which he could disobey.[14]

In view of the above, it seems clear that from Gordon Clark's perspective, bad things happen to good people because *God has decreed it.* This means that my nephew Greg was violently hit by a high-speed car and killed simply because God decreed it. My brother Paul consequently suffered inconsolable grief simply because God decreed it. And yet, in this view, God is still believed to be "good."

Case Study 2: Islam's Arbitrary God

One of the more controversial aspects of the Muslim view of God, whose name is Allah, relates to his absolute sovereignty. The Quran tells us, "God hath power over all things" (Sura 3:165). In the Muslim view, God brings about both good and evil. God can guide men in righteousness, or he can lead them to evil. In some 20 passages of the Quran, Allah is said to lead men astray. Abdiyah Akbar Abdul-Haqq makes this observation: "Even if a person desires to choose God's guidance, he cannot do so without the prior choice of God in favor of his free choice."[15] Everything that happens in the universe, whether good or bad, is foreordained by the unchangeable decrees of Allah. Muslims believe all our thoughts, words, and deeds (good or evil) were foreseen, foreordained, determined, and decreed from all eternity. Allah is thus variously described as the bringer-down, the Compeller, the Tyrant, or the Haughty.[16] One Muslim theologian, Al-Ghazzali, put it this way:

> He willeth also the unbelief of the unbeliever and the irreligion of the wicked and, without that will, there would neither be unbelief nor irreligion. All we do we do by His will: what He willeth not does not come to pass. If one should ask why God does not will that men should believe, we answer, "We have no right to inquire about what God wills or does. He is perfectly free to will and to do what He pleases." In creating unbelievers, in willing that they should remain in that state; in making serpents, scorpions and pigs: in willing, in short, all that is evil, God has wise ends in view which it is not necessary that we should know.[17]

Another Muslim theologian, Risaleh-i-Barkhawi, goes so far as to say this:

> Not only can he (God) do anything, he actually is the only one who does anything. When a man writes, it is Allah who has created in his mind the will to write. Allah at the same time gives power to write, then brings about the motion of

the hand and the pen and the appearance upon paper. All other things are passive, Allah alone is active.[18]

There is thus a very strong strain of determinism and even fatalism in Islam. A frequent statement one hears among devout Muslims is *im shallah*—if God wills it.[19] This strong sense of fatalism can lead to irresponsible actions. Bruce McDowell and Anees Zaka speak of children in apartment buildings in Teheran, Iran, who would fall over low balcony railings to their deaths, and because of the belief that this must have been the will of Allah, nothing was done to heighten the railings to prevent such tragedies in the future.[20] Fatalism thus leads to a diminished sense of moral responsibility. John Gilchrist summarizes the Muslim mindset this way: "If no one can resist [Allah's sovereign will], why strive for one's own advancement at all? Simply take what comes for it will surely come just as he purposes."[21] This attitude pervades the mentality of many Muslims.

Some Muslims try to explain this contradiction in Allah (causing both good *and* evil) as relating not to his *nature* but rather to his *will*. However, such an explanation seems less than satisfactory in view of the fact that actions that stem from a will are rooted in a person's nature. Or, as Christian apologists Norman Geisler and Abdul Saleeb put it, "Salt water does not flow from a fresh stream."[22]

One cannot help but notice that the Allah of the Quran seems to act in a quite arbitrary fashion. He can choose good, but he can just as easily choose evil. He can choose mercy, but he might just as easily choose severity. He can choose love, but he can just as easily choose hate. This is nowhere more evident than in Sura 11:118-19: "If the Lord pleased, He had made all men of one religion...but unto this has He created them; for the word of the Lord shall be fulfilled: verily I will fill hell altogether with genii and men." In other words, Allah makes some people believe in other (false) religions for the very purpose of populating hell.

Despite the heavy emphasis on God's absolute sovereignty, the Quran also teaches that human beings will be held morally account- able for the evil they engage in. Allah will judge them on that future Day of Judgment. It is never adequately explained how humans can be held accountable for that which Allah arbitrarily and sov- ereignly decreed from all eternity, but Muslims nevertheless believe it.

Because the Quran teaches that Allah engages in both good and evil, we are not surprised that the Quran never suggests that Allah is holy. The Quran seems to emphasize Allah's power rather than his purity, his omnipotence rather than his holiness. This, of course, is completely different from the God of the Bible, for the pivotal attribute of Yahweh is holiness (see Exodus 3:5; 1 Peter 1:16).

Answering Challenges to God's Goodness

We need to make sense of what one might call the threefold dilemma—that is, God is all-powerful, God is all-good, and yet evil exists. But the solution is not to be found in compromising or redefining God's goodness.

The Bible teaches that our all-good God has a good purpose for allowing evil—at least on a temporary basis. Between eternity past and eternity future is a tiny dot of time in which humans live on a temporal earth. During this tiny dot of time, God allows (not deterministically causes) evil for some eternal good.

I will address God's specific purposes for allowing evil through- out the rest of this book. At present, we will limit our attention to a biblical response to the views of Gordon Clark and of the Islamic religion.

The Biblical God Is Singularly Good

The Bible strongly emphasizes the absolute unity of God's moral character. By *unity*, I mean that God is not both good and evil, merciful and mean. God is *singularly* good, just, and righteous. The God of the Bible abhors evil, does not create moral evil, and does not lead men astray.

Christian apologists have noted that in Islamic teaching, God is not *essentially* good but is only *called* good because He *does* good. He is named for His actions. Obviously, this line of thinking is fatally flawed. If we call God good because He does good, then should we call God evil because He does evil? This conclusion seems unavoidable.[23]

Further, if God does evil, doesn't this reveal something about His nature? Doesn't an effect resemble its cause? As Thomas Aquinas pointed out, one cannot produce what one does not possess.[24] In this light, we can hardly escape the conclusion that evil is a part of Allah's nature.

Contrary to this, the Bible is clear that both good and evil cannot stem from one and the same essence (God). God is light, and "in him there is no darkness at all" (1 John 1:5; compare with Habakkuk 1:13; Matthew 5:48). First John 1:5 is particularly cogent in the Greek, which translates literally, "And darkness there is not in Him, *not in any way*." John could not have said it more forcefully.

Related to this is a warning from the prophet Isaiah: "Woe to those who call evil good and good evil" (Isaiah 5:20). Saying that good and evil stem from the same essence of God is the same as

calling evil good and calling good evil. The Scriptures are emphatic
that God is *entirely* good:

> How great is your goodness,
>   which you have stored up for those who fear you,
> which you bestow in the sight of men
>   on those who take refuge in you (Psalm 31:19).

> Taste and see that the LORD is good;
>   blessed is the man who takes refuge in him (Psalm
>   34:8).

> Good and upright is the LORD;
>   therefore he instructs sinners in his ways (Psalm 25:8).

> For the LORD is good and his love endures forever;
>   his faithfulness continues through all generations
>   (Psalm 100:5).

> Praise the LORD. Give thanks to the LORD, for he is good;
>   his love endures forever (Psalm 106:1).

> The LORD is good,
>   a refuge in times of trouble.
> He cares for those who trust in him (Nahum 1:7).

In the previous chapter, I briefly touched on God's attributes
of righteousness and holiness. Without repeating that earlier material, consider how the following verses on these attributes contrast with the Islamic view of God:

> For the LORD is righteous,
>   he loves justice;
>   upright men will see his face (Psalm 11:7).

> The LORD loves righteousness and justice;
>   the earth is full of his unfailing love (Psalm 33:5).

Righteousness and justice are the foundation of your
throne;
> love and faithfulness go before you (Psalm 89:14).

You are always righteous, O LORD (Jeremiah 12:1a).

Who is like you, majestic in holiness? (Exodus 15:11).

There is no one holy like the LORD;
> there is no one besides you;
> there is no Rock like our God (1 Samuel 2:2).

Exalt the LORD our God
> and worship at his holy mountain,
> for the LORD our God is holy (Psalm 99:9).

He provided redemption for his people;
> he ordained his covenant forever—
> holy and awesome is his name (Psalm 111:9).

And they [the angels] were calling to one another:
> "Holy, holy, holy is the LORD Almighty;
> the whole earth is full of his glory" (Isaiah 6:3).

Who will not fear you, O Lord,
> and bring glory to your name?
For you alone are holy.
> All nations will come
> and worship before you,
> for your righteous acts have been revealed (Revelation
> 15:4).

According to the Quran, the primary attributes of Allah are transcendence and sovereignty. While the Bible does portray God as being transcendent and sovereign, the foundational attribute of God's holiness is a thread that runs through the entire Bible. God never does *anything* that violates His intrinsic holiness in any way.

Our Sovereign God Allows for Free Will

You will recall from the previous chapter that God is sovereign in the sense that He rules the universe, controls all things, and is Lord over all. Nothing can happen in this universe that is beyond the reach of His control. All forms of existence are within the scope of His absolute dominion (Psalm 50:1; 66:7; 93:1; Isaiah 40:15; 1 Timothy 6:15).

Contrary to the views of Gordon Clark and Islam, Scripture also portrays man as having a free will (Genesis 3:1-7), a will that is not deterministically controlled by an outside force (like God). It is certainly inscrutable to man's finite understanding *how* both divine sovereignty and human free will can both be true, but both doctrines are taught in Scripture. In fact, they are often seen side by side in a single Scripture verse.

For example, in Acts 2:23 we read this of the crucified Jesus: "This man was handed over to you by God's set purpose and foreknowledge; and you, with the help of wicked men, put him to death by nailing him to the cross." Here we see *divine sovereignty* ("by God's set purpose and foreknowledge") and *human free will* ("you, with the help of wicked men, put him to death").

We also see both doctrines in Acts 13:48: "When the Gentiles heard this, they were glad and honored the word of the Lord; and all who were appointed for eternal life believed." God's sovereignty is clear ("all who were appointed for eternal life") as is man's free will ("believed").

Scripture includes numerous indicators that human beings have a free will. In Matthew 23:37 Jesus speaks to Jews who had rejected Him: "O Jerusalem, Jerusalem, you who kill the prophets and stone those sent to you, how often I have longed to gather your children together, as a hen gathers her chicks under her wings, *but you were not willing*" (emphasis added). Christ (God) was willing to affectionately gather these Jews close to Him, but they volitionally (without compulsion from God) chose not to draw near to Him.

Likewise, we see man's free will illustrated in Genesis following Adam and Eve's sin. After they had committed their rebellious act by eating the forbidden fruit, God came into the Garden and asked, "What is this *you* have done?" (Genesis 3:13, emphasis added). Adam and Eve could not pass the buck back to God and say, "You decreed me to do it." They were guilty of their own act of rebellion against the Lord.

Reconciling human freedom and divine sovereignty is not an easy task. Some people have suggested that divine sovereignty and human free will are like parallel railroad tracks that run side by side in Scripture. The tracks never come together on this side of eternity. When we enter glory, we will no doubt come to a fuller understanding of these biblical doctrines. Now we see but a poor reflection as in a mirror; then we shall see clearly (1 Corinthians 13:12).

A.W. Tozer gives this well-known but still very helpful illustration regarding how both divine sovereignty and human freedom can be true at the same time:

> An ocean liner leaves New York bound for Liverpool. Its destination has been determined by proper authorities. Nothing can change it. This is at least a faint picture of sovereignty.
>
> On board the liner are several scores of passengers. These are not in chains, neither are their activities determined for them by decree. They are completely free to move about as they will. They eat, sleep, play, lounge about on the deck, read, talk, altogether as

they please; but all the while the great liner is carrying them steadily onward toward a predetermined port.

Both freedom and sovereignty are present here and they do not contradict each other. So it is, I believe, with man's freedom and the sovereignty of God. The mighty liner of God's sovereign design keeps its steady course over the sea of history. God moves undisturbed and unhindered toward the fulfillment of those eternal purposes which He purposed in Christ Jesus before the world began. We do not know all that is included in those purposes, but enough has been disclosed to furnish us with a broad outline of things to come and to give us good hope and firm assurance of future well-being.[25]

We must conclude, in view of the above, that Gordon Clark and Islam are simply incorrect in asserting that God deterministically causes evil. I do not believe for an instant that when a man gets drunk and shoots his family, God deterministically caused this travesty. Rather, the man used his free will in a perverted way, grossly violated one of the Ten Commandments (Exodus 20:13), and thereby grieved God by this horrendous act (see Ephesians 4:30).

God Does Not Create Evil

Occasionally I come across people who argue that the Bible itself indicates that God creates evil or is involved in evil in some way. For example, in Isaiah 45:7 God says, "I form the light and create darkness, I bring prosperity and create disaster; I, the LORD, do all these things." In Proverbs 16:4 we read, "The LORD works out everything for his own ends—even the wicked for a day of disaster." Exodus 4:21 indicates that God hardened Pharaoh's heart. Romans 9:13 says that God hated Esau (and hate is evil). What do these verses mean? Do they really teach that God is involved in evil? Let's take a closer look.

Isaiah 45:7. In this verse, God said, "I form the light and create darkness, I bring prosperity and create disaster; I, the LORD, do all these things." In this verse, the Hebrew word for disaster does not mean "moral evil." In fact, Hebrew linguists tell us that the word need not have any moral connotations at all.[26] This word would be perfectly fitting for the plagues that God inflicted on the Egyptians through Moses. The plagues were not morally evil. God engineered these calamitous events to bring the Egyptians to repentance. God as the Judge of the earth can rightly inflict such plagues on sinful human beings without having His character impugned with accusations of evil. Certainly such plagues may *seem* evil to those experiencing them, but these people were experiencing due justice. Norman Geisler adds this insight:

> The Bible is clear that God is morally perfect (cf. Deuteronomy 32:4; Matthew 5:48), and it is impossible for Him to sin (Hebrews 6:18). At the same time, His absolute justice demands that He punish sin. This judgment takes both temporal and eternal forms (Matthew 25:41; Revelation 20:11-15). In its temporal form, the execution of God's justice is sometimes called "evil" because it seems to be evil to those undergoing it (cf. Hebrews 12:11).[27]

Again, there is no *moral* evil on God's part. In the case of the Egyptians, God was merely bringing just judgment on unrepentant sinners. God's good end—that is, the Israelites' deliverance from Egyptian bondage—was the result of this judgment.

Proverbs 16:4. In this verse, we read: "The LORD works out everything for his own ends—even the wicked for a day of disaster." This verse does not mean that God specifically created certain wicked people for the sole purpose of destroying them or sending them to hell. Scripture assures us that God does not want *any* to perish (2 Peter 3:9) and that God loves the whole world of humanity (John 3:16). God "wants all men to be saved and to come to a knowledge of the truth" (1 Timothy 2:4). The price of redemption that Christ paid at the cross is made available to *all* people (1 John 2:2). These verses provide an important backdrop to the proper interpretation of Proverbs 16:4, for if we learn anything from such verses, it is that God cares for and loves all people.

The Expositor's Bible Commentary notes that the primary thrust of the passage is that, in the end, there will be commensurate justice corresponding to human actions:

> God in his sovereignty ensures that everything in life receives its appropriate retribution....The point is that God ensures that everyone's actions and their consequences correspond—certainly the wicked for the day of calamity. In God's order there is just retribution for every act, for every act includes its answer or consequence.[28]

Old Testament expositors C.F. Keil and F. Delitzsch add that when this retribution comes upon the wicked, it will make God's holiness "manifest in the merited punishment, and thus also making wickedness the means of manifesting His glory."[29] What an awesome and sobering day that will be!

Exodus 4:21. In this verse we are informed that God hardened the Egyptian Pharaoh's heart. More broadly, ten times the text of Scripture states that the Pharaoh hardened *his own* heart (Exodus 7:13,14,22; 8:15,19,32; 9:7,34,35; 13:15), and ten times that God hardened Pharaoh's heart (4:21; 7:3; 9:12; 10:1,20,27; 11:10; 14:4,8, 17). The Pharaoh hardened his own heart seven times before God first hardened it, though the *prediction* that God would do it preceded all.

It would seem, from the whole of Scripture, that God hardens on the same grounds that He shows mercy. If men will *accept* mercy, He will give it to them. It they will not, thus hardening themselves, He is only just and righteous in judging them. *Mercy* is the effect of a right attitude; *hardening* is the effect of stubbornness or a wrong attitude toward God. It is like the clay and the wax in the sun. The same sunshine hardens one and softens the other. The responsibility is with the materials, not with the sun. Scholars have suggested that the danger of resisting God is that He will eventually give us over to our own choices (see Romans 1:24-28).

Romans 9:13. In this verse we read that God hated Esau. Contextually, the word "hate" should not be taken to mean that God had the human emotional sense of disgust, disdain, and a desire for revenge against Esau. God did not have a negative psychological emotion that burned against Esau. Rather the word should be understood as the Hebrew idiom it is—a word that means "to love less" (compare with Genesis 29:30-33).

We gain insights into this meaning of the word in Luke 14:26 where Jesus said: "If anyone comes to me and does not hate his father and mother, his wife and children, his brothers and sisters—yes, even his own life—he cannot be my disciple." This word does not communicate the emotional feeling of hate. Keep in mind that in Jesus' ethic, we do not have the prerogative of hating *anyone.* We are to love even our enemies (Luke 6:27). As well, the fifth commandment instructs us: "Honor your father and your mother" (Exodus 20:12), a commandment repeated in the New Testament (Ephesians 6:1-3; Colossians 3:20). Jesus certainly was not instructing His followers to disobey God's holy law. Rather, the word *hate* clearly communicates the idea, "to love less." In other words, we are to love our parents less than we love Jesus.

Thus we might paraphrase Romans 9:13 this way: "In comparison to my great love for Jacob, my feeling for Esau, whom I 'love less,' may *seem* like hatred." God's sovereign purposes for His people related to Jacob and his descendants alone.

We must conclude that God is not, nor ever has been, involved in committing any evil acts. God's actions have always been in perfect harmony with His holy, righteous, and just nature.

God Does Not Condone Lying

Gordon Clark suggested that God in Old Testament times caused prophets to lie. However, I believe this is a distortion of the biblical picture. Let us not forget that Scripture forbids lying (Exodus 20:16). Lying is a sin (Psalm 59:12) and is an abomination to God (Proverbs 12:22). Numbers 23:19 explicitly tells us that "God is not a man, that he should lie." Clark's view violates the spirit of such passages.

In 2 Chronicles 18:20-21 God does *permit* the activity of a "lying spirit." However, there is a distinction between what God *causes* and what He *allows*. For example, God allowed Adam's sin in the Garden of Eden, but He did not cause it. God allowed Lucifer's rebellion against Him, but He did not cause it. God allowed Ananias and Sapphira to lie to Peter, but He did not cause them to do so. Likewise, God permitted the activity of a lying spirit, but He did not cause it. Therefore, God's character cannot be impugned.

Healing Hearts

If I thought that God deterministically caused all the bad things that happen in my life, I would have an awfully hard time feeling close to Him. The more I think about it, the more I am repulsed by such an idea. I cannot conceive of the pain I would have caused my brother Paul had I told him, "Well, Paul, it must have been God's will that Greg be hit by a high-speed car, thrown 100 feet, and then run over by two more cars. But I think you should trust Him nevertheless." I believe it is more accurate biblically to recognize that while God is completely sovereign, He has also allowed us to make free choices, and a great deal of the evil that falls on us is due to making wrong choices. (More on this later in the book.)

My friend, the next time life throws you a hard punch, please do not succumb to doubting the goodness of God. That will only cause you more pain and suffering. His goodness is truly abundant (Psalm 31:19), and He seeks only your highest good. He loves you and desires to nurture you in all your hurts.

Based on years of experience, my best advice to you is to begin by memorizing some key passages on the goodness of God. My personal favorites are Psalm 34:8; Psalm 100:5; Psalm 106:1; and Nahum 1:7. Open up your Bible and let these verses soothe your soul. As you reflect on God's goodness, offer praise to God for all the good things that are still in your life. I say this because when we suffer, we have a tendency to focus only on the negative things in our lives. By bringing to mind and meditating on the good things that remain in our lives, we can transform our attitudes and place our suffering in proper perspective.

We can also put our suffering in proper perspective by remembering the silver lining: Suffering can help keep the world, and all that is in the world, from becoming too attractive to us. We might speculate that without suffering, people would be perfectly content with this world and would want nothing further. No one would yearn for an eternal home, nor would they feel compelled to make preparations for eternity.

God, I believe, wants us to know that this life is not all there is. Our short years on this planet are preparing us for all eternity. This earth is not our true home. As Christians, we are simply "pilgrims" and "sojourners" passing through (see 1 Peter 2:11 NKJV). We are on our way to another country—a *heavenly* country (see Hebrews 13:14). This is the country that the saints of old yearned for:

> All these people were still living by faith when they died. They did not receive the things promised; they only saw them and welcomed them from a distance. And they admitted that they were aliens and strangers on earth. People who say such things show that they are looking for a country of their own. If they had been thinking of the country they had left, they would have had opportunity to return. Instead, they were longing for a better country—a heavenly one. Therefore God is not ashamed to be called their God, for he has prepared a city for them (Hebrews 11:13-16).

These individuals had an eternal perspective. And whenever they encountered suffering, this eternal perspective pulled them through. We would do well to imitate their forward gaze toward eternity. Joseph Stowell points us in the right direction:

> Eternity is primary. Heaven must become our first and ultimate point of reference. We are built for it, redeemed for it, and on our way to it. Success demands that we see and respond to *now* in the light of *then*. All that we have, are, and accumulate must be seen as resources by which we can influence and impact the world beyond. Even our tragedies are viewed as events that can bring eternal gain.[30]

In maintaining our forward gaze on eternity, we should revel in such Bible passages as Revelation 21:3-5:

> I heard a loud voice from the throne saying, "Now the dwelling of God is with men, and he will live with them. They will be his people, and God himself will be with them and be their God. He will wipe every tear from their eyes. There will be no more death or mourning or crying or pain, for the old order of things has passed away." He who was seated on the throne said, "I am making everything new!" Then he said, "Write this down, for these words are trustworthy and true."

If we go about our lives thinking that this life is all there is, we will surely be easily discouraged. But if our assurance is that a blissful eternal state awaits us, and that what we do on earth counts for eternity, we will find plenty of divine wind gusting into our earthly sails, enabling us to face any rough seas that may be ahead of us. If we know for sure that dying is gain—that the moment we pass from this life we will be with Christ in heaven—then we will not be shaken when things go awry on this transitory earth. We will not succumb to challenging God's goodness. Rather, we will realize that the sufferings of the present are not worthy to be compared with the glory that will be revealed in the heavenly estate (Romans 8:18).

Hermann Lange's life perfectly illustrates what I am talking about. Lange was a young German preacher who stood among the Christians who spoke out against Adolf Hitler's repression of the gospel. Like many others, Lange was arrested, interrogated, tried as a criminal, and condemned to die before a firing squad. Instead of questioning God's goodness, Lange maintained a perpetual

forward gaze on eternity. On the last day of his life, he wrote a
farewell letter to his parents:

> When this letter comes to your hands, I shall no longer
> be among the living. The thing that has occupied our
> thoughts constantly for many months, never leaving them
> free, is now about to happen.
>
> If you ask me what state I am in, I can only answer: I
> am, first, in a joyous mood, and second, filled with great
> anticipation. As regards the first feeling, today means the
> end of all suffering and all earthly sorrow for me—and "God
> will wipe away every tear" from my eyes. What consolation,
> what marvelous strength emanates from faith in Christ, who
> has preceded us in death. In him, I have put my faith, and
> precisely today I have faith in him more firmly than ever...
>
> And as to the second feeling [of anticipation], this day
> brings the greatest hour of my life! Everything that till now
> I have done, struggled for, and accomplished has at bottom
> been directed to this one goal, whose barrier I shall pene-
> trate today. "Eye hath not seen, nor ear heard, neither have
> entered into the heart of man, the things which God hath
> prepared for them that love him" (1 Corinthians 2:9)...
>
> Until we meet again above in the presence of the Father
> of Light, Your joyful Hermann.[31]

DOES EVIL PROVE GOD IS FINITE?

The word "finite" means "having a limit; limited in quantity, degree, or capacity."[1] Some people have considered the problem of evil and concluded that God must be limited in power, that He is finite. They suggest that God may *want* to do away with the problem of evil (that is, He is a good God), but He simply does not have the power to carry out His wishes. The view that God is limited in power is known in theological circles as finite godism.

In this chapter, we will briefly consider three modern manifestations of finite godism: (1) Rabbi Harold Kushner's view that God is good but not all-powerful; (2) the view of process theology, which holds that God is still growing and is not in sovereign control of the universe but rather seeks to "lure" it toward goodness; and (3) the view of open theism, which holds that God is finite in the sense that He does not know the future and therefore does not know whether good will conquer evil. Contrary to these views, I will provide biblical evidence that God is both all-powerful *and* all-knowing, and I will demonstrate why a finite god is unworthy of worship.

The Finite God of Rabbi Kushner

Finite godism was popularized in the early 1980s by Rabbi Kushner, author of the bestselling book *When Bad Things Happen to Good People.* Kushner found himself face-to-face with the problem of evil in the premature death of his son.

> I believed that I was following God's ways and doing his work. How could this be happening to my family? If God existed, if he was minimally fair, let alone loving and for-giving, how could he do this to me? And even if I could per-suade myself that I deserved this punishment for some sin of neglect or pride that I was not aware of, on what grounds did [my son] Aaron have to suffer?[2]

Kushner concluded that God simply cannot control some things. God is good, but He is not powerful enough to bring about all the good things He desires. In short, God is finite.[3] "God wants the righteous to live peaceful, happy lives, but sometimes even He can't bring that about. It is too difficult even for God to keep cru-elty and chaos from claiming their innocent victims."[4]

Kushner suggests that God is limited by the laws of nature and by the reality of human moral freedom.[5] He laments that even God has a hard time "limiting the damage that evil can do."[6] He cites the Holocaust as an example. This was a horrible event, and God surely wanted to stop it, but He simply was not strong enough to stand against it. He didn't even have the power to relieve Job of his afflictions.

The Finite God of Process Theology

Another form of finite godism is process theology. This theological system involves a highly philosophical view of God advocated by such thinkers as Alfred North Whitehead, Charles Hartshorne, and John Cobb. Process theology is not for the faint of heart. This is deep stuff, and one can easily get a headache while contemplating it. Nevertheless, because this has been a highly influential theological viewpoint, it is worth brief consideration.[7] To make things easier for you, I have translated the main (difficult) teachings of process theology into "plain English":

1. All of reality is constantly changing. It is always in a state of *process.*

2. Everything in the universe is related to everything else and influences everything else. Nothing exists in isolation. Nothing is an "island."

3. Reacting against the idea that God is transcendent (above and beyond the universe), advocates of process theology believe God is intimately related to the universe. Indeed, the universe is viewed as God's body. All things are said to occur "within God." God is organically related to the whole of reality. He is interdependent with the world. And, like the rest of the universe, God is characterized by process and change rather than fixity and absoluteness.[8]

4. God is not sovereign over the world. He is not a controlling or coercive being. Rather, He simply seeks to *lure* the world in positive directions. He seeks to persuade the world toward the good and inspire human beings toward their best. He is the dynamic behind evolution.[9]

5. God is not omnipotent (all-powerful). Things take place in creation that He cannot alter. As noted above, He works interdependently with the creation, not by coercing human beings to carry out His wishes but by trying to lure them to actualize the goals He has set for them.[10]

6. Human beings can freely resist God's lure. They can choose not to conform to the divine persuasions that God sets in motion.[11]

As such, the divine activity involves risk.[12] There is no guarantee that God will succeed.

7. Because God is not in absolute control and He only lures and influences people, the problem of evil is easily solved. Process theologian John Cobb comments that "since God is not in complete control of the events of the world, the occurrence of genuine evil is not incompatible with God's beneficence toward all his creatures."[13]

8. God is not omniscient (all-knowing). The future is radically open, for God is not directing us toward a predetermined end. God does not foreknow future contingent events. He knows as much as *can* be known (embracing the past up to the present moment), but His knowledge continues to grow as future unforeseen events unfold. Every moment, new unforeseen events take place that then and only then become known by God.

9. God is in the process of growth and development. He grows as a result of personal relationships and as a result of events that take place on earth. God is moved by the events that transpire on this planet. He can be either enriched or saddened by what He encounters. God, for example, was saddened by the Holocaust, and regretted that Hitler and his Nazi thugs chose to ignore His lure toward the positive.

Certainly there is more to process theology, but this shows that the process God is finite in a number of ways.

The Finite God of Open Theism

A close cousin of process theology is a more recent view known in theological circles as open theism.[14] Like process theology, open theism posits that God does not have exhaustive foreknowledge of the future. The evil things human beings do catch God by surprise just as much as they catch us by surprise. God knows whatever is *possible* to know, which includes all events of the past and the present. But it is *not possible* for God to infallibly know the future free acts of human beings.[15] Open theist John Sanders writes, "Though God's knowledge is coextensive with reality in that God knows all that can be known, the future actions of free creatures are not yet reality, and so there is nothing to be known."[16]

God therefore takes risks because He does not fully know the future.[17] God *can*, however, accurately predict what humans might do, because He knows the character of the people engaging in the acts.[18]

Not surprisingly, open theists argue that God's sovereign control is also limited. Open theist Greg Boyd says that God "chooses to leave some of the future open to possibilities, allowing them to be resolved by the decisions of free agents."[19]

In this viewpoint, then, we must conclude that much of the evil that has emerged in our world was (1) not foreseen by God and (2) was caused by free agents over whom God was not in sovereign control. This would include such events as Hitler's murder of millions of Jews in the Holocaust and the terrorists' flight into the Twin Towers.

Another point worth mentioning in regard to open theism is its view that God is in some sense a temporal being. Because God performs acts in the temporal world (a world where there is time, with "befores" and "afters"), God Himself must be a temporal being who undergoes change.[20] The argument can be summed up this way: "1) God is related to a changing world. 2) Whatever is related to a changing world undergoes change. 3) Therefore, God undergoes change."[21]

Open theists see the Incarnation as a perfect example of the temporality of God. After all, God became a human being in the Incarnation. Because human beings are temporal beings, God became a temporal being in the Incarnation. Therefore, God is subject to time. As events unfold in the world—that is, as time passes—God can be surprised when some horrible event occurs. It is perfectly feasible, in this viewpoint, that God had virtually no idea that Al Qaeda terrorists would fly planes into the Twin Towers on 9–11. This terrorist act took God by surprise every bit as much as it took American citizens by surprise.

There is much more to open theism than what I've summarized. But this summary is enough to demonstrate its concept of a finite God.

How Kushner's View Fails

Traditional historic Christianity has always proclaimed the biblical teaching that God is infinite and that the universe is contingent because it depends upon Him for its very existence. If God Himself is finite, then He Himself is a contingent being who must depend on someone or something greater for His existence.[22] Such a God is not worthy of our worship.

Nor is this finite God worthy of our trust, for we have no guarantee that He will be able to defeat evil in the future. We have no guarantee, for example, that the world will survive the next 20 years. We have no guarantee that terrorists won't take over the entire planet and inflict horror upon it, that a horrible plague like AIDS will not wipe out all humankind, or that Satan and his horde of demons will be restrained from inflicting great (even lethal) harm upon Christians in the future. Bible scholar John Wenham suggests that a finite concept of God "profoundly affects everyday

Christian living, for it means that we cannot turn to him confident of his power to intervene if he wishes to do so; we cannot entrust anything to him."[23]

Kushner's finitism fails to consider that God's timing is not human timing. The fact that God has not defeated evil *today* does not mean He is not eliminating it *in the future* (see 2 Peter 3:7-12; Revelation 21–22). It is shortsighted to conclude that because something evil has happened today, God must be limited in power. God may have reasons for allowing something evil to happen today, reasons that we know nothing about and that God is using to bring about some greater good in the future. I noted earlier in the book that when we get to heaven, we will likely say, "Ahhhh, I get it now," and we will understand why God allowed certain things to happen.

Finitism clearly goes against the biblical testimony of God. Contrary to the impotent God of Rabbi Kushner, Scripture portrays God as being omnipotent—He is all-powerful. He has the power to do all that He desires and wills. Some 56 times, Scripture declares that God is the Almighty (for example, Revelation 19:6).[24] God is abundant in strength (Psalm 147:5) and has incomparably great power (2 Chronicles 20:6; Ephesians 1:19-21). No one can hold back God's hand (Daniel 4:35). No one can reverse God (Isaiah 43:13), and no one can thwart Him (Isaiah 14:27). Nothing is impossible with God (Matthew 19:26; Mark 10:27; Luke 1:37), and nothing is too difficult for Him (Genesis 18:14; Jeremiah 32:17,27). The Almighty reigns (Revelation 19:6), and He will one day overthrow all evil.

Further, contrary to Kushner's view, God is not limited by or subject to the laws of nature. The laws of nature are merely observations of uniformity or constancy in nature—a constancy that God Himself built into the universe. These laws describe the

way nature behaves when its course is not affected by a superior power. But our omnipotent God is not prohibited in the
slightest degree from taking action in the world if He so desires.

Scripture tells us that God is the Sustainer and Governor of
the universe (Acts 14:16-17; 17:24-28). The Bible describes Jesus
as "sustaining all things by his powerful word" (Hebrews 1:3) and
the one in whom "all things hold together" (Colossians 1:17). That
which from a human vantage point is called the "laws of nature"
is in reality nothing more than God's normal cosmos-sustaining
power at work! Bottom line: *God is not limited by the laws of
nature—He controls the laws of nature.*

One further point bears mentioning in regard to Rabbi
Kushner's book, *Why Bad Things Happen to Good People*. R.C.
Sproul was once asked, "Why do bad things happen to good
people?" His response was short and to the point: "I haven't met
any good people yet, so I don't know."[25] Of course, Sproul was not
denying that some people are more virtuous than others, but he
was referring to the very important theological point that every
one of us is fallen in sin, and every one of us suffers the effects
of that fallenness (Isaiah 53:5-6; Romans 3:23; 5:12). We would
do well to keep in mind that sin is a major culprit when it comes
to understanding why bad things happen to people. I will discuss
this further later in the book.

How Process Theology and Open Theism Fail

In what follows, I offer summaries of the ten most significant
criticisms that show the weakness of both process theology and
open theism.

**1. What would happen to the God of process theology if the
world did not exist?** Without a world (a body for God) with which

God could interdependently interact and grow, what would happen to His being? This God seems to be dependent on the creation. As theologian Millard Erickson put it, "dependence on the processes of the world compromises quite seriously the absolute or unqualified dimensions of God. While the Bible does picture God as involved with the world, it also pictures him as antedating the creation and having an independent status."[26] Process theology undermines God's absolute transcendence by making the creation essentially necessary to His being.

One must also wonder how this relates to the second law of thermodynamics. This law says that in an isolated system (a system, like our universe, that neither loses nor gains energy from outside of itself), the natural course of things is to degenerate. The universe is running down, not evolving upward. Scientist Isaac Asimov noted that this law basically means that the universe is getting increasingly disorderly. Clean up a room and it quickly becomes messy again. Clean up a kitchen and watch how fast it becomes disorderly again. "How difficult to maintain houses, and machinery, and our own bodies in perfect working order; how easy to let them deteriorate. In fact, all we have to do is nothing, and everything deteriorates, collapses, breaks down, wears out, all by itself—and that is what the second law is all about."[27] What does this say about the God of process theology? After all, if the world is the "body" of God, and God and the world are interdependent, is God Himself subject to the second law of thermodynamics? Is He too "running down"?

2. God can interact with the world (and with human beings) without changing in His essential nature. Contrary to process theology and open theism, the Bible is clear that God in His essential nature is immutable (unchanging). In Malachi 3:6 God affirms,

"I the LORD do not change." Psalm 102:25-27 says of God, "In the beginning you laid the foundations of the earth, and the heavens are the work of your hands. They will perish, but you remain; they will all wear out like a garment. Like clothing you will change them and they will be discarded. But you remain the same, and your years will never end." James 1:17 speaks of "the Father of the heavenly lights, who does not change like shifting shadows."

Scripture is also clear that God's eternal plans do not change. In Psalm 33:11 we read, "The plans of the LORD stand firm forever, the purposes of his heart through all generations." God affirms, "I make known the end from the beginning, from ancient times, what is still to come. I say: My purpose will stand, and I will do all that I please" (Isaiah 46:10). In Hebrews 6:17 we read of "the unchanging nature of his purpose."

Despite the fact that God is unchanging in His essential nature and His eternal purposes, He nevertheless *can* and *does* engage in changing relationships in the world. Sometimes process theologians and open theists speak of mainstream theists (like myself) as if we do not believe God personally interacts with the world, but they are in error. Indeed, mainstream theists believe that while God never changes in His *attributes*, He is enriched relationally by His *interactions* with the world. Norman Geisler explains it this way:

> God is really unchanging in nature but changing only in activity. For example, God *acts* in wrath when the condition of man's rejection prevails, and He *acts* in mercy when this condition is changed to repentance. But in both cases there is a changeless consistency in His nature as holy-love. The difference in activity does not signal a change in the *attributes* of God. It indicates rather a change in the creatures who are the recipients of God's activity, which activity is wholly in accord with His unchanging nature.[28]

So, while God is unchanging in terms of His absolute deity, He is nonetheless a personal being with whom personal relationships can be established and enjoyed. A person is a conscious being—one who thinks, feels, purposes, and carries these purposes into action. A person engages in active relationships with others. You can talk to a person and get a response from him. You can share feelings and ideas with him. You can argue with him, love him, and even hate him if you so choose. Surely by this definition God must be understood as a person. After all, God is a conscious being who thinks, feels, and purposes—and He carries these purposes into action. He engages in relationships with others. You can talk to God and get a response from Him.

The biblical picture of God is that of a loving personal Father to whom believers may cry, *"Abba"* (Romans 8:15). Abba is an Aramaic term of great intimacy, loosely meaning "daddy." He is also the "Father of compassion" of all believers (2 Corinthians 1:3). He is often portrayed in Scripture as compassionately responding to the personal requests of His people. (A few good examples may be found in Exodus 3:7-8; Job 34:28; Psalm 81:10; 91:14-15; and Philippians 4:6-7.) Yet all the while God's essential nature is unchanging.

3. While God is transcendent, He is also immanent. The theological phrase "transcendence of God" refers to God's otherness or separateness from the created universe and from humanity. The phrase "immanence of God" refers to God's active presence within the creation and in human history (though all the while remaining distinct from the creation). While process theologians and open theists often falsely characterize the historic Christian view of God as being radically transcendent, with little or no true interaction among His creatures, the God of the Bible has always been viewed as both transcendent *and* immanent, high above His creation, but at the same time intimately involved among His creatures.

A plethora of verses in both the Old and New Testaments speak of God's transcendence. For example, in 1 Kings 8:27 Solomon says, "But will God really dwell on earth? The heavens, even the highest heaven, cannot contain you. How much less this temple I have built!" In Psalm 113:5-6 the psalmist asks, "Who is like the LORD our God, the One who sits enthroned on high, who stoops down to look on the heavens and the earth?"

Likewise, many verses in Scripture speak of God's immanence. In Exodus 29:45-46 God states, "I will dwell among the Israelites and be their God. They will know that I am the LORD their God, who brought them out of Egypt so that I might dwell among them." Deuteronomy 4:7 asks, "What other nation is so great as to have their gods near them the way the LORD our God is near us whenever we pray to him?"

Some verses in the Bible teach both God's transcendence *and* immanence. For example, Deuteronomy 4:39 says, "Acknowledge and take to heart this day that the LORD is God in heaven above and on the earth below. There is no other." Isaiah 57:15 affirms, "For this is what the high and lofty One says—he who lives forever, whose name is holy: 'I live in a high and holy place, but also with him who is contrite and lowly in spirit, to revive the spirit of the lowly and to revive the heart of the contrite.'" In Jeremiah 23:23-24 we read, "'Am I only a God nearby,' declares the LORD, 'and not a God far away? Can anyone hide in secret places so that I cannot see him?' declares the LORD."

Clearly, God is above and beyond the creation, yet He is simultaneously active in the midst of the creation. Contrary to process theology and open theism, God is both transcendent and immanent.

4. God is omniscient (all-knowing). God knows all things, both actual and possible (Matthew 11:21-23). He knows all things past (Isaiah 41:22), present (Hebrews 4:13), and future (Isaiah 46:10). And because He knows all things, His knowledge cannot increase or decrease. Psalm 147:5 affirms that God's understanding "has no limit." God's knowledge is infinite (Psalm 33:13-15; 139:11-12; 147:5; Proverbs 15:3; Isaiah 40:14; 46:10; Acts 15:16-18; Hebrews 4:13; 1 John 3:20). Therefore, contrary to process theology and open theism, which argue that God does not know future contingent events until they occur, Scripture is clear that God knows all things simultaneously—past, present, and future.

Numerous scriptural examples show that God knows the freewill decisions human beings will make. One example is John 13:38, where Jesus indicated to Peter that before the cock crowed, Peter would disown Jesus three times. Notice the specificity of Jesus' prediction. He did not say Peter would disown Jesus "a few times," or "many times," or even two times or four times, but specifically *three* times. One must wonder how Jesus can be so specific if God (and therefore Jesus) is unaware of the future freewill actions of human beings. Of course, things unfolded just as Jesus had predicted.

Jesus also knew that Judas would make the freewill decision to betray Him (John 13:18-19). This was not a mere educated guess on Jesus' part. Jesus omnisciently knew what Judas intended to do. The biblical text gives no indication that Jesus was rendering a guess based on Judas's character.

Note that God's foreknowledge of these events does not mean that God *caused* them, as if Peter and Judas had no choice in the matter. As theologian Lewis Sperry Chafer put it,

> If the question be asked whether the moral agent has free-
> dom to act otherwise than as God foresees he will act, it may
> be replied that the human will because of its inherent
> freedom of choice is capable of electing the opposite course
> to that divinely foreknown; but he will not do so. If he did
> so, *that* would be the thing which God foreknew. The divine
> foreknowledge does not *coerce;* it merely *knows* what the
> human choice will be.[29]

Therefore, while God is fully aware of the freewill acts that humans will commit (including all evil acts), God's foreknowledge is not causally related to those events. God is therefore not responsible for the evil acts committed by freewill agents.

5. Because God exhaustively knows the future, His prophecies of the future are accurate and certain. If, as open theists argue, God is unaware of future decisions by freewill agents, then prophecy is uncertain at best. After all, many prophecies set forth in Scripture involve or relate to future decisions by freewill agents. There are many examples of this. For example, Zechariah 11:12 prophesies that Jesus would be betrayed for 30 shekels of silver, which was fulfilled in the person of Judas (Matthew 26:15). But what if Judas chose not to betray Jesus? What if he had a last-minute change of heart? The prophecy would have failed.

There is also the prophecy of Jesus being born in Bethlehem (Micah 5:2; see also Matthew 2:6). What if Joseph, because of Mary's pregnancy, decided not to go to Bethlehem to take part in the required census ordered by Caesar Augustus (Luke 2:1)? The prophecy would have failed, for Jesus would not have been born in Bethlehem.

Contrary to open theism, Scripture is clear that God *exhaustively* foreknows the future, and therefore His prophecies of the future are both accurate and certain. According to the book of Isaiah, God's ability to foretell the future is one of the things that separates Him from all the false gods. God proclaimed:

> Who then is like me? Let him proclaim it.
> Let him declare and lay out before me
> what has happened since I established my ancient people,
> and what is yet to come—
> yes, let him foretell what will come (Isaiah 44:7).

> Do not tremble, do not be afraid.
> Did I not proclaim this and foretell it long ago?
> You are my witnesses. Is there any God besides me?
> No, there is no other Rock; I know not one (Isaiah 44:8).

> Declare what is to be, present it—
> let them take counsel together.
> Who foretold this long ago,
> who declared it from the distant past?
> Was it not I, the LORD?
> And there is no God apart from me,
> a righteous God and a Savior;
> there is none but me (Isaiah 45:21).

> I foretold the former things long ago,
> my mouth announced them and I made them known;
> then suddenly I acted, and they came to pass (Isaiah 48:3).

> Therefore I told you these things long ago;
> before they happened I announced them to you
> so that you could not say, "My idols did them;
> my wooden image and metal god ordained them"
> (Isaiah 48:5).

6. God is eternal, not temporal. Contrary to process theology and open theism, which both argue that God is a temporal being,

Scripture teaches that God transcends time altogether. He is above the space-time universe. As an eternal being, He has always existed. God is the King eternal (1 Timothy 1:17), who alone is immortal (6:16). God is the "Alpha and Omega" (Revelation 1:8) and is the "first and the last" (see Isaiah 44:6; 48:12). God exists "from eternity" (Isaiah 43:13), and "from everlasting to everlasting" (Psalm 90:2). He lives forever from eternal ages past (Psalm 41:13; 102:12,27; Isaiah 57:15).

Because God transcends time—because He is *above* time—He can see the past, present, and future in a single intuitive act. "God's knowledge of all things is from the vantage point of eternity, so that the past, present, and future are all encompassed in one ever-present 'now' to Him."[30] The entire panoramic sweep of all human history—past, present, and future—lies before the all-seeing eye of God.

However, simply because God is *beyond* time does not mean that He cannot act *within* time. "The theistic God can be beyond time and yet act in the temporal world. God's being is eternal, but His creative activity is temporal."[31] From a biblical perspective, God acts within the realm of time but from the realm of eternity. God is eternal, but He does temporal things. God's acts take place within time, but His attributes remain beyond time.[32]

7. God did not become temporal in the Incarnation. The Incarnation is that event in which Jesus—the second person of the Trinity—took on human flesh. The open theist argument that the Incarnation means that God became temporal is based on a complete misunderstanding of what took place at the Incarnation, for indeed, the divine did not ontologically[33] become human. The divine nature did not change into a human nature. Please allow me to get a little theological with you.

To properly understand the Incarnation, we must clarify what is meant by the word *nature*. This word is commonly used to designate the divine or human elements in the person of Christ. In other words, *nature*, when used of Christ's divinity, refers to all that belongs to deity, including all the attributes of deity. *Nature*, when used of Christ's humanity, refers to all that belongs to humanity, including all the attributes of humanity. Another way to describe nature is that it refers to "the sum-total of all the essential qualities of a thing, that which makes it what it is."[34]

Before the Incarnation, Jesus was one person with one nature (a divine nature). In the Incarnation, Jesus was still one person, but now He had two natures—a divine nature and a (distinct) human nature. I must emphasize that though the incarnate Christ had both a human and a divine nature, He was only one person—as indicated by His consistent use of "I," "me," and "mine" in reference to Himself. Jesus never used the words "us," "we," or "ours" in reference to His human-divine person. Nor did the divine nature of Christ ever carry on a verbal conversation with His human nature.

While the attributes of one nature in the incarnate Christ are never attributed to the other, the attributes of both natures are properly attributed to His one person. Thus Christ at the same moment in time had what seem to be contradictory qualities. He was finite and yet infinite, weak and yet omnipotent, increasing in knowledge and yet omniscient, limited to being in one place at one time and yet omnipresent. In the Incarnation, the person of Christ is the partaker of the attributes of both natures, so that whatever may be affirmed of either nature—human or divine—may be affirmed of the one person.

How could two different natures—one infinite and one finite—exist within one person? Or, as Robert Gromacki asks,

"Would not one nature be dominated by the other? Would not each nature have to surrender some of its qualities in order for each to coexist beside each other? Could Jesus Christ be truly God and truly man at the same time?"[35]

The early church did not understand how such incompatible natures could be joined in one person without one or the other losing some of its essential characteristics. The discussion that resulted from this confusion, however, led to the orthodox statement that the two natures are united without mixture and without loss of any essential attributes, and that the two natures maintain their separate identities without transfer of any property or attribute of one nature to the other.[36] As theologian Robert Lightner put it,

> In the union of the human and divine in Christ each of the natures retained its own attributes. Deity did not permeate humanity, nor did humanity become absorbed into deity. The two natures retain their complete identity even though they have been joined together in a personal union. Christ is thus *theanthropic* (God-man) in person. Embracing perfect humanity made him no less God, and retaining his undiminished deity did not make him less human.[37]

Jesus' human and divine natures did not mix to form a third compound nature. The human nature always remained human, and the divine nature always remained divine. "To rob the divine nature of God of a single attribute would destroy His deity, and to rob man of a single human attribute would result in destruction of a true humanity. It is for this reason that the two natures of Christ cannot lose or transfer a single attribute."[38]

All of this leads up to my point that the Incarnation does not constitute proof that God became temporal in the Incarnation, as open theists argue. God's nature did not change at all in the

Incarnation. Rather, Jesus as eternal God took on an additional nature (a human nature) that remained forever distinct from His divine nature.

8. God is absolutely sovereign over His creation. Earlier in the book I noted that God is sovereign in the sense that He rules the universe, controls all things, and is Lord over all (see Ephesians 1). Nothing can happen in this universe that is beyond the reach of His control. All forms of existence are within the scope of His absolute dominion (Psalm 50:1; Psalm 66:7; Psalm 93:1; Isaiah 40:15; 1 Timothy 6:15).

This is a far cry from the God of process theology, who seeks only to inspire people toward goodness. The God of the Bible is in sovereign control over the world, whereas the God of process theology merely works in cooperation with the world. The biblical God is independent of the world, whereas the God of process theology is interdependent with the world.[39] There's a world of difference between the two!

9. Because God is sovereign, His promises are trustworthy. If the open theism view is true—if God limits His sovereign control and is not aware of our future decisions—then we can't put much stock in the many promises of God found in the Bible. Contrary to this view, it is precisely because God is absolutely sovereign and exhaustively knows the future that we can trust in His promises. Numbers 23:19 asserts, "God is not a man, that he should lie, nor a son of man, that he should change his mind. Does he speak and then not act? Does he promise and not fulfill?" Prior to his death, an aged Joshua declared, "Now I am about to go the way of all the earth. You know with all your heart and soul that not one of all the good promises the LORD your God gave you has failed. Every promise has been fulfilled; not one has failed" (Joshua

23:14). Solomon later proclaimed: "Praise be to the LORD, who has given rest to his people Israel just as he promised. Not one word has failed of all the good promises he gave through his servant Moses" (1 Kings 8:56; see Joshua 21:45).

10. **Process theology offers no guarantee of a better world.** I've alluded to this earlier, but it bears repeating. In process theology, God is neither totally sovereign nor all-knowing, so we have no guarantee that God will succeed in luring the world toward goodness. In open theism, God does not know the future for sure and rarely intervenes against the choices of free agents, so we have no guarantee of ultimate victory over evil. If I believed in process theology or open theism, I'd be worried right now because our world seems to be sinking deeper and deeper into sin and rebellion against God.

Healing Hearts

How could one conceivably want to turn to the God of process theology and open theism when things go wrong in life? Let's face it. Such a God is unworthy of our worship and unworthy of our trust. He is impotent in the face of catastrophe. We can expect no real help from Him in times of trouble. A God who is not totally sovereign over the affairs of men can hardly cause all things to work together for good to those who love Him (Romans 8:28).

The good news is that the God of the Bible is nothing like the God of process theology or open theism. The God of the Bible is all-powerful, all-knowing, and sovereign over the affairs of humanity. The God of the Bible definitely can cause all things to work together for good for those who love God (Romans 8:28).

My former associate Walter Martin used to say, "I've read the last chapter in the Bible, and we win!" The point he was making is that our sovereign and almighty God *will* bring about an end to evil and establish His perfect kingdom forever. You can count on it. Don't let any doubt creep into your mind. In the end, God will have caused all things to work for good for all believers, and believers will enjoy an eternity with Him, never again to be interrupted by pain or suffering.

Meanwhile, during your short time on earth, I suggest that you keep certain biblical truths in mind:

- While God is transcendent, He is also immanent—right there with you. He's at your side every moment of every day (see Jeremiah 23:23-24).

- God is omniscient (all-knowing) and is therefore aware of all of your hurts. Nothing escapes His notice (see Psalm 33:13-15; 139:11-12; 147:5).

- God is omnipotent (all-powerful) and is therefore able to bring you deliverance in His perfect timing (Psalm 147:5; Matthew 19:26).

- God is sovereign, and nothing can happen in this universe that is beyond the reach of His control (Psalm 93:1; 1 Timothy 6:15). Therefore, no circumstance can touch you unless God sovereignly allows it in order to bring about some greater good.

- Because God is sovereign, you can trust in His promises (Numbers 23:19; Joshua 23:14). I believe this so much that I've written a book you might find helpful entitled *The Complete Book of Bible Promises*, published by Harvest House Publishers. (It's available at your local Christian bookstore.)

WHY DOESN'T GOD ABOLISH EVIL IMMEDIATELY?

When atheists, agnostics, and skeptics talk about the problem of evil, they often say that if there really is a God, He ought to be about the business of abolishing evil. He ought to get rid of it now—in fact, He ought to have already gotten rid of it. Annie Besant (1847–1933) is representative of this viewpoint:

> A railway accident happens, in which a useful man, the main-stay of a family, is killed, and from which a profligate [a shameless person of lesser virtue] escapes. An explosion in a mine slays the hardworking breadwinners at their toil, and the drunken idler—whose night's debauchery has resulted in heavy morning sleep—is "providentially" saved as he snores lazily at home in bed. The man whose life is invaluable to a nation perishes in his prime, while the selfish aristocrat lives on to a green old age. The honest conscientious trader keeps with difficulty out of the bankruptcy court, and sees his smart, unscrupulous neighbor pile up a fortune by tricks that just escape the meshes of the law.[1]

Besant's point is that if there really were a God, He would be involved in the affairs of earth. He would be involved *in the now,* making sure that bad things do not happen to good people. At the same time, He would make sure that evil people experienced pain and suffering. The fact that good people suffer and evil people prosper, she reasons, undermines belief in the God of Christianity.

A Shortsighted View

Besant's argument is typical among unbelievers, but it is unfounded. To begin, only a false dichotomy divides human beings into two camps: "good people" who should be exempt from evil, and "bad people" who should have their fill of evil. The biblical reality is that *all* human beings are "bad" in the sense of being fallen. To be sure, some are more righteous and virtuous than others, but all are deeply infected by sin—so deeply infected that none of us can do anything to commend ourselves to God.

Human sin always shows up clearly in the presence of God's holiness. In the light of His holiness, the "dirt" of sin shows up crystal clear. Remember what happened to the prophet Isaiah? He was a relatively righteous man. But when he beheld God in His infinite holiness, Isaiah's own personal sin came into clear focus, and he could only say, "Woe to me!...I am ruined! For I am a man of unclean lips, and I live among a people of unclean lips" (Isaiah 6:5).

When we measure ourselves against other human beings, we may come out looking okay. In fact, to measure ourselves against other human beings might lead us to believe that we are fairly righteous and deserve to have good things happen to us. But other human beings are not our moral standard. God is. And as we measure ourselves against God in His infinite holiness and righteousness, our sin shows up in all of its ugliness, and we begin to doubt whether we deserve anything good at all.

Billy Graham once told a story that well illustrates how human sin shows up best in the light of God's holiness. Consider his words:

Several years ago I was to be interviewed at my home for a well-known television show and, knowing that it would appear on nationwide television, my wife took great pains to see that everything looked nice. She had vacuumed and dusted and tidied up the whole house and had gone over the living room with a fine-tooth comb since that was where the interview would be filmed.

When the film crew arrived with all the lights and cameras, she felt that everything in that living room was spic and span. We were in place along with the interviewer when suddenly the television lights were turned on and we saw cobwebs and dust where we had never seen them before. In the words of my wife: "That room was festooned with dust and cobwebs which simply did not show up under ordinary light."

The point is, of course, that no matter how well we clean up our lives and think we have them all in order, when we see ourselves in the light of God's Word, in the light of God's holiness, all the cobwebs and all the dust do show up.[2]

Romans 3:23 is quite clear that "all have sinned and fall short of the glory of God." The words *fall short* translate a single present tense word in the Greek. The present tense indicates continuing action. Human beings *perpetually* fall short of God's glory. The word *glory* here refers not just to God's splendor but to the outward manifestation of His attributes, including His righteousness, justice, and holiness. Human beings fall short of God in these and other areas.

Paul later explains that "sin entered the world through one man, and death through sin, and in this way death came to all men, because all sinned" (Romans 5:12). Even when we think we're not sinning, we are just deceiving ourselves. Jeremiah 17:9 affirms that "the heart is deceitful above all things and beyond cure. Who can understand it?" In the eyes of God, even man's "righteous" deeds are as filthy garments (Isaiah 64:6). Understandably, 1 John 1:8 asserts: "If we claim to be without sin, we deceive ourselves and the truth is not in us." Sin is a universal condition.

Sin was universal even among the biblical saints. Noah got drunk (Genesis 9:21). Abraham lied about his wife (Genesis 20:2). Peter denied the Lord three times (Luke 22:61). And the great apostle Paul lamented, "What a wretched man I am! Who will rescue me from this body of death?" (Romans 7:24). Obviously, dividing human beings into two camps—the good and the bad— is an idea that has no scriptural support.

In view of the fact that we're all sinners and that we've all been contaminated by evil, one would be wise to rethink the idea that God should simply get rid of all evil immediately. We would all die. As Christian apologist Paul Little put it,

> If God were to stamp out evil today, he would do a complete job. His action would have to include our lies and personal impurities, our lack of love, and our failure to do good. Suppose God were to decree that at midnight tonight all evil would be removed from the universe—who of us would still be here after midnight?[3]

Would I still be here? Not a chance. Would my wife and children still be here? I don't think so, even though their commitment to God is matched by few. Would Billy Graham still be here? I'm sure he'd tell you not to hold your breath. Would Chuck Swindoll still be here? I'm sure he'd just laugh and shake his head. *Reality check: None of us would be here!*

Let us be clear on this: Creating a universe in which God brings about instant and total justice has the definite downside of yielding a people-less universe. Absent the cross,[4] you and I and everyone else would be absolute goners. *Show over!* God would be the only one left![5] After all, each of us has committed *some* evil, whether by commission or by omission, by word, deed, or thought.[6] In the interest of self-preservation, I'm glad God *doesn't* wipe out all evil immediately!

But What If…

What if God dealt with evil, not by instantly snuffing all human beings out of existence but by simply stopping them from sinning the moment before they were about to commit the act? Would such a scenario be possible?

This would mean that God, just in the nick of time, would stop the car of the drunken driver so that it would not crash into the bus full of schoolchildren. Even before that, God would have prevented the man from making the decision to get drunk in the first place. Even before that, God might have distracted the man away from visiting the liquor store so that he would not even be tempted to imbibe later on.

Likewise, God would, just in the nick of time, deflect the bullets of the would-be murderer so that the woman under attack survived unscathed. Even before that, God would have providentially worked so that the man would never even have thought to buy a gun. Still further, one might argue that God would work in his heart to deal with any underlying hostilities that might make him want to shoot someone in the first place.

Likewise, just before the abusive husband is about to verbally lash his wife, God numbs his mouth, throat, and tongue so he can't say a word (at least until he calms down). God removes His restraint only when the man is in a saner state of mind. One might also argue that God would have worked providentially in the man's life so that he had a healthy upbringing by a loving mother and father who set good examples in interpersonal relationships. On and on it goes.

Can you see where I am going with this? Such a scenario would ultimately mean that human beings would no longer be free to make choices, and their personal responsibility would evaporate since God would be thwarting all evil before it erupts. The world would be even more unpredictable because we'd never know when God was about to step in out of the blue and intervene in the affairs of humanity. Such a world would be chaos.[7]

God Is Not Finished Yet

Scripture is clear that God is not finished yet. It is simply wrong to conclude that God is not dealing with the problem of evil because He has not once-for-all dealt with it in the present moment. God's definitive dealing with evil is yet future (I will address judgment, heaven, and hell later in the book). Christian philosopher Peter Kreeft suggests that "since the solution is future, it is *not yet*. We are in a story, and only the end of the story explains the rest of it, just as only the conclusion of an argument explains why the premises are selected as they are."[8] When we read a good novel, we often do not understand everything that's taken place in the story until the very end of the book. That's when our perspective on the story becomes complete. That's when we say, "Oh, I get it now!" Likewise, one day in the future, we will come to the last chapter in the human story, and all will become clear. Kreeft explains:

> On this day, the mystery of suffering and the deeper and more original mysteries of sin and death will be solved, not just in theory but in practice; not just explained but removed. God will tie up the loose ends of the torn tapestry of history, and the story which now seems to be a tortured tangle will appear as a masterpiece of wisdom and beauty.[9]

Robert Morey, in like manner, suggests that God is dealing with the problem of evil in a progressive way that will not be complete until the future Day of Judgment. Speaking to an atheist, Morey argues:

> You assume that God can solve the problem only in one single act. But why can't He deal with evil in a progressive way? Why does He have to deal with it all at once? Can't He deal with it throughout time as we know it and then bring it to climax on the Day of Judgment? You are assuming that the only way for God to deal with evil is in one single act. This is an erroneous assumption on your part. I am not saying that evil no longer exists. I am saying that God has solved the problem but in a long-term way, in stages.[10]

All this, of course, calls for the need for faith now. As long as the believer is at home in the body and away from the Lord (2 Corinthians 5:8), he must live in this fallen, sinful, temporal world by faith and not by sight (5:7). Focusing only on what is seen leads to a distorted understanding of human pain and suffering. Such a perspective is reminiscent of human existence "under the sun" as described by Solomon in Ecclesiastes, resulting in meaninglessness and despair (see Ecclesiastes 1:2,14; 2:1,11,15,17,19,21, 23,26; 3:19; 4:4,7). Only by focusing on the unseen realities of the spiritual realm and future glory are we able to keep pain and suffering in proper perspective.

Meanwhile, God Puts Boundaries on Evil

Even though God's ultimate solution to the problem of evil awaits the future, God has even now taken steps to ensure that evil does not run utterly amok. Consider:

- ✍ God has given us human government to withstand law-lessness (Romans 13:1-7).

- ✍ God founded the church to be a light in the midst of the darkness, to strengthen God's people, and to help restrain the growth of wickedness in the world through the power of the Holy Spirit (see, for example, 1 Timothy 3:15; Acts 16:5).

- ✍ God has given us the family unit to bring stability to society (see, for example, Proverbs 22:15; 23:13).

- ✍ God has in His Word given us a moral standard to guide us and keep us on the right path (Psalm 119).[11]

- ✍ God has promised a future day of accounting in which all human beings will face the divine Judge (Hebrews 9:27). For Christians, this future day serves as a deterrent to committing evil acts.

Healing Hearts

This might be a good time for all of us to meditate for a few moments on the wonderful patience of God. After all, if it weren't for God's great patience, none of us would be here. All of us would have already been judged and executed. Not only does God *not* judge us instantly, He patiently and mercifully gives us the opportunity to receive the free gift of salvation so that we can live with Him forever in heaven.

God's patience is obvious in many passages of Scripture. Meditating on such verses is helpful, for they not only help us see why God doesn't judge all evil instantly in our world, but they also help us to be thankful when God doesn't judge *our own* evil instantly. Here are some of my favorites:

- ✐ The LORD is slow to anger and great in power (Nahum 1:3a).

- ✐ Return to the LORD your God, for he is gracious and compassionate, slow to anger and abounding in love, and he relents from sending calamity (Joel 2:13).

- ✐ You, O Lord, are a compassionate and gracious God, slow to anger, abounding in love and faithfulness (Psalm 86:15).

- ✐ The LORD, the LORD, the compassionate and gracious God, slow to anger, abounding in love and faithfulness (Exodus 34:6).

- ✐ The LORD is slow to anger, abounding in love and forgiving sin and rebellion (Numbers 14:18a).

- ✐ For my own name's sake I delay my wrath; for the sake of my praise I hold it back from you, so as not to cut you off (Isaiah 48:9).

- ✐ The Lord is not slow in keeping his promise, as some understand slowness. He is patient with you, not wanting anyone to perish, but everyone to come to repentance (2 Peter 3:9).

5

THE PROBLEM
WITH FREE WILL

The original creation was "very good" (Genesis 1:31). It was without sin, evil, pain, and death. The Edenic paradise was perfect! Yet today, the world is permeated with sin, evil, pain, and death. As Cornelius Plantinga put it, "the whole range of human miseries, from restlessness and estrangement through shame and guilt to the agonies of daytime television—all of them tell us that things in human life are not as they ought to be."[1] What brought about the change?

Scripture indicates the turn downward came for humanity when Adam and Eve used their God-given free wills to choose to disobey God. Prior to man's misuse of free will, Lucifer and a number of other angels had already misused their free wills to rebel against God (Isaiah 14:12-15; Ezekiel 28:11-19; Revelation 12:4). Lucifer then tempted Eve in the Garden of Eden (Genesis 3:1-7). The first human couple chose wrongly, and humans have been suffering ever since, continuing to misuse their free wills.

Human free will can wreak havoc in many ways. For example, George's free choice to smoke cigarettes can bring about the evil of lung cancer into his life. George's free choice can also bring evil upon others. For example, the secondhand smoke of the cigarettes can harm the health of George's wife and children. As well, George smoking in bed in the middle of the night might end up killing everyone in the house if he falls asleep and the cigarette ignites the bed. This, in turn, might cause the flames to jump from his house to a neighbor's house and kill all of its occupants. The smoke from these fires might then cause the person down the street with severe asthma to choke up and have to be rushed to the hospital for a breathing treatment. See what a mess George's free will caused? And George is just one man. The free wills of humans worldwide accumulate to form a *major* reason why bad things happen to people.

One theologian compares our decisions and actions to ripples in a pond. Every action we take causes a ripple. The decisions and actions of other people also cause ripples in that pond. Those ripples run into each other, affecting each other in various ways. (In other words, our actions affect the actions of other people, like the asthmatic person being rushed to the hospital due to the fire caused by George's cigarette.) Ripples of the past—say, from our parents—often affect the ripples we make in the present. (For example, my father's choice to move to Texas in the 1970s eventually influenced my decision to attend Dallas Theological Seminary.) As well, angelic beings—both holy and evil (demons)—can cause ripples. (Lucifer's "ripple" in tempting Eve has affected all of us because we're all now fallen in sin.)

The problem is that most of us will never know more than an infinitesimally small fraction of the decisions and actions various people (and angels) have made that have caused the ripples that affect our lives. Because of our massive ignorance, we are often unsure why certain things happen to us. (The mailman had no idea that the dog that bit him had just suffered abuse by a young boy who slammed a door on its tail. Of course, the dog was completely unaware that the boy's mother had just previously yelled at him for forgetting to take out the garbage, and the boy, angry and hurt, slammed the door to vent his anger, not intending to target the dog's tail. Mother doesn't normally yell at her boy for such minor infractions, but just previous to all this, she received an angry phone call from her husband, who had just been fired by his boss, the same boss that had just been yelled at by the board of directors.) Things can seem completely arbitrary when all the while we are simply unaware of their causes. "We are the heirs to an incomprehensibly vast array of human, angelic, and natural ripples throughout history about which we know next to nothing but which nevertheless significantly affect our lives."[2] People often ask, Why did this particular bad thing have to happen to that good person? Much evil is a result of someone's (or a bunch of people's) wrong use of free will!

Even natural evils—earthquakes, tornados, floods, and the like—are rooted in our wrong use of free choice. We must not forget that we are living in a fallen world, and because of that, we are subject to disasters in the world of nature that would not have occurred had man not rebelled against God in the beginning (Romans 8:20-22).[3] Sid Litke comments that natural disasters are

> part of a sinful world. God lowered the perfection of creation (from the perfect Garden of Eden) to match the spiritual state of those who live here (Romans 8:20-22). God graciously has sustained people on this earth (allowing them to reproduce, to develop governments and systems to deal with the effects of sin). He has graciously sustained the fallen creation (providing sun and rain for food to sustain life—Colossians 1:17). But the natural effect of a fallen creation is that even good things can have evil byproducts (water can drown someone; gravity can kill someone; lightning can burn and kill).[4]

The Garden of Eden had no natural disasters or death until after the sin of Adam and Eve (see Genesis 1–3). The good news is that God will put an end to natural disasters, death, and all evil when He creates the new heavens and a new earth (see Revelation 21:4).[5]

Why Did God Create Humans with the Capacity for Evil?

Some people wonder why God couldn't have created humans in such a way that they would never sin, thus avoiding evil altogether. But a scenario in which people never had the possibility of sinning would necessitate that those people be no longer truly human. They would not have the capacity to make choices and to freely love. This scenario would require that God create robots who act only in programmed ways—like one of those chatty dolls with a string on its back that says, "I love you."[6] Apologist Paul Little notes that with such a doll,

> there would never be any hot words, never any conflict, never anything said or done that would make you sad! But who would want that? There would never be any love, either. Love is voluntary. God could have made us like robots, but we would have ceased to be men. God apparently thought it worth the risk of creating us as we are.[7]

In a similar vein, Christian philosopher Peter Kreeft observes that love is the highest value in the universe, and in a world of robots, such love would be entirely missing. "Real love—our love of God and our love of each other—must involve a choice. But with the granting of that choice comes the possibility that people would choose instead to hate."[8]

Love cannot be programmed; it must be freely expressed. Unless human beings can freely choose *not to* love, they can't freely choose *to* love. The possibility of the one necessitates the possibility of the other. Love simply cannot be programmed into people in a coercive way.[9]

God wanted Adam and Eve and all humanity to show love by *freely* choosing obedience. That is why God gave human beings a free will. My friend Norman Geisler is correct in saying that "forced love is rape; and God is not a divine rapist. He will not do *anything* to coerce their decision."[10] Yet, a free choice, as noted above, always leaves the possibility of a wrong choice. As J.B. Phillips once put it, "Evil is inherent in the risky gift of free will."[11]

God Cannot Do Certain Things

Consider that God simply cannot do certain things.[12] For example, God cannot make square circles. Nor can He make round squares. It is impossible for God to lie because such an act would violate His holy nature. And it is impossible for God to eliminate all evil without eliminating free choice. Because free choice is necessary to the existence of a moral universe—a universe that includes the free expression of love—God cannot eliminate evil without also eliminating this good moral universe.[13]

The only way God could guarantee that His free creatures would never choose wrongly would be to tamper with their freedom in some way. I noted in a previous chapter that every time someone was about to commit a crime, He could supernaturally distract that person away from the crime just in the nick of time so that no evil results. But if this were the case, God would be in the business of full-time distraction, setting forth virtually billions of distractions per hour all over the world to prevent evil from happening.

Such a scenario does not involve true freedom. Further, God's distraction of humans about to commit evil does not take care of the evil in the human heart that prompts the evil act. So in reality, the distraction has not prevented evil; it has only stopped the outward manifestation of evil that was already inwardly present in the human heart.

It comes down to this: God either gives free will to humans or He does not. If He gives them freedom, then they must maintain the capacity to actually *use* that freedom, rightly or wrongly. Judy Salisbury is right when she says:

> He cannot give human beings free choice sometimes and not other times. He cannot create beings as free moral agents, then snap His fingers and make them robots whenever they stray from His will. God cannot create beings with free choice and then force them to make right choices. If that were the case, they would not be free moral agents who have the responsibility and capacity to choose to bless or curse Him.[14]

God Is Not Responsible for Man's Wrong Choices

I strongly doubt anyone would say that God's bestowal of freedom on humans is a bad thing. Can you imagine people picketing in the street with signs that say, "Down with Freedom, Back to Bondage"?[15] God's gift of freedom to the human race is a wonderful gift, but as I've said, it is a gift that carries risks. The fact that God has given us the gift of free will does not mean that God is responsible for how we *use* that free will.

God's plan had the potential for evil from the very beginning when He bestowed upon humans the freedom of choice. But the actual origin of evil came as a result of a man who directed his will away from God and toward his own selfish desires.[16] "Whereas God created the *fact* of freedom, humans perform the *acts* of freedom. God made evil *possible;* creatures make it *actual.*"[17] Ever since Adam and Eve made evil actual on that first occasion in the Garden of Eden, a sin nature has been passed on to every man and woman (Romans 5:12; 1 Corinthians 15:22), and it is out of the sin nature that we today continue to use our free wills to make evil actual (Mark 7:20-23). God is not responsible for the evil humans commit.

Theologians Gordon R. Lewis and Bruce A. Demarest give us an illustration in the person of Henry Ford: "Henry Ford is the final cause of all Ford cars, for there would not be any if he had not invented them to provide transportation. But Henry Ford, who could well have envisioned misuses of his automobiles, apparently felt it wiser, in a kind of benefit-evil analysis, to invent them than not."[18] However, when a person who has had one too many drinks gets in his car and ends up in a head-on collision that kills innocent people, Henry Ford does not thereby become guilty of a crime. By analogy, we cannot blame the evil in the world on God simply because God gave humans a free will, for it was the creatures' wrong use of free will that has caused such evil. Lewis and Demarest conclude:

> Although God has not told us specifically why he chose to create, we suggest that in infinite wisdom, taking into account all the data of omniscient foreknowledge in a kind of foreseen benefits-evils analysis, he concluded that it was better to create than not to create. Analogously, although some married couples may hesitate to bring children into a fallen world

with all the known risks or evils, most do have children. Apparently they conclude that the evils are far outweighed by the inestimable value of enduring loving relationships with children (and possibly grandchildren) throughout their lives.[19]

It Will Be Worth It in the End

The fact that humans used their God-given free choice to disobey God did not take God by surprise. God, in His omniscience, knew it would happen. In His wisdom, God knew that in the end, the temporary allowance of evil in the world would be worth it. As C.S. Lewis put it, God in His omniscience "saw that from a world of free creatures, even though they fell, he could work out...a deeper happiness and a fuller splendor than any world of automata [robots] would admit."[20]

As things are now, our present world is not the best of all possible worlds. However, in accordance with God's sovereign plan, it is the best way *to* the best possible world:

> If God is to both preserve freedom *and* defeat evil, then this is the best way to do it. Freedom is preserved in that each person makes his own free choice to determine his destiny. Evil is overcome in that, once those who reject God are separated from the others, the decisions of all are made permanent. Those who choose God will be confirmed in it, and sin will cease. Those who reject God are in eternal quarantine and cannot upset the perfect world that has come about. The ultimate goal of a perfect world with free creatures will have been achieved, but the way to get there requires that those who abuse their freedom be cast out.[21]

One day, God *will* completely overthrow all evil. And on that glorious day, no one will doubt that the existence of evil in the world of free creatures is compatible with the existence of an all-good and all-powerful God. Moreover, those who enter eternity without having used their free wills to trust in Christ for salvation will understand just how effectively God has dealt with the problem of evil.

Healing Hearts

My friends, since a great deal of suffering in our world is rooted in a wrong use of free will, wisdom dictates that we make every effort to use our free wills wisely. The way to do this is to line up our free wills, as much as possible, with what God has revealed in the Bible.

When I teach, I often use metaphors to demonstrate to students how critically important the Bible is in our lives.

The Bible is like a *manufacturer's handbook* that instructs us how to operate our lives. Our lives will "break" if we live in violation of the Creator's instructions. But if we follow the instructions, we will operate with optimal efficiency.

The Bible is also like an *eyeglass*. Without the eyeglass, we do not see clearly. We see only a blurred reality. But with the eyeglass, all comes into clear focus. If you want to see your way clearly through life, allow God's Word to sharpen your focus.

Further, the Bible is like a *lamp*. It sheds light on our path and helps us to see our way clearly. Psalm 119:105 says, "Your word is a lamp to my feet and a light for my path." Do you want an enlightened free will? Expose it daily to the Word of God!

The Bible is also like an *anchor*. Just as an anchor keeps a boat from floating away, so the Bible is an anchor for our lives. It prevents us from being swept away when a tidal wave of adversity surges into our lives.

Finally, the Bible is like *food*. It gives us spiritual nourishment. If we don't feed on God's Word, we become spiritually malnourished. The way to maintain spiritual health is to drink richly from God's Word.

The point is that living our lives according to the Bible is in our own best interest. It is especially important that we govern our free wills according to the wisdom that is in God's Word. One particular book in the Bible is especially helpful in this regard—the book of Proverbs.

The book of Proverbs is a "wisdom book" and contains maxims of moral wisdom. These maxims were engineered to help the young in ancient Israel acquire mental skills that promote wise living (including wise freewill choices).

The majority of the proverbs were written by Solomon, the wisest man who ever lived (1 Kings 3; 4:29-34). Solomon spoke some 3000 proverbs during his life. His wisdom was unparalleled.

In Solomon's thinking, wise living was essentially synonymous with godly living, for one who is godly or righteous in his daily behavior is wise in God's eyes. By contrast, a wicked or unrighteous person is foolish. Indeed, Solomon often equates the "path of wisdom" with the "path of righteousness," and the "path of folly" with the "path of wickedness" (see Proverbs 2–4; 6:1-19).

Linguists tell us that the main Hebrew word for *wisdom* in the Old Testament is *hokmah*. It was used commonly for the skill of craftsmen, sailors, singers, administrators, and counselors. *Hokmah* pointed to the experience and efficiency of these various workers in using their skills in their respective fields of expertise. Similarly, a person who possesses *hokmah* in his spiritual life and relationship to God is one who is both knowledgeable and experienced in following God's way. Biblical wisdom involves skill in the art of godly living. This wisdom, which makes for skilled living, is broad in its scope, teaching students how to be successful at home, at work, and in human relationships, regarding money, regarding death and the afterlife, and much more. In the book of Proverbs, the reader learns how to think and act wisely in all of these areas.

The word *proverb* literally means "to be like," or "to be compared with." A proverb, then, is a form of communicating truth by using comparisons or figures of speech. The proverbs, in a memorable way, crystallize and condense Solomon's experiences and observations about life. The reward of "chewing on" these maxims is wisdom, including the ability to make wise freewill choices.

Here, then, is what I suggest. The book of Proverbs has 31 chapters. If you go through one chapter a day, you can be done in a month. That means that in just one month, you can learn from Solomon about the best way (the wisest way) to use your free will in your family relationships, your friendships, your attitude toward money, your sexual purity, and much more. I can tell you from personal experience that taking this exercise seriously will pay rich dividends in your life.

Please allow me to whet your appetite. Following is some of Solomon's wisdom on some key issues in life. Take a few moments to look up some of these verses, and you'll quickly see how relevant they are to making wise choices in the future.

Your relationship with God—
Proverbs 2:7-8; 3:5-6; 10:3,22,27; 14:26,31; 16:2,7; 17:3,5; 19:23; 20:27; 22:2; 28:25; 29:25.

How you should respond to people who treat you wrongly—
Proverbs 20:22; 24:17-18; 25:21-22.

Your family—
Proverbs 10:5; 13:24; 14:26; 18:22; 19:14,18; 20:7; 22:6,15; 23:13,14; 27:15-16; 28:7; 30:17; 31:10-31.

Your friends—
Proverbs 3:27-28; 11:13; 12:26; 17:9,14,17; 18:24; 19:11; 20:3; 22:11; 25:17; 27:9,10.

People to avoid—
Proverbs 15:18; 16:28; 18:1; 20:19; 22:24-25; 23:6-8; 25:19-20; 26:18-19,21.

Your sexual purity—
Proverbs 5:3,7-14; 6:25-26,30-35; 7:6-27.

Your need for humility—
Proverbs 3:7; 16:18; 18:12; 22:4; 25:27; 26:12; 27:2.

Your work—
Proverbs 6:6-9; 10:26; 15:19; 20:4; 21:25; 22:13; 24:30-34; 26:16.

Your speech—
Proverbs 10:19; 12:25; 16:24; 17:9,27; 18:8,13; 24:26; 25:11; 28:23; 29:5; 31:8-9.

Your money—
Proverbs 8:18,21; 10:4,22; 11:1,4,24-25; 13:11; 14:23,31; 19:17; 20:13,17; 21:5,17; 22:7,9,26-27; 23:21; 28:19,22,25,27.

Take it from me: *Live wisely, and you'll save yourself a lot of grief!*

6

SATAN
AND SUFFERING

Remember the ripples? In the previous chapter I noted that one theologian compares our choices and actions to ripples in a pond. All our choices and actions cause ripples. The decisions and actions of other people and of angelic beings (both holy and evil) also cause ripples in that pond. Those ripples run into each other, affecting each other in various ways, whether for good or bad.

Satan and the demonic spirits who follow his perverted lead are relentless in sending one ripple after another toward us, each one strategically engineered to wreak as much havoc in our lives as possible. There can be no doubt that from a scriptural perspective, Satan and the powers of darkness are responsible for a great deal of the suffering that takes place on planet earth. This is in keeping with what I've said earlier in the book. Some suffering comes upon us as a result of *our own* misuse of free will. In other cases we can suffer as a result of *other beings* misusing their free wills—whether human beings or demonic beings. In what follows I will narrow our attention to Satan and demons, and I will point the spotlight on some of the specific ways they generate suffering.

Satan's Misuse of Free Will

Satan, though possessing creaturely limitations, is nevertheless pictured in Scripture as being extremely powerful and influential in the world. He is the "prince of this world" (John 12:31), "the god of this age" (2 Corinthians 4:4), and the "ruler of the kingdom of the air" (Ephesians 2:2). He deceives the whole world (Revelation 12:9; 20:3). He has power in the governmental realm (Matthew 4:8-9; 2 Corinthians 4:4), the physical realm (Luke 13:11,16; Acts 10:38), the angelic realm (Jude 9; Ephesians 6:11-12), and the ecclesiastical (church) realm (Revelation 2:9; 3:9). Clearly, Christians should be very concerned about Satan. He can cause much suffering!

Many scholars believe Ezekiel 28 and Isaiah 14 show that Lucifer, once an important angel, wrongly used his free will by rebelling against God, and his name was changed to Satan. The being described in Ezekiel 28 is portrayed as having been full of wisdom and perfect in beauty, and having the seal of perfection (verse 12). He is also described as having the nature of a cherub (which is an angel, verse 14), as being initially blameless and sinless (verse 15), as being on the Holy Mount of God (verses 13-14), and as being cast out of the mountain of God and thrown to the earth (verse 16). Since such things cannot be said of a mere human being, many believe this is a reference to Lucifer.

One theologian has suggested that Lucifer

> awoke in the first moment of his existence in the full-orbed beauty and power of his exalted position; surrounded by all the magnificence which God gave him. He saw himself as above all the hosts in power, wisdom, and beauty. Only at the throne of God itself did he see more than he himself possessed...Before his fall he may be said to have occupied the role of prime minister for God, ruling possibly over the universe but certainly over this world.[1]

Our text tells us that Lucifer was created in a state of perfection (Ezekiel 28:12,15), and he remained perfect in his ways until iniquity was found in him (verse 15b). What was this iniquity? We read in verse 17, "Your heart became proud on account of your beauty, and you corrupted your wisdom because of your splendor." Lucifer apparently became so impressed with his own beauty, intelligence, power, and position that he began to desire for himself the honor and glory that belonged to God alone. The sin that corrupted Lucifer was self-generated pride. This seems to be confirmed in Isaiah 14:12-17, which describes the five boastful "I wills..." of Lucifer:

"I will ascend to heaven" (Isaiah 14:13). Apparently Lucifer wanted to abide in heaven and desired equal recognition alongside God Himself.

"I will raise my throne above the stars of God" (Isaiah 14:13). The "stars" likely have reference to the angels of God. Lucifer apparently desired to rule over the angelic realm with the same authority as God.

"I will sit enthroned on the mount of assembly, on the utmost heights of the sacred mountain" (Isaiah 14:13). Scripture elsewhere indicates that the "mount of assembly" is a reference to the center of God's kingdom rule (see Isaiah 2:2; Psalm 48:2). The phrase is sometimes associated with the Messiah's future earthly rule in Jerusalem during the millennial kingdom. So we may say that Satan desired to rule over human beings in place of the Messiah.[2]

"I will ascend above the tops of the clouds" (Isaiah 14:14). Clouds often metaphorically represent the glory of God in the Bible (Exodus 13:21; 40:28-34; Job 37:15-16; Matthew 26:64; Revelation 14:14). Apparently Lucifer sought a glory equal to that of God Himself.

"I will make myself like the Most High" (Isaiah 14:14). Scripture describes God as being the possessor of heaven and earth (Genesis

14:18-19). Apparently Lucifer sought the supreme position of the universe for himself. "Satan wanted to be as powerful as God. He wanted to exercise the authority and control in this world that rightfully belongs only to God. His sin was a direct challenge to the power and authority of God."[3]

God rightfully judged this mighty angelic being: "I threw you to the earth" (Ezekiel 28:17). As a result of this heinous sin, Lucifer was banished from living in heaven (Isaiah 14:12). He became corrupt, and his name changed from Lucifer ("morning star") to Satan ("adversary"). His power became completely perverted (Isaiah 14:12,16-17).

Lucifer's rebellion represents the actual beginning of sin in the universe—preceding the fall of Adam and Eve. Sin originated when Lucifer freely chose to rebel against the Creator—with full understanding of the issues involved.

Apparently, one-third of the angels freely chose to follow Lucifer in his rebellion. Many scholars believe the first five verses of Revelation 12 contain a mini-history of Satan. Revelation 12:4 seems to refer to the fall of the angels who followed Satan: "His [Satan's] tail swept a third of the stars out of the sky and flung them to the earth."[4] The word *stars* is sometimes used of angels in the Bible (see Job 38:7). If *stars* refers to angels in Revelation 12:4, it would appear that after Lucifer rebelled against God, he was able to draw a third of the angelic realm after him in this rebellion. When he sinned, he did not sin alone but apparently led a massive angelic revolt against God.

The demons are highly committed to their dark prince, Satan. Indeed, as Merrill Unger puts it,

> these spirits, having [made] an irrevocable choice to follow Satan, instead of remaining loyal to their Creator, have

become irretrievably confirmed in wickedness, and irreparably abandoned to delusion. Hence, they are in full sympathy with their prince, and render him willing service in their varied ranks and positions of service in his highly organized kingdom of evil.[5]

Demons are portrayed in Scripture as being evil and wicked. They are designated "unclean spirits" (Matthew 10:1, rendition from the Greek), "evil spirits" (Luke 7:21), and "spiritual forces of evil" (Ephesians 6:12). All these terms point to the immoral nature of demons. It is not surprising, then, that many people involved in the occult are involved in immorality.[6]

Satan's Names

The names used of Satan throughout Scripture show us the damage he can do. Following is a sampling of these names:

Satan is called the *accuser of the brethren* (Revelation 12:10). The Greek of this verse indicates that accusing God's people is a continuous, ongoing work of Satan. He never lets up. This verse indicates that Satan accuses God's people "day and night." Thomas Ice and Robert Dean note that Satan opposes God's people in two ways. "First, he brings charges against believers before God (Zechariah 3:1; Romans 8:33). Second, he accuses believers to their own conscience."[7] Some of the emotional guilt believers suffer is rooted in the work of Satan.

Satan is called our *adversary* (1 Peter 5:8 NASB). This word indicates that Satan opposes us and stands against us in every way he can.

Satan is called *Beelzebub* (Matthew 12:24). This word literally means "lord of the flies," carrying the idea of "lord of filth." The devil corrupts everything he touches. No doubt he is behind the filth of pornography, which tempts not only unbelievers but believers as well. Bondage to pornography is a hideous form of suffering.

Satan is called the *devil* (Matthew 4:1). This word carries the idea of "adversary" as well as "slanderer." The devil was and is the adversary of Christ; he is the adversary of all who follow Christ. Satan slanders God to man (Genesis 3:1-7), and man to God (Job 1:9; 2:4). (A slanderer is a person who utters maliciously false reports that injure the reputation of another.[8])

Satan is called our *enemy* (Matthew 13:39). This word comes from a root meaning "hatred." It characterizes Satan's attitude— he hates both God and His children.

Satan is called the *evil one* (1 John 5:19). He is "the opposer of all that is good and the promoter of all that is evil."[9] Indeed, he is the very embodiment of evil.

Satan is called the *father of lies* (John 8:44). The word *father* is used here metaphorically of the originator of a family or company of persons animated by a deceitful character. Satan was the first and greatest liar. His lies no doubt encompass the world of the cults and false religions, which have caused immeasurable suffering among multitudes of people.

Satan is called a *murderer* (John 8:44). This word literally means "man killer" (compare with 1 John 3:12,15). Hatred is the motive that leads one to commit murder. Satan hates both God and His children, so he has a genuine motive for murder. The late Ray Stedman notes that

> because he is a liar and a murderer, the Devil's work is to deceive and to destroy. There you have the explanation for

all that has been going on in human history throughout the whole course of the record of man...Whom the Devil cannot deceive, he tries to destroy, and whom he cannot destroy, he attempts to deceive.[10]

Satan is called the *god of this age* (2 Corinthians 4:4). Of course, this does not mean that Satan is deity. It simply means that this is an evil age, and Satan is its "god" in the sense that he is the head of it. As well, Satan is in "back of the false cults and systems that have cursed the true church through the ages."[11]

Satan is called the *prince of this world* (John 12:31; 14:30; 16:11). The key word here is *world*. This word refers not to the physical earth but to "a vast order or system that Satan has promoted which conforms to his ideals, aims, and methods."[12]

Satan is called a *roaring lion* (1 Peter 5:8-9). This graphic simile depicts Satan's strength and destructiveness. He seeks to mutilate Christians.

Satan is called the *tempter* (Matthew 4:3). Theologian Henry Thiessen says "this name indicates his constant purpose and endeavor to incite man to sin. He presents the most plausible excuses and suggests the most striking advantages for sinning."[13]

Satan is called a *serpent* (Genesis 3:1; Revelation 12:9). This word symbolizes the origin of sin in the Garden of Eden, as well as the hatefulness and deadly effect of sin. The serpent is characterized by treachery, deceitfulness, venom, and murder.

From this brief survey of names, we can see that Satan's purpose is to thwart the plan of God in every area and by every means possible. Toward this end, Satan promotes a world system of which he is the head and that stands in opposition to God and His rule in this universe. In the process, he causes vast and immeasurable suffering among human beings, especially Christians.

Satan as the "Ape" of God

It was Augustine who called the devil *Simius Dei*—"the ape of God." Satan is the great counterfeiter.[14] He mimics God in many ways. "The principal tactic Satan uses to attack God and His program in general is to offer a counterfeit kingdom and program."[15] This is hinted at in 2 Corinthians 11:14, which makes reference to Satan masquerading as an "angel of light."

In what ways does Satan act as "the ape of God"? Consider the following:

- Satan has his own *church*—the "synagogue of Satan" (Revelation 2:9).

- Satan has his own *ministers*—ministers of darkness that bring false sermons (2 Corinthians 11:4-5).

- Satan has formulated his own *system of theology* called "doctrines of demons" (1 Timothy 4:1 NASB; Revelation 2:24).

- His ministers proclaim his *gospel*—"a gospel other than the one we preached to you" (Galatians 1:8).

- Satan has his own *throne* (Revelation 13:2) and his own *worshippers* (13:4).

- Satan inspires *false Christs* and *self-constituted messiahs* (Matthew 24:4-5).

- Satan employs *false teachers* who bring in "destructive heresies" (2 Peter 2:1).

- Satan sends out *false prophets* (Matthew 24:11).

- Satan sponsors *false apostles* who imitate the true apostles of Christ (2 Corinthians 11:13).

In view of such mimicking, one theologian has concluded that "Satan's plan and purposes have been, are, and always will be to seek to establish a rival rule to God's kingdom. He is promoting a system of which he is the head and which stands in opposition to God and His rule in the universe."[16]

Later in the book I will show that one source of suffering among human beings is false beliefs, particularly those related to the kingdom of the cults. Satan is busy promoting doctrines of demons and false gospels through his false teachers and false prophets, and his work as an "ape of God" has caused incalculable suffering among human beings.

Fallen Angels Among Unbelievers

Second Corinthians 4:4 indicates that Satan blinds the minds of unbelievers to the truth of the gospel. This passage indicates that Satan inhibits the unbeliever's ability to think or reason properly in regard to spiritual matters.[17] One of the ways Satan seems to do this is by leading people to think that any way to heaven is as acceptable as another. In other words, Satan promotes the idea that one does not need to believe in Jesus Christ as the only means to salvation.

Satan also seeks to snatch the Word of God from the hearts of unbelievers when they hear it (Luke 8:12). Demons, under Satan's lead, seek to disseminate false doctrine (1 Timothy 4:1). As well, they wield influence over false prophets (1 John 4:1-4) and seek to turn men to the worship of idols (see Leviticus 17:7; Deuteronomy 32:17; Psalm 106:36-38). In short, fallen angels do all they can to spread spiritual deception.

Scripture also portrays demons as inflicting physical diseases on people (such as dumbness, Matthew 9:33; blindness, 12:22; and epilepsy, 17:15-18). Further, they afflict people with mental disorders (Mark 5:4-5; 9:22; Luke 8:27-29; 9:37-42), cause people to be self-destructive (Mark 5:5; Luke 9:42), and are even responsible for the deaths of some people (Revelation 9:14-19).

Of course, we must be careful to note that even though demons can cause physical illnesses, Scripture distinguishes natural illnesses from demon-caused illnesses (Matthew 4:24; Mark 1:32; Luke 7:21; 9:1; Acts 5:16). Theologian Millard J. Erickson notes that in the case of numerous healings no mention is made of demons. "In Matthew, for example, no mention is made of demon exorcism in the case of the healing of the centurion's servant (8:5-13), the woman with the hemorrhage of twelve years' duration (9:19-20), the two blind men (9:27-30), the man with the withered hand (12:9-14), and those who touched the fringe of Jesus' garment (14:35-36)."[18]

Fallen Angels Among Believers

Fallen angels are also very active causing suffering among believers in various ways.

- ✿ Satan tempts believers to sin (Ephesians 2:1-3; 1 Thessalonians 3:5).
- ✿ Satan tempts believers to lie (Acts 5:3).
- ✿ Satan tempts believers to commit sexually immoral acts (1 Corinthians 7:5).
- ✿ Satan accuses and slanders believers (Revelation 12:10).
- ✿ Satan hinders the work of believers in any way he can (1 Thessalonians 2:18).

- Satan and demons seek to wage war against and defeat believers (Ephesians 6:11-12).
- Satan sows tares among believers (Matthew 13:38-39).
- Satan incites persecutions against believers (Revelation 2:10).
- Demons hinder answers to the prayers of believers (Daniel 10:12-20).
- Satan opposes Christians with the ferociousness of a hungry lion (1 Peter 5:8).
- Satan plants doubt in the minds of believers (Genesis 3:1-5).
- Satan fosters spiritual pride in the hearts of Christians (1 Timothy 3:6).
- Satan leads believers away from "sincere and pure devotion to Christ" (2 Corinthians 11:3).
- Demons instigate jealousy and faction among believers (James 3:13-16).
- Demons would separate the believer from Christ if they could (Romans 8:38).
- Demons work with Satan against believers (Matthew 25:41; Ephesians 6:12; Revelation 12:7-12).

Satan's Domain: The World

I read a story about a flock of wild geese that was flying south for the winter. As they were en route, one of the geese looked down and noticed a group of domestic geese by a pond on a farm. He saw that they had plenty of grain to eat, so he went down to join them. The food was so good, he decided to stay with the domestic geese until spring, when his own flock would fly north again.

When spring came, he heard his old flock going by and flew up to join them. The goose had grown fat, however, and flying was difficult. So he decided to spend one more season on the farm and join the wild geese on their next winter migration.

The following fall, when his former flock flew southward, the goose flapped his wings a little, but kept eating his grain. And by the time they passed overhead yet again, the now-domesticated goose didn't even notice them.[19] This illustrates what can happen to the Christian in the world. The Christian can slowly become so comfortable in the world system that he or she loses sight— even loses interest—in his or her true calling and life as a Christian.

The word *world*, when used in Scripture, often refers not to the physical planet (earth) but to an anti-God system headed by Satan. Indeed, 1 John 5:19 tells us that "the whole world is under the control of the evil one [Satan]." Before we were Christians, you and I followed the ways of the world without hesitation (Ephesians 2:2). But when we became Christians, we obtained another master—Jesus Christ—who calls us to be separate from the world. Scripture portrays the world as a seducer. It perpetually seeks to divert our attention and devotion away from God (Romans 12:2; 1 John 2:15-17). It seeks to eclipse our view of heavenly things. It can subtly trap us and lead us astray. For this reason the New Testament instructs us not to love the world or anything in the world (1 John 2:15-16).

Numerous things in the world appeal to our sin nature. If we give in to these things, our attention is drawn away from God, and we can be led into suffering. Embracing the world and its ways will inevitably drive our affections away from God. There is no neutral ground.

Among the things of the world that may entice us away from God are money, material possessions, fame, a career, entertainment, pleasure, and many other things. None of these items are necessarily wrong or evil in themselves. But used wrongly, they have the potential to shift our attention away from Christ as our first priority. Any of these items can effectively sidetrack us into the web of worldliness. When an insect is stuck in a spider web, the spider can easily move in for the kill. The world system is like a web that would entrap us. This web allows Satan to move in and harm us.

Satan's Ally: Man's Flesh

Another subtle enemy of the Christian that can contribute to great suffering is the flesh. The Bible uses the term *flesh* to describe that force within each of us that is in total rebellion against God. This sin nature was not a part of man when God originally created him. Rather, it entered Adam and Eve the moment they disobeyed God. Since the time of Adam and Eve, all human beings have been born into the world with a fleshly nature or sin nature that rebels against God.

Manifestations of the flesh include hatred, discord, jealousy, fits of rage, selfish ambition, dissensions, factions, envy, drunkenness, and the like (Galatians 5:20-21). These kinds of things greatly hinder our relationship with God.

It is critical to understand that when you and I become Christians, the flesh or sin nature in us is not done away with. It stays with us until we die and go to heaven (or until the Rapture, whichever comes first). Until that day, the flesh is ever-present. As J. Dwight Pentecost notes, "We all live in an unredeemed body in the midst of an unredeemed creation, with an unredeemed nature within us. We have an enemy without who constantly oppresses us, and an enemy within that is ever present with us."[20] That's a recipe for suffering if I ever heard one!

Lessons from Job

Perhaps the most potent example of undeserved pain and suffering is Job, a truly upright and godly man (Job 1:1). One minute, everything was fine in Job's life; the next, he had lost nearly everything—his family, his wealth, and his health (1:6–2:10). Consider two key insights from the first two chapters of Job that relate to our present study.

First, Job had no idea that his life was a spiritual battleground between God and Satan. He was blind to the fact that his suffering was caused by an insidious assault by the powers of darkness, an assault purposefully allowed by God. Let us not forget that Job did not have the book named after him, which gives us a behind-the-scenes glimpse of the spiritual warfare that caused his afflictions. Warren Wiersbe observes:

> It seemed that all of the calamities in [Job's] life had perfectly natural explanations: the Sabeans took the oxen and donkeys; fire from heaven (perhaps lightning) burned the sheep; the Chaldeans took the camels; and a great wind (a tornado?) wrecked his oldest son's house and killed all of Job's children. But Satan was behind all of them![21]

What we learn from this is that certain sufferings that may appear to have natural explanations may be caused by a satanic or demonic attack. The problem is, of course, that we are limited in our perspective and rarely know whether spiritual warfare is going on behind the scenes or not. Our best policy is therefore to trust in God and depend on Him in every situation. You see, our painful circumstances may or may not be related to a demonic attack. But God always knows why things happen, and He always has a good purpose for allowing whatever circumstances come our way. So, maintain your trust in God whether you're aware of any spiritual warfare or not.

The second insight is that Satan cannot freely do whatever he wishes to do. Satan is on a leash. God has set borders around him beyond which he is not free to go (see Job 1:12; 2:6). If those borders did not exist, you and I would surely be dead right now because Satan hates both God and His children, and he would delight in murdering us (see John 8:44).

In view of these protective borders, you don't need to spend a lot of time worrying about being attacked by demons. Rather, focus your attention on the God who loves you, for He is the One who always is and forever will be in control of all things in the universe.

Healing Hearts

Christians should be very thankful that God has made provisions for our defense against Satan and his fallen angels. This means we can limit the amount of suffering they can cause in our lives. In this "Healing Hearts" section, I want to provide eight scriptural insights about our defense.

1. *Each believer must be informed and thereby alert to the attacks of Satan* (1 Peter 5:8). To defeat an enemy, we must know as much as possible about the enemy—including his tactics. The apostle Paul says, "We are not unaware of his schemes" (2 Corinthians 2:11). We find all the information we need about this enemy and his schemes in the Word of God.

2. *We are to take a decisive stand against Satan.* James 4:7 says, "Resist the devil, and he will flee from you." This is not a one-time resistance. Rather, on a day-to-day basis we must steadfastly resist the devil. And when we do, he will flee from us. Ephesians 6:14 likewise tells us to "stand firm" against the devil. This we do, not in our own strength but in the strength of Christ. After all, it was Christ who "disarmed the powers and authorities...[and] made a public spectacle of them, triumphing over them by the cross" (Colossians 2:15).

3. *Realize that the power of the flesh to operate in the life of the Christian has been effectively neutralized by our unity with Christ's death to sin.* The flesh has no right to reign in the Christian's life any longer, and its power is broken in our lives when by faith we count this as true (Romans 6:1-14).

The story is told of Handley Page, a pioneer in aviation, who once landed in an isolated area during his travels. Unknown to him, a rat got onboard the plane there. On the next leg of his flight, Page heard the sickening sound of gnawing. Suspecting it was a rodent, his heart began to pound as he visualized the serious damage that could be done to the fragile mechanisms that controlled his plane. Such damage would be extremely difficult (and expensive) to repair. What could he do? He remembered hearing that a rat cannot survive at high altitudes, so he pulled back on the stick. The airplane climbed higher and higher until Page himself found it difficult to breathe. He listened intently and finally sighed with relief. The gnawing had stopped. And when he arrived at his destination, he found the rat lying dead behind the cockpit![22]

Often we, as God's children, are plagued by sin that gnaws at our lives simply because we are living at too low a spiritual level. To defeat sin, we must move up and away from the world to a higher level where the things of this world cannot survive. In other words, by faith we need to count on our spiritual union with Christ to break the power of sin in our lives. Jesus gives us the victory. Keep your eyes on Him!

Closely related to this, we need to walk in the power of the Holy Spirit (Galatians 5:16). To walk in the Spirit means to have a continuing attitude of dependence upon the Spirit and not on our own human resources. As we walk in dependence upon the Spirit, the power of the flesh is rendered inoperative. But if we walk in our own strength, the flesh will surely gain the upper hand. Let us never fall into the folly of thinking that just because we have become Christians, and we've enjoyed a few spiritual "highs" with the Lord, we are immune to the sins of the flesh. Nothing could be further from the truth. The fact is, a true Christian can and does experience fleshly sins. Therefore, walking in the spirit is a *must*. Walking in the flesh, by contrast, makes one easy prey for Satan.

4. *God has provided powerful spiritual armor for our defense* (Ephesians 6:11-18). Each piece of armor is important and serves its own special purpose. But you and I must choose to put on this armor. God doesn't force us to dress in it. Read Paul's description of this armor:

> Put on the *full armor of God* so that you can take your stand against the devil's schemes. For our struggle is not against flesh and blood, but against the rulers, against the authorities, against the powers of this dark world and against the spiritual forces of evil in the heavenly realms. Therefore put on the *full armor of God,* so that when the day of evil comes, you may be able to stand your ground, and after you have done everything, to stand. Stand firm then, with the *belt of*

> *truth* buckled around your waist, with the *breastplate of righteousness* in place, and with your feet fitted with the readiness that comes from the *gospel of peace.* In addition to all this, take up the *shield of faith,* with which you can extinguish all the flaming arrows of the evil one. Take the *helmet of salvation* and the *sword of the Spirit,* which is the word of God. And pray in the Spirit on all occasions with all kinds of prayers and requests. With this in mind, be alert and always keep on praying for all the saints (Ephesians 6:11-18, emphasis added).

Without wearing this spiritual armor, you and I don't stand a chance against the forces of darkness. But with this armor on, victory is ours. Wearing this armor is not a complicated thing. It means that our lives will be characterized by such things as righteousness, obedience to the will of God, faith in God, and an effective use of the Word of God. These are the things that spell defeat for the devil in your life. These are the things that help immunize you against his germs.[23]

5. *Effective use of the Word of God is especially important for spiritual victory.* Jesus used the Word of God to defeat the devil during His wilderness temptations (Matthew 4). We must learn to do the same. Ray Stedman urges:

> Obviously, the greater exposure there is to Scripture the more the Spirit can use this mighty sword in our lives. If you never read or study your Bible, you are terribly exposed to defeat and despair. You have no defense; you have nothing to put up against these forces that are at work. Therefore, learn to read your Bible regularly.[24]

6. *We must not give place to the devil by letting sunset pass with us having unrighteous anger in our hearts toward someone*

(Ephesians 4:26-27). An excess of wrath in our heart gives the devil opportunity to work in our lives.

7. *We should pray for ourselves and for each other.* Jesus set an example for us in the Lord's Prayer by teaching us to pray, "Deliver us from the evil one" (Matthew 6:13). This should be a daily prayer. Jesus also set an example of how to pray for others in His prayer for Peter: "Simon, Simon, Satan has asked to sift you as wheat. But I have prayed for you, Simon, that your faith may not fail" (Luke 22:31-32). We should pray for each other that we will maintain a strong faith in the face of adversity.

8. *Finally, the believer should never dabble in the occult.* Occultic activities (including such things as reading horoscopes, playing with Ouija boards, and playing with Tarot cards) give the devil opportunity to work in our lives (Deuteronomy 18:10-11; see also Romans 16:19). Don't do it!

By following disciplines such as these, we will have victory over Satan and his host of demons, who seek to bring us down. And the more victory we have, the less suffering we will experience from these malevolent spirits.

DIVINE DISCIPLINE
AND SUFFERING

Anyone who studies Scripture for long cannot get away from the fact that some of the suffering Christians experience on earth is a result of divine discipline. Of course, punishment and discipline are very different things. Punishment involves retribution for wrongdoing. It involves paying the penalty for what one has done. Scripture emphatically teaches that Jesus paid the price for our sin on the cross. Jesus took our punishment upon Himself (2 Corinthians 5:21). If God punished Jesus for our sins and then punished us as well, He would be exacting a double payment. This is something God would never do. God does not punish His children for their sins. Rather, He disciplines them, and the motive for this discipline is not anger but love. If we can keep this fundamental fact in mind, it will give us an entirely different attitude regarding our experiences.[1]

The twelfth chapter of Hebrews instructs us that God disciplines those whom He loves. In verses 7 through 11 we read this:

> Endure hardship as discipline; God is treating you as sons. For what son is not disciplined by his father? If you are not disciplined (and everyone undergoes discipline), then you are illegitimate children and not true sons. Moreover, we have all had human fathers who disciplined us and we respected them for it. How much more should we submit

to the Father of our spirits and live! Our fathers disciplined
us for a little while as they thought best; but God disciplines
us for our good, that we may share in his holiness. No discipline seems pleasant at the time, but painful. Later on,
however, it produces a harvest of righteousness and peace
for those who have been trained by it.

This tells us that when God disciplines His children, He does
not act out of anger or revenge but out of immeasurable love and
concern. God loves us far too much to allow us to remain in unrepentant sin. Because He cares for us, He chastens us. As Warren
Wiersbe put it, "Chastening is not the work of an angry judge as
He punishes a criminal. It is the work of a loving Father as He
perfects a child."[2]

Are we not much the same way with our own children? If I
saw my son engaging in a sinful lifestyle that was damaging to him,
the most *un*loving thing I could do would be to leave him alone
and allow him to continue on that path of destruction. The most
loving thing I could do would be to confront him with his sin. If
he resisted, then I would have no choice but to discipline him. All
the while, my motive would be heartfelt love, not vengeance. I only
want what is best for my son. Likewise, God wants only what is
best for us, and for that reason He disciplines us as His own children. His desire is to take some things away (sin, for example) so
that He can replace it with something better (holiness). Like a gar-
dener prunes a vine so that it will be more fruitful, so the Father
prunes His children to make them more fruitful (John 15:2). God
works in the life of each believer in such a way as to "cut out" all
that is bad so that he or she will bear more spiritual fruit.

Here is a basic principle to keep in mind: To minimize divine
discipline, minimize unrepentant sin. To avoid some of the pain
of discipline, we need to take the initiative to judge our own sin.

After all, Scripture teaches that if we would judge ourselves, we would not be judged (1 Corinthians 11:31).

This is not to say, of course, that the righteous are never disciplined by God. They most certainly are. God is constantly molding *all* His children into the image of Christ. God may accordingly discipline a believer who is not necessarily engaged in conscious disobedience but who still has an area in his life that falls short of God's ideal. Or God may discipline a believer to shake loose his or her earthly perspective so He can replace it with a heavenly (eternal) perspective.

Martyn Lloyd-Jones once suggested that "God's great concern for us primarily is not our happiness but our holiness. In His great love to us He is determined to bring us to that, and He employs many differing means to that end."[3] God knows precisely what kinds of circumstances to allow into our lives to discipline us. And the result of God's discipline in our lives is that we share in His holiness. In other words, we start to take on the family likeness.

A Reflection on God's Character?

I want to emphasize God's motive of love when He allows painful circumstances to come our way for the purpose of discipline. Some people have questioned God's character for allowing suffering into our lives. They act as if God is somehow evil if He permits us to encounter pain. One theologian asks, "Must one believe that God is cruel, compassionless, impotent, or nonexistent in order to deal with the reality of evil in the world?"[4] The answer, of course, is no.

God's allowance of suffering is perfectly compatible with His love and does not cast God in a bad light. C.S. Lewis once commented that he would very much like to live in a universe governed

by God where "a good time was had by all." But since it is clear
that a good time is not had by all, and since Lewis nevertheless
believes that God is love, Lewis concludes that "my conception of
love needs correction."[5]

Returning to the parent-child metaphor, a son might conclude
that his father is unloving for disciplining him. But exactly the
opposite is true. The father disciplines his son precisely because
he loves him. It is the same with God. Our concept of God's love
must grow if we are to recognize that His love is behind all His
interactions with us.

Case Study 1: The Israelites in Exile

As a means of disciplining His rebellious children, God in 597
B.C. allowed Israel to go into exile in hostile Babylon, ruled by
Nebuchadnezzar. Jerusalem and the temple were obliterated (Lamentations 1:1-7). Then, after God accomplished His sovereign purpose, He delivered Israel from this exile.

The backdrop to all this is that in the book of Deuteronomy,
God through Moses promised great blessings if the nation lived
in obedience to the covenant God made with them. God also
warned that if the nation disobeyed His commands, it would experience disciplinary action—including exile from the land (Deuteronomy 28:15-68).

Israel consistently broke God's law, and in the first chapter of
Isaiah, we find the nation in court. The Lord indicts Judah (through
Isaiah) for "breach of contract" in breaking the Sinai Covenant,
which God gave the Israelites at the time of the Exodus from Egypt.
In this courtroom scene, the Lord calls upon heaven and earth to
act as witnesses to the accusations He levels against the nation

(Isaiah 1:2). The whole universe bears witness that God's judgments are just.

The Lord indicted Judah for rebelling against Him. The Hebrew word for "rebel" in Isaiah 1:2 was often used among the ancients in reference to a subordinate state's violation of treaty with a sovereign nation. In Isaiah 1, the word points to Judah's blatant violation of God's covenant. Therefore, Israel went into captivity.

In this case, the Babylonian captivity was God's means of chastening Judah. This discipline, of course, was intended as a corrective. Throughout both the Old and New Testaments, we find that God disciplines His children to purify them. Just as an earthly father disciplines his children, so God the Father disciplines His children to train and educate them (Hebrews 12:1-5). God loved the Israelites far too much to remain passive when they strayed from their commitment to Him. A lack of action on God's part would have been an indication that He did not love His children.

We learn some very interesting insights about God's love in Psalm 107, which was written right after Israel's return from the Babylonian exile. Indeed, God's love is said to endure forever in Psalm 107:1-3, despite the fact that He had purposefully allowed Israel to go into captivity in Babylon:

> Give thanks to the LORD, for he is good;
>   his love endures forever.
> Let the redeemed of the LORD say this—
>   those he redeemed from the hand of the foe,
> those he gathered from the lands,
>   from east and west, from north and south.

The psalm shows this loving God responding to the cries of His people. Indeed, verse 6 informs us that the Israelites cried out to God once they went into exile, much like young children cry when their parents discipline them. God then responded to their tears with great compassion, according to verses 6-9:

> They cried out to the LORD in their trouble,
>   and he delivered them from their distress.
> He led them by a straight way
>   to a city where they could settle.
> Let them give thanks to the LORD for his unfailing love
>   and his wonderful deeds for men,
> for he satisfies the thirsty
>   and fills the hungry with good things.

After an appropriate time of suffering under His disciplining hand, God delivered His people and fully restored them. Even in the midst of their discipline, God intended all the while to restore them. Let me repeat again that God *never* disciplines to get even with His children. God allows suffering to restore His people. God wants them rehabilitated, rejuvenated, and reinvigorated. God's love and His discipline are perfectly compatible.

Case Study 2: David's Hard Lesson

David was a man after God's own heart (Acts 13:22), but in middle age he fell deeply into sin and *remained* in sin for almost a full year. God had no choice but to discipline him, and then David, in desperation, finally confessed his sin to God and repented.

Here is the way it happened:

> In the spring, at the time when kings go off to war, David sent Joab out with the king's men and the whole Israelite army. They destroyed the Ammonites and besieged Rabbah. But David remained in Jerusalem.

> One evening David got up from his bed and walked around on the roof of the palace. From the roof he saw a woman bathing. The woman was very beautiful, and David sent someone to find out about her. The man said, "Isn't this Bathsheba, the daughter of Eliam and the wife of Uriah the Hittite?" Then David sent messengers to get her. She came to him, and he slept with her. (She had purified herself from her uncleanness.) Then she went back home. The woman conceived and sent word to David, saying, "I am pregnant" (2 Samuel 11:1-5).

How easily and how quickly a great man can fall. And what pain is caused when great men fail to repent! David could have saved himself a lot of trouble and pain by repenting and confessing his sin immediately to God. He still would have had consequences to deal with, but at least he could have gotten on the healing path immediately instead of waiting almost a year.

Second Samuel 11:6-17 indicates that David compounded his problem, digging his hole ever deeper—and causing himself more pain.

> So David sent this word to Joab: "Send me Uriah the Hittite." And Joab sent him to David. When Uriah came to him, David asked him how Joab was, how the soldiers were and how the war was going. Then David said to Uriah, "Go down to your house and wash your feet." So Uriah left the palace, and a gift from the king was sent after him. But Uriah slept at the entrance to the palace with all his master's servants and did not go down to his house.
>
> When David was told, "Uriah did not go home," he asked him, "Haven't you just come from a distance? Why didn't you go home?"
>
> Uriah said to David, "The ark and Israel and Judah are staying in tents, and my master Joab and my lord's men are camped in

the open fields. How could I go to my house to eat and drink and lie with my wife? As surely as you live, I will not do such a thing!"

Then David said to him, "Stay here one more day, and tomorrow I will send you back." So Uriah remained in Jerusalem that day and the next. At David's invitation, he ate and drank with him, and David made him drunk. But in the evening Uriah went out to sleep on his mat among his master's servants; he did not go home.

In the morning David wrote a letter to Joab and sent it with Uriah. In it he wrote, "Put Uriah in the front line where the fighting is fiercest. Then withdraw from him so he will be struck down and die."

So while Joab had the city under siege, he put Uriah at a place where he knew the strongest defenders were. When the men of the city came out and fought against Joab, some of the men in David's army fell; moreover, Uriah the Hittite died.

During this episode, David ended up breaking four of the Ten Commandments: "You shall not murder" (Exodus 20:13), "you shall not commit adultery" (verse 14), "you shall not steal" (verse 15), "you shall not covet your neighbor's wife..." (verse 17).[6] These "thou shalt nots" are not in the Bible to make our lives more miserable. They are there for our own good. God created us, and by living as He intended us to live (obeying His commands), we are on the path of blessing and the abundant life. But if we choose to remove ourselves from this path, choosing instead a path bristled by thorns, we have no one to blame but ourselves when we are painfully pricked.

Because David remained in sin for almost a full year, God had no choice but to discipline him. Following this discipline, David finally repented and confessed his sin to God. This repentance is recorded for us in Psalm 51. Consider the first 12 verses:

A psalm of David. When the prophet Nathan came to him
after David had committed adultery with Bathsheba.

Have mercy on me, O God,
    according to your unfailing love;
according to your great compassion
    blot out my transgressions.
Wash away all my iniquity
    and cleanse me from my sin.

For I know my transgressions,
    and my sin is always before me.
Against you, you only, have I sinned
    and done what is evil in your sight,
so that you are proved right when you speak
    and justified when you judge.
Surely I was sinful at birth,
    sinful from the time my mother conceived me.
Surely you desire truth in the inner parts;
    you teach me wisdom in the inmost place.

Cleanse me with hyssop, and I will be clean;
    wash me, and I will be whiter than snow.
Let me hear joy and gladness;
    let the bones you have crushed rejoice.
Hide your face from my sins
    and blot out all my iniquity.

Create in me a pure heart, O God,
    and renew a steadfast spirit within me.
Do not cast me from your presence
    or take your Holy Spirit from me.
Restore to me the joy of your salvation
    and grant me a willing spirit, to sustain me.

God's discipline in David's life was apparently severe. David speaks of "bones you have crushed" (Psalm 51:8). His suffering involved a physical affliction of some sort. David also asks God to restore to him the joy of salvation (verse 12), which implies that as a result of his sin and God's subsequent discipline, he had lost that joy. We can see, then, that there are physical, emotional, and spiritual consequences of sin.

My pastor once said, "You will either respond to God's *light* or you will respond to His *heat*." His point was that we will either respond to God's Word and follow it voluntarily, or we will be forced to respond to the heat of God's discipline. David made the wrong choice! Let us learn from his failure.

Do Not Judge

As we learn about God's discipline in the lives of believers, we can easily conclude that whenever we see brothers or sisters in the Lord suffering, God must be disciplining them for their sin. *Let us not be quick to judge, for we do not know all the facts.* Recall what I said earlier in the book: Sometimes people bring suffering on themselves because they've used their free wills in an inappropriate way, but people can also suffer because of the consequences of freewill decisions made by other people. At still other times, people suffer because of spiritual warfare or something else.

I hope that when you see a Christian sister with cancer (for example), you will not automatically conclude that God's disciplining her for some sin. After all, we live in a fallen world brimming with disease and pain. As theologian Millard Erickson put it, "We must be mindful that if God sends his sunshine and rain on the unjust and the just alike, then in a world in which sin has brought ravages of nature and disease, misfortune may also fall on the just and unjust alike."[7] So, *judge not!* Instead, pour your efforts into ministering to the suffering (see 2 Corinthians 1:4).

Healing Hearts

As I ponder the truth that God sometimes disciplines us as His children, I realize that sometimes we may allow the pain of discipline to distract us away from the broader, comforting truth that we are *forever* in the family of God. I believe that one of the greatest blessings of salvation is that believers have been adopted into God's forever family. We literally become "sons of God" (a biblical term that generically means "children of God") (Romans 8:14).

Adopted into God's family, we enjoy a relationship of privilege and responsibility. As children of God, we are called to live in a manner that reflects our new family relationship. We are called to reflect the family likeness (Matthew 5:48). God's loving discipline helps us to achieve this likeness.

As children of God, we have no need to be fearful about approaching God. Scripture assures us that we can boldly approach His throne and say, "*Abba*, Father" (Romans 8:15). *Abba* is an Aramaic term of great affection and intimacy—similar to the English word "daddy." Therefore, let not your concept of God be one of *stern divine discipliner* but rather *loving heavenly father*, who disciplines out of the depths of His love.

Because of this new family relationship with God, believers are called "heirs of God" and "co-heirs with Christ" (Romans 8:17). In a typical family, each child receives a share in their parents' estate. This makes each child an heir, and the children together are coheirs. As God's children we are heirs, and collectively we are coheirs with Christ (Galatians 4:7).

Scripture informs us that as believers we inherit "every spiritual blessing" in Christ (Ephesians 1:3). And upon entering heaven, we will inherit all the riches of God's glorious kingdom (1 Corinthians 3:21-23). *What a magnificent future awaits us!* During times of suffering, it is wise to keep before our minds this magnificent future. Because we know the end of our own personal stories, we have hope during the trials of life.

Never forget that your primary identity is your membership in God's forever family. This should affect your attitude, your behavior—everything in your life. Let your identity as a child of God be a source of strength and encouragement to you.

CAN GOD BRING GOOD OUT OF EVIL?

The first time I took my young son, David, to the dentist, he did not appreciate it. He did not like having to open his mouth wide so the dental hygienist could pick around and clean his teeth with sharp instruments. He did not like the process of being x-rayed. He especially did not like the idea of his teeth being drilled on.

When we arrived back home, he informed my wife and I, in no uncertain terms, that he was not going back to the dentist again. I think he was truly shocked that his parents would allow him to go through such a horrible ordeal. But as you would expect, I have continued to take him to the dentist year after year despite his objections and despite the temporary discomfort it causes for him.

Of course, the long-term good that comes from going to the dentist far outweighs the short-term pain. The same is often true with God's dealings with us. God sometimes allows us to experience short-term pains because of the long-term benefits.[1]

After I became a Christian at age 17, one of the first Christian biographies I read was *Joni* by Joni Eareckson. That book profoundly impacted the way I view human pain and suffering. It also demonstrated to me how God can bring tremendous good out of something that seemed to be utterly horrible.

Her story is famous. Joni dove into the waters of Chesapeake Bay, and her head hit something hard and unyielding. Her body sprawled out of control as she heard what sounded like loud buzzing. It was an odd sensation, almost like an electrical shock. She said she felt no pain. She also couldn't move a muscle. She wasn't sure what had happened.

She later recalled how, at that moment, she began to panic. She tried to get up, tried to break free from whatever was holding her down, but nothing budged. The only thing moving her body at all was the tidal swell that gently lifted and rolled her a little.

Thoughts flooded into her mind. She wondered if she was conscious. She wondered if someone would see her. She worried about drowning. *She needed to breathe.* Then she heard a voice. Her sister Kathy was calling her name, asking her if she was all right. If she could have spoken, she would have yelled, "Get me out of here!" *She desperately needed to breathe.* She heard her sister ask if she dove into this shallow water. Struggling, stumbling, and trying her best, Kathy managed to pull Joni out of the water. And when Joni's head broke the water's surface, she took in a huge lungful of air.

As the ambulance rushed Joni to the hospital, she prayed the Lord's Prayer, looking out the window as they passed cars and pedestrians. Upon arriving at the hospital, she was rushed through doors with a sign, "Emergency Entrance."

Soon enough, Joni was told she had total quadriplegia—the result of a diagonal fracture between the fourth and fifth cervical levels.[2] She was also told that the injury was permanent. This was not something she would "get well" from.[3] How overwhelmingly devastating this must have initially seemed!

One might naturally think that this tragic event would mark the end of a meaningful life for Joni Eareckson. But this was not to be the case. Far from it! Because of what Joni went through, she now has a ministry—Joni and Friends—that reaches millions of people around the globe. This ministry exists to "communicate the gospel and equip Christ-honoring churches worldwide to evangelize and disciple people affected by disability."[4] This important ministry would not exist had it not been for Joni's accident.

As for her frail body, her words inspire me: "The Bible indicates that our bodies are temporal. Therefore, my paralysis is temporal. When my focus shifted to this eternal perspective, all my concerns about being in a wheelchair became trivial."[5] In Joni's case, God brought a great good out of a terrible evil that she suffered.

Trusting God When You Hurt

I heard a story from a Christian philosopher about a hunter and a bear that illustrates how we must learn to trust in God even when He seems to be purposely allowing us to suffer. The story shows how suffering can easily be misunderstood:

> Imagine a bear in a trap and a hunter who, out of sympathy, wants to liberate him. He tries to win the bear's confidence, but he can't do it, so he has to shoot the bear full of drugs. The bear, however, thinks this is an attack and that the hunter is trying to kill him. He doesn't realize that this is being done out of compassion.
>
> Then, in order to get the bear out of the trap, the hunter has to push him further into the trap to release the tension on the spring. If the bear were semiconscious at that point, he would be even more convinced that the hunter was his enemy who was out to cause him suffering and pain. But the bear would be wrong. He reaches this incorrect conclusion because he's not a human being.[6]

Consider this little story as an analogy between us and God. Sometimes we can't comprehend why God allows us to go through such tough circumstances. Just as the bear questioned the hunter's motivations, so we sometimes question God's motivations. However, just as the hunter was bringing about a great good through his hard dealings with the bear, so God brings about great good through our sufferings. Just as the bear should have trusted in the hunter, so we should trust in God in the midst of our trials.[7]

The big problem for most people is that they tend to respond to the five senses. And since the spiritual world is not subject to any of these, the faith of many people is often weak and impotent. *We tend to focus on external circumstances.*

The eye of faith, however, perceives the unseen reality where God operates. The spiritual world lies all about us, enclosing us, embracing us, altogether within our reach. God Himself is here, awaiting our response to His presence. He is here to comfort us. And this spiritual world will come alive to us the moment we begin to reckon upon its reality and believe what He has promised in His Word (Hebrews 11:1; see also 2 Corinthians 5:7).

Conditioning the Faith Muscle

Great Christian thinkers have often commented that faith is like a muscle. A muscle has to be repeatedly stretched to its limit of endurance in order to build more strength. Without increased stress in training, the muscle simply will not grow.

In the same way, faith must be repeatedly tested to the limit of its endurance in order to expand and develop. God often allows His children to go through trying experiences in order to develop their faith muscles (1 Peter 1:7). God's children need to learn to trust Him (just as the bear needed to learn to trust the hunter). This learning process takes place in the school of real life—with all of its difficult trials and tribulations.

This fact jumps out to me from the book of Exodus. Following Israel's deliverance from Egypt, God first led them to Marah, a place where they had to trust God to heal the water to make it drinkable. Notice that God led them to Marah before leading them to Elim, a gorgeous oasis with plenty of good water (Exodus 15:22-27). God could have bypassed Marah altogether and brought them directly to Elim if He had wanted to. But, as is characteristic of God, He purposefully led them through the route that would yield maximum conditioning of their faith muscles, where they would be forced to trust in His promises of sustenance. God does the same thing with us. He often governs our circumstances so they yield maximum conditioning of our faith muscles (1 Peter 1:7). God takes us through the school of hard knocks to teach us that He is reliable.

Certainly this is illustrated in the life of Joseph, who was sold into slavery by his own brothers (see Genesis 38–39). Joseph suffered at the time, but God was always in control. God used these negative circumstances to bring Joseph to Egypt, where He elevated Joseph to a position of great authority (Genesis 41). But we must remember that during the time of suffering itself, Joseph had *no idea* what God's intentions were. He did not know that God was using these dire circumstances to bring him to a position of prominence. Joseph's story illustrates why trusting God is so important, regardless of the circumstances. In Joseph's case, God truly did bring about a greater good through the pain he suffered. Joseph summarized the matter when he later told his brothers, "You intended to harm me, but God intended it for good"

(Genesis 50:20). Our faith must ever rest upon God, who brings a greater good out of any evil that befalls us.

We also see this in the life of the apostle Paul, who trusted God as few others have. Paul was thrown into prison time and time again during his work of ministry (see, for example, Acts 16:23-37; Ephesians 3:1; Philippians 1:7; Colossians 4:10; Philemon 9). This must have been painful at the time, but Paul wrote Ephesians, Philippians, Colossians, and Philemon (four very important New Testament books) while he was in prison. Truly God did bring about a greater good through Paul's suffering. No wonder Paul wrote, "We know that in all things God works for the good of those who love him" (Romans 8:28).

And what about the death of Jesus on the cross of Calvary? At the time that Jesus was crucified, a bystander would likely see no good in the unjust execution. Yet, all the while, God was unfolding His wonderful plan of redemption, accomplishing the greater good of human salvation through this death on the cross (2 Corinthians 5:21; 1 Peter 2:24; 1 John 2:2). What appeared to be the worst tragedy of all turned out to be the greatest blessing of all.

We must keep in mind that if God was able to bring good from evil in the lives of Joseph, Paul, and Jesus, He can do the same in our lives. God invites us, "Trust Me." How will you respond to that invitation?

Saving Faith—One of the Greatest Goods of All

I can think of another way God often brings about a greater good from the suffering people go through. I am referring to the suffering that often brings people to saving faith in God. Each of us can think of unbelievers who endured horrible times of suffering and eventually trusted in God for salvation as a result. Unfortunately, people often do not turn to God until they feel their need for Him.

I know a man who was an unbeliever (I will call him Tim) who was strong, self-willed, proud, and independent. Tim was a type A personality who was always in control. When he was not pleased with someone, he gave him or her the third degree. He was not a man who was pleasant to be around when he was angry, and he got angry a lot.

Tim's wife eventually decided to divorce him, and she sought custody of their children. Tim's whole life came crashing to the ground. As the divorce proceedings drug along month after month, he sunk lower and lower in despair. During the midst of this mess, I shared the gospel with him. When he finally hit rock bottom, he was open to the gospel. I was with him when he prayed and verbalized to God his faith in Jesus Christ for salvation. It is the first time I ever saw Tim cry.

Not only did Tim become a Christian, but by God's grace, his family was restored. Tim and his wife canceled the divorce proceedings. I would never presume to be able to discern the thoughts and the methods of the Almighty, but in this case, God apparently knew that the only thing that would get Tim's attention was the possible loss of his family. Is this case, God brought a tremendous good out of what seemed to be a horrible evil.

Recognizing that God sometimes uses painful circumstances to draw people to salvation, one scholar suggests that

> God's overriding aim is for people to come to the knowledge of Himself in a free, uncoerced way. Perhaps it is just a fact that only in a world containing pointless natural suffering would people turn to God. Who knows? It may be

that God has created a world containing natural evils that
don't contribute to any higher good in this life but which
serve as the context in which He knew people would believe
and trust in Him.[8]

Whether or not this scholar is correct, many people do not
choose to trust in and follow God *until* they encounter suffering
in life. Without a doubt, every time a suffering person comes to
God in faith, good has been brought out of evil.

Pain as a Warning Sign

I'll never forget it as long as I live. I was on a Boy Scout camping
trip during the winter months in New Jersey. It was very, very cold
outside. I happened to be on dinner detail one night, so some
fellow Scouts and I got busy cooking dinner.

I was cooking stew in a plain metal pot with a plain metal
handle. It had been sitting over the open fire for probably 15 min-
utes or so when I mindlessly decided to pick it up to stir the stew.
In less than a second, the stew along with the pan was dumped
on the ground, and I was howling in agony from the burning pain
that shot through my hand. I still cannot believe I was so stupid
to have done that. But I'll tell you one thing: *I never did it again.*
I learned my lesson once and for all. That one small "evil" served
to prevent me from making any similar mistakes in the future that
would possibly cause even greater evils.[9]

Our capacity to experience pain through the nerves God has
built into the human body is a blessing. To lose those nerves—
and the capacity to experience pain as a warning signal—would
be terrible. This is illustrated by those who have leprosy. Lepers
often lose toes and fingers, not as a direct result of the disease itself

but because they lack the nerves that cause warning pains. They can't feel any pain in their extremities. A leper may inadvertently pick up a cooking pot as I did, but in his case he would not feel it on his hand, and he would cause severe damage to his fingers without even knowing it. We can all praise God for pain that accomplishes the greater good of helping us avoid more severe pain and damage to our bodies.[10] Our God is a wise, wise God!

Healing Hearts

Charles Durham, in his book *Temptation: Help for Struggling Christians*, tells an astonishing story of the importance of struggle:

> A man once found a cocoon of an Emperor moth and kept it with the purpose of watching the beautiful creature emerge. Finally the day came and it began to struggle through the small opening at one end of the cocoon. The struggle continued for hours, but the moth could never force its body beyond a certain point.
>
> Finally believing that something was wrong and that the opening should have been larger, the man took a pair of scissors and carefully clipped the restraining threads. The moth emerged easily, and crawled out onto the windowsill. Its body was large and swollen, its wings small and shriveled. He supposed that in a few hours the wings would develop into the beautiful objects that he had expected. But it did not happen. The moth that should have been a thing of great beauty, free to float and fly, spent its short life dragging around the swollen body and shriveled wings.
>
> The constricting threads and the struggle necessary to pass through the tiny opening had been God's method of forcing fluids from the body into the wings. The "merciful" snip of the threads was the most cruel thing possible.[11]

My friend, God has a very good reason for allowing each of us to go through struggles. These struggles ultimately bring about changes in us that otherwise would not have occurred. Our struggles can help force the fluids into our wings so that we can eventually fly.[12]

Of course, from our limited vantage point, we may not be aware of the purpose God has for a particular difficulty He has allowed us to pass through. But in His inscrutable providential workings, He invariably allows such hurts only to bring about some greater good.

Are you going through a time of suffering right now? *Trust your divine parent.* God knows what He is doing. He has your best interests at heart. He seeks only your highest good. If you do not know why certain things are going wrong in your life, simply resolve to trust Him (Psalm 5:11; 37:5; 40:4; 50:15; 62:8; 118:8; Proverbs 3:5-6; 28:25; 28:26; John 14:1; Hebrews 4:15; 10:35). Do not insist on understanding everything. This will lead only to frustration, for on this side of eternity, we will *never* understand everything. Instead follow the advice of the wise man Solomon: "Trust in the LORD with all your heart and lean not on your own understanding; in all your ways acknowledge him, and he will make your paths straight" (Proverbs 3:5-6). Trust in the Lord with all your heart that God is doing something important in your life right now through your present struggles.

9

THE SCHOOL OF SUFFERING

In the previous chapter, we explored the idea that God can bring good out of evil. Now let's take the discussion one step further and consider God's use of suffering as a teaching tool. We will build on what we have already learned as we look at Lazarus' death, recorded in John 11. We find some amazing insights in this chapter.

In John 11:3, Jesus hears that His dear friend Lazarus is ill. We learn in verse 4 that Lazarus' situation would ultimately bring much glory to God. So far, so good.

But then something very interesting takes place. Jesus did not rush off to be at Lazarus' side as soon as He heard the news that His beloved friend was seriously ill. Rather, He waited a few days (John 11:6). And He waited *despite* the intensity of His love for Lazarus and his sisters, Mary and Martha. A principle we can derive from this is that God sometimes allows His children to go through a period of suffering even though He deeply loves them, because in the end, He will somehow be glorified following their time of suffering.

As you ponder this passage, try to put yourself in Mary's and Martha's shoes. They had no idea why Jesus would choose to wait several days before coming to see Lazarus. They might have felt that Jesus turned a deaf ear to their predicament. Of course, all the while Jesus knew what He was doing and what the outcome of the situation would be. Likewise, when we go through times of suffering and God seems to be silent, we must remember that God knows what He is doing and that He may be planning a scenario that will, in the end, surprise us and bring much glory to God. We need to keep in mind that our timing is not necessarily God's timing and that God's timing is always the best timing.

Pay particular attention to Jesus' words to the disciples in John 11:4: "This sickness will not end in death. No, it is for God's glory so that God's Son may be glorified through it." Notice that Jesus did not say that Lazarus would not die but only that the *final outcome* of this sickness would not be death. This episode was to glorify (or show the divine perfection of) Jesus in a big way. Though no one knew precisely what He meant when He spoke the words recorded in verse 4, Christ would eventually raise Lazarus from the dead—something only God can do. Everyone who saw it would be confronted with Christ's deity.

Human love would no doubt have rushed to the scene of Lazarus' sickness. But divine love—Jesus' love—acts with divine wisdom. Christ deliberately waited. He had something to accomplish that no one else was aware of. Jesus' love and His two-day delay are perfectly compatible in view of His divine purpose.

Another gem we can mine from this passage is that God knows perfectly well all that we are going through. In John 11:7,11, Jesus informed His disciples that Lazarus had in fact died. No one told Him this. Rather, Jesus in His divine all-knowingness—His omniscience—simply knew that Lazarus had died. I point this out because sometimes we might get the feeling that God is not aware of what we're going through. Be assured, He knows everything that is going on in your life. He is all-aware, but He may be slow in responding to your prayer for deliverance because He has a greater purpose in mind. Remember, we are only small threads in the tapestry of life, and we can't see the whole tapestry at once. God *does* see the whole tapestry. So He calls on us to trust Him in the midst of our trials, even when we are unsure why certain things are happening in our lives.

We should also remember that God cares deeply about the hurts that we encounter. In the present case, we read that Jesus, upon finally arriving at Lazarus' house, was "deeply moved in spirit and troubled" (John 11:33), and He wept (verse 35). The people who witnessed Jesus cry said, "See how he loved him!" (verse 36). It is important for you to understand that God's magnificent love abides, even when He allows His children to suffer, or delays their deliverance. God's timing is always based on divine wisdom.

In John 11:38-44, notice a faith conflict that is similar to what many people experience today when something goes wrong. Some of the people said: "Could not he who opened the eyes of the blind man have kept this man from dying?" (John 11:37). Evidently, Jesus purposely allowed this faith conflict to occur because He intended to teach those present to have faith in God even in the face of conflict. Ponder the following words:

> Jesus, once more deeply moved, came to the tomb. It was a cave with a stone laid across the entrance. "Take away the stone," he said.
>
> "But, Lord," said Martha, the sister of the dead man, "by this time there is a bad odor, for he has been there four days."
>
> Then Jesus said, "Did I not tell you that if you believed, you would see the glory of God?"
>
> So they took away the stone. Then Jesus looked up and said, "Father, I thank you that you have heard me. I knew that you always hear me, but I said this for the benefit of the people standing here, that they may believe that you sent me."

> When he had said this, Jesus called in a loud voice,
> "Lazarus, come out!" The dead man came out, his hands and
> feet wrapped with strips of linen, and a cloth around his face.
> Jesus said to them, "Take off the grave clothes and let
> him go" (John 11:38-44).

Martha's conflict was between *walking by sight* and *walking by faith.* By sight, Martha recognized that Lazarus' body had been in the tomb four days, and the body was decaying and stinking. Moreover, to open the tomb would involve the risk of becoming defiled, according to Jewish law. But Martha overcame any doubts and, rallying her faith, obeyed Jesus.

The final outcome of this ordeal was that God was greatly glorified. But in the midst of the trial, the people did not know that this would be the outcome. This is why trusting God when things go wrong is so critically important. God may be planning a glorious outcome that you are completely unaware of. I have learned not to get discouraged by what seems to be a delay on God's part. He has perfect timing, as evidenced in the story of Lazarus.

Of course, our much-desired deliverance often may not come on this side of eternity. Even then, we must maintain our faith in God, knowing with full assurance that He is at our side as our faithful sustaining companion through every trial. We never go it alone. He is our divine Comforter. He never fails to give us the grace we need in all our trials (2 Corinthians 12:9).

Happiness Is Not God's Goal

We must dispel the popular myth that God's primary goal for humanity is happiness.[1] Gordon R. Lewis and Bruce A. Demarest are right when they observe that the greatest good of the Christian life *is not* freedom from pain, but Christlikeness. God planned to work all things together for good, not for our ease, but for our conformity to Christ's characteristics. So he planned to permit discipline ("for our good"), that those who are trained by it might enjoy the "peaceable fruit of righteousness" (Hebrews 12:10-11).[2]

God cares for our righteous character far more than He cares for mere comforts of life. After all, our character has eternal ramifications. Our personal level of comfort does not!

Our problem is that we tend to interpret events in our lives strictly from an earthly perspective. Evil often feels devastating to us because our mind-set seems to be that God's purpose for us is happiness. If that is God's purpose, we wonder, then why is this horrible thing happening to me?[3]

We must understand that God is operating from the perspective of eternity. He cares more about holiness than He does about happiness.[4] Christian author Paul Powell suggests that "God's goal is not primarily to make us comfortable but to conform us to the image of His Son, Jesus Christ. And in the pursuit of that goal He can and does use all of life's experiences."[5] God may therefore allow us to go through a season of hurt that has no apparent earthly benefit but has immense eternal benefit. Miles Stanford writes that "God does not hurry in His development of our Christian life. He is working from and for eternity."[6] God is infinitely wise in allowing events to come into our lives that will mold us in ways that will optimize our future life in heaven. God has an agenda, and He is working in our lives to fulfill that agenda.

Here's a little story that well illustrates what I am talking about:

A little piece of wood once complained bitterly because its owner kept whittling away at it, cutting it, and filling it with holes, but the one who was cutting it so remorselessly paid no attention to its complaining. He was making a flute out of that piece of ebony, and he was too wise to desist from doing so, even though the wood complained bitterly. He seemed to say, "Little piece of wood, without these holes, and all this cutting, you would be a black stick forever—just a useless piece of ebony. What I am doing now may make you think that I am destroying you, but, instead, I will change you into a flute, and your sweet music will charm the souls of men and comfort many a sorrowing heart. My cutting you is the *making* of you, for only thus can you be a blessing in the world."[7]

When God cuts away at us by allowing us to go through times of suffering, we must ever keep in mind that He is changing us and molding us for our own good. While we may hurt at the time, the silver lining is that we become more Christlike. As Charles Swindoll put it,

God works away in our being and chips away everything that doesn't look like Christ—the impatience, the short temper, the pride, the emotional drives that lead us away from our Father. He's shaping us into His image. That's His predetermined plan. And He's committed to it. Nothing we can do will dissuade Him from that plan. He stays at it. He is relentless. And He never runs out of creative ideas.[8]

Healing Hearts: Take Up Your Cross and Follow Jesus

So far in this chapter, I've explored how God sometimes uses suffering as a teaching tool in our lives. In this "Healing Hearts" section, I want to expand on what I said about how God's goal for us is not *happiness* but *holiness*. A verse closely related to this is Mark 8:34, where Jesus instructed His disciples: "If anyone would come after me, he must deny himself and take up his cross and follow me." As we will see, such a life may involve suffering, but it is also a life of profoundly deep joy.

Jim Elliot was a missionary who worked among the Auca Indians, at whose hands he was eventually murdered. Following his death, his wife, Elisabeth, continued the work and made successful contact with the tribe. Jim had taken Jesus at His word when He said, "If anyone would come after me, he must deny himself and take up his cross and follow me" (Mark 8:34; see also Matthew 16:24; Luke 14:27). In obedience to these words, Jim gave up his physical life, but he considered it a small sacrifice in view of the eternal life that lay before him. He once mused, "He is no fool who gives up that which he cannot keep to gain that which he can never lose."[9]

Corrie Ten Boom was speaking at a church service in Munich when she beheld a former Nazi policeman—one of her former jailers—in the congregation. He came up to Corrie after the service and said, "How grateful I am for your message, Fräulein. To think that, as you say, He has washed my sins away!" He thrust his hand out to shake her hand. She kept her hand at her side. How could she forgive him? Yet, as she pondered that Jesus had even died for this man—as she pondered Christ's call on her to deny herself and forgive this man—she prayed silently for the Lord to enable her to forgive him. After an immense inner struggle, she resolved to respond God's way and then sensed the love of Christ flooding her whole being. She reached out to a former enemy. She learned the truth that taking up one's cross is often very hard to do.[10]

German theologian Dietrich Bonhoeffer, who was executed by the direct order of Nazi Heinrich Himmler in April, 1945, once made this statement: "When Christ calls a man, He bids him come and die." He said that suffering

> is the badge of true discipleship. The disciple is not above his master....That is why Luther reckoned suffering among the marks of the true Church....Discipleship means allegiance to the suffering Christ, and it is therefore not at all surprising that Christians should be called upon to suffer.[11]

Jesus often made revolutionary statements. And His words often served to revolutionize the lives of those who chose to follow Him. Certainly His words about taking up one's cross and following Him (Mark 8:34) would have made more sense to His first-century hearers than to modern readers because the cross as a tool of execution was quite common in those days. When a man had been condemned to die and the time of execution had arrived, the Roman executioners required the man to carry his own cross to the place of execution. So it was with Jesus when the time of His execution came: "Carrying his own cross, he went out to the place of the Skull (which in Aramaic is called Golgotha)" (John 19:17).

What does taking up our cross and following Jesus mean? Jesus' primary point seems to be related to living a life of self-denial and submission to Jesus Christ in all things. Jesus is quite obviously calling for a total commitment. The idea is this: If you really want to follow Me, do not do so in word only, but put your life on the line and follow Me on the path of the cross—a path that will involve sacrifice, self-denial, and possibly even suffering and death for My sake.

The disciples had been quite busy telling Jews in every city that salvation was only available in Jesus Christ. They no doubt encountered resistance and ridicule in the process. After all, they had given up their jobs and were following a revolutionary. Some might have considered them mad to do such a thing. But Jesus assured them they had done the right thing. One must deny self—including the yearning for approval from others and the desire for self-exaltation before others—and perpetually follow Jesus.

Before going further, I should clarify the distinction between becoming saved and perpetually following Christ as a disciple. Scripture is clear that we become saved by placing personal faith in Jesus Christ. Close to 200 times in the New Testament, salvation is said to be by faith alone—with no works in sight (John 5:24; 11:25; 12:46). Further, we must not miss the fact that Jesus' words about taking up one's cross and following Him are addressed to His (already saved) disciples (as Matthew 16:24 makes clear). We would be wrong, then, to conclude that Jesus was saying that a life of self-denial and taking up one's cross is a condition of final salvation. Following a person is an ongoing process—a progression—but entrance into God's family is a singular event that begins at the new birth, which hinges on faith in Christ. So while salvation is free, discipleship is costly. In salvation, Christ pays the price (on the cross); in discipleship, the believer pays the price (by taking up his cross and following Jesus). Salvation involves a new birth; discipleship involves a lifetime of growth *following* the new birth.

Jesus calls His followers to a life of sacrifice and commitment. The disciple is to deny himself. The Christian is thus no longer to live his life with *self* on the throne of his heart; *Christ* must reign supreme. As Bible scholar William Lane put it, "Jesus stipulated that those who wish to follow him must be prepared to shift the center of gravity in their lives from a concern for self to reckless abandon to the will of God. The central thought in self-denial is a disowning of any claim that may be urged by the self, a sustained willingness to say *No* to oneself in order to be able to say *Yes* to God."[12] Jesus was thus calling for a radical denunciation of all self-idolatry and of every attempt to establish one's life in accordance with the dictates of self (see Romans 14:7-9; 15:2-3).

One must be careful not to confuse self-denial with asceticism, whereby one overtly denies oneself things and the enjoyment of life as God intended it. It is not a denial of objects but rather the authority over one's life that Jesus speaks about. Jesus calls His followers to turn from the idolatry of self-centeredness.

Notice the three key verbs in Mark 8:34—*deny, take up,* and *follow.* The first two verbs are aorist imperatives, which indicate a decisive action. We must decisively deny ourselves and take up our crosses! The word *follow,* however, is a present imperative. The present tense indicates continuous action. We are to perpetually and unceasingly follow Jesus, day in and day out. (It is not just a Sunday thing.) Following Jesus is a process, not a single event. The imperative indicates it is a command. It is not merely optional. Those who seek to be Jesus' disciples *must* take up their crosses and follow Jesus daily. Those who do so can count on Jesus' perpetual presence in their lives, even in the midst of life's worst storms. And that presence makes all the difference.

Ironically, even paradoxically, Scripture indicates that the enjoyment of the good life—the truly abundant life—requires taking up one's cross and selflessly following Jesus day to day. The life that is sold out to Jesus is truly the joyful life, regardless of the external circumstances one encounters in life. Do you seek inner peace in the midst of the storms of life? My friend, give yourself entirely over to Jesus, and it will be yours.

WHEN GOD SAYS NO

Have you read the book of Deuteronomy lately? If you have, I am sure you will recall that after God forbade Moses to cross the Jordan into the Promised Land as a result of his disobedience at Meribah (Numbers 20:12), Moses pleaded with God to change His mind. But God responded, "That is enough....Do not speak to me anymore about this matter...You are not going to cross this Jordan" (Deuteronomy 3:26-27). Moses, one of the greatest spiritual giants in the history of the human race, was handed a big *no* from God.

Most Christians receive a *no* from God more often than they care to admit. In this way, God is like human parents who must often say no to their children for their own good. God always has His children's highest good in mind when He says no. Moreover, He always gives them the grace to accept it. Christian pastor Blaine Allen is right when he says that

> never will the Lord say no to a petition without instantly supplying the grace to accept the answer....He will not stock-pile it in us in advance, but he will not allow it to be depleted either. Whatever burden he places on us, he will moment by moment carry for us as well.[1]

The apostle Paul also received a big *no* from God, and he learned all about the grace of which Allen speaks. Consider these words from 2 Corinthians 12:2-9:

> I know a man in Christ who fourteen years ago was caught up to the third heaven. Whether it was in the body or out of the body I do not know—God knows. And I know that this man—whether in the body or apart from the body I do not know, but God knows—was caught up to paradise. He heard inexpressible things, things that man is not permitted to tell. I will boast about a man like that, but I will not boast about myself, except about my weaknesses. Even if I should choose to boast, I would not be a fool, because I would be speaking the truth. But I refrain, so no one will think more of me than is warranted by what I do or say. To keep me from becoming conceited because of these surpassingly great revelations, there was given me a thorn in my flesh, a messenger of Satan, to torment me. Three times I pleaded with the Lord to take it away from me. But he said to me, "My grace is sufficient for you, for my power is made perfect in weakness." Therefore I will boast all the more gladly about my weaknesses, so that Christ's power may rest on me.

Apparently, the apostle Paul saw "the third heaven," the resplendently beautiful dwelling place of Christ and the saints. This glorious, awe-inspiring experience would likely have tempted him to boast about it pridefully, especially when some in the city of Corinth challenged his apostleship. So God gave him a "thorn" to keep him humble. God had a purpose for allowing him to suffer.

Our text specifies that this thorn was "in the flesh" (2 Corinthians 12:7). The word *flesh* is the normal word in the Greek language used to denote the physical substance of which the body is composed. Whatever Paul suffered from, it was apparently physical in nature. And it *hurt.*

The word for "thorn" carries the idea of "a sharpened wooden shaft," "a stake," or "a splinter." This gives us at least some indication of the pain Paul was forced to endure—a pain that God would not take away. Bible expositor J. Dwight Pentecost observes this:

When Paul talked about the thorn in the flesh, it wasn't a little prick such as one gets from a rosebush. He wouldn't have talked about being buffeted had it been something insignificant. This was a very serious and grievous suffering. It extended over a period of time because he said he prayed to the Lord three times that this thorn might be taken away; but God chose to deny his request.[2]

Many scholars believe Paul may have suffered from a severe eye disease that lasted a considerable time. We all know how uncomfortable a little dust in the eye can be, but perhaps the idea of a thorn in the eye better captures the kind of pain Paul suffered. Such an eye affliction may be the reason why Paul did not travel alone throughout Asia Minor (see Acts 15:40; 16:1-3). He apparently needed a guide.

Whether or not this was the case, our text tells us that a messenger of Satan was behind this thorn that tormented Paul (2 Corinthians 12:7). The Greek word for "torment" literally means "to strike," "to beat," "to harass," or "to trouble." This is the same word used for the soldiers violently striking and beating Jesus during His trial (Matthew 26:67). Paul's physical ailment was beating him down. Despite this, God's response to Paul's request for the thorn's removal was no. God's refusal was not in any way related to a sin on Paul's part nor to any lack of faith. In fact, the affliction was not for *punishment* but for *protection*—that is, protection from a self-inflated attitude. Because of this, Paul accepted God's verdict on the matter without hesitation.

We might speculate that prior to Paul becoming a Christian, he probably boasted about being a Hebrew of Hebrews, and he likely gloried in keeping the law. But now, as an apostle of Christ, we find him boasting in his weakness, for when he is weak, Christ showers His power on him all the more abundantly. Experiences he formerly would have abhorred (like his present physical affliction), he could now welcome supernaturally because the evidence of Christ's power in the midst of them brought glory to God, not Paul.

Paul thus said, "That is why, for Christ's sake, I delight in weaknesses, in insults, in hardships, in persecutions, in difficulties. For when I am weak, then I am strong" (2 Corinthians 12:10). The word *delight* in this verse means "to approve" or "to be well pleased with." It refers to an active delighting in God's ways, regardless of the outward circumstances in life. You see, through his suffering, Paul learned all about God's full sufficiency in all things. Just as God intended, the "thorn" produced in Paul a dependence that revealed Christ's power.

Might I suggest that, even though we are all spiritual toddlers next to the apostle Paul, God may do the same with us on occasion? God may allow you and me to encounter certain painful circumstances with the sole goal of causing us to become dependent on His strength. God may allow us to suffer so that we might be humbled and so that His strength might be made manifest through our weakness.

This has certainly been true in my own life. In fact, the more I grow and mature as a Christian, the more acutely aware I am of my weaknesses and my need to depend on God and His strength. The truth of the matter is that the Christian life is a dependent life—and God often engineers our circumstances to teach us this pivotal truth.

Saved *in* Suffering, Not *from* It

Related to the many times I have received a *no* from God through the years is an important lesson I have learned: God often does not save us *from* painful circumstances, but He sustains us *in* our painful circumstances. Christian pastor Paul Powell once said that "though God does not exempt us from suffering and He does not explain to us why our suffering comes, He does enter into our experiences with us and helps us through them. God doesn't save us *from* trouble; he saves us *in* trouble."[3] I think Powell is right.

Consider the case of Shadrach, Meshach, and Abednego in Daniel 3. These three companions of Daniel refused to worship the image of gold set up by King Nebuchadnezzar, so the king threatened to throw them into a blazing fire (Daniel 3:15). The three brave lads responded by informing the king that God was perfectly able to rescue them (verse 17). This made the king so mad that he heated the furnace seven times hotter than usual and commanded his strongest soldiers to toss Daniel's three friends into the flames (verses 19-20).

As the King was observing what should have been an instant incineration, he was suddenly startled by what he saw and exclaimed: "Look! I see four men walking around in the fire, unbound and unharmed, and the fourth looks like a son of the gods" (Daniel 3:25). The king then commanded the three to come out of the flames, and after seeing that they were completely unharmed, exclaimed: "Praise be to the God of Shadrach, Meshach and Abednego, who has sent his angel and rescued his servants! They trusted in him and defied the king's command and were willing to give up their lives rather than serve or worship any god except their own God" (verse 28).

Of course, if God had wanted to, He certainly could have intervened early on and prevented the three youths from being thrown into the furnace. But He chose not to do this. He allowed the three to be mistreated! But He did *not* allow them to go through this ordeal alone. Indeed, God sent His angel—perhaps the Angel of the Lord, which many theologians interpret to be a preincarnate appearance of Christ[4]—to sustain them in the midst of the flames. This illustrates my point that God often does not exempt His children *from* suffering, but He sustains them *in* the suffering. God's children are never alone in their trials.

Scripture is brimming with other examples of this:

- God did not prevent Hagar from being mistreated by Sarah, but He was with Hagar in her time of suffering (Genesis 16).

- God did not keep Joseph from being sold into slavery and taken to Egypt, but He was with Joseph in his unfair circumstances (Genesis 27–50).

- God did not keep Moses from being mistreated by the Egyptians, but He was with Moses in his trials (Hebrews 11:24-27).

- God did not keep David from being severely persecuted by Saul, but God did sustain and rescue David in these persecutions (1 Samuel 19:1–26:25).

- God did not keep Daniel from the lion's den, but He was with Daniel in the lion's den (Daniel 6).

- God did not keep the apostle Paul from going to jail, but He was with Paul in his jail experiences (Ephesians 3:1; Philippians 1:7; Colossians 4:10).

- God did not keep the apostle John from being exiled on the island of Patmos, but He was with John in his time of exile (Revelation 1:9-10).

It seems obvious that God's pattern is often to save *in*, not *from*. This means that you and I may not be exempt from trials, but we can be sure that God is with us through all of them.

This brings to mind Psalm 23:4, in which David reflected: "Even though I walk through the valley of the shadow of death, I will fear no evil, for you are with me; your rod and your staff, they comfort me." The "valley of the shadow of death" refers to a treacherous, dreadful place. In fact, many scholars believe the phrase is more accurately translated "the valley of deep darkness." It may be that David was thinking of an actual place in Palestine— "a chasm among the hills, a deep, abrupt, faintly lighted ravine with steep sides and a narrow floor."[5] This place is a home for vultures by day and a haven for wolves and hyenas by night. The danger for defenseless sheep is obvious.

Because he knew the Lord was with him, David feared no evil while passing through the valley of the shadow of death. The truth we draw from this verse is that while God may not keep us from going through such dark circumstances, God is with us in our circumstances, and we need not ever fear. Just as a shepherd with his rod and staff comforts his sheep, so God—or more specifically, Christ our Shepherd—comforts us, even in the midst of distressing circumstances.

The instruments used by ancient shepherds were highly effective. The *rod* is a great oak club about two feet long. It had a round head in which the shepherd pounded sharp bits of metal. This rod was specifically used to protect the sheep from wild animals. "A skillful shepherd not only swung the club to smash the head of an attacker but he could also hurl the club like a missile over the heads of his flock to strike a wolf lurking in the distance."[6]

The *staff* was bent or hooked at one end. It was often used by shepherds to restrain a sheep from wandering off from the flock or to hook its legs to pull it out of a hole. At other times, the shepherd would use the staff to pull branches aside when a sheep got entangled in the brush. By using the rod and the staff, the shepherd brought "comfort" to the sheep (Psalm 23:4). The Hebrew word for "comfort" literally means "to give strength" or "empower." In the presence of their shepherd, the sheep were strengthened and empowered because they knew they were secure in his presence.

The same is true of each of us as Christ's sheep. Knowing that He is with us every step of the way and that we are never alone, we have strength to cope with whatever might come our way. We will never find ourselves in situations the Lord is not aware of, and He will never leave or forsake us (Hebrews 13:5). The divine shepherd does not exempt us from such situations, but He is always with us in such situations.

Healing Hearts: It Is Well with My Soul

Every time I hear the story, my heart swells in praise to God for His faithfulness.

Horatio Gates Spafford was a personal friend of the great evangelist, Dwight Moody. Spafford and his family decided to go to England in November, 1873, to join Moody and Ira Sankey on an evangelistic crusade, and then travel in Europe. Spafford had to attend to some last-minute business before he could leave, so he sent his family on ahead on a great ship—a French steamer called the Ville de Havre.

Tragically, the ship never made it to its destination. It collided with another ship off the coast of Newfoundland and quickly sank. Only 47 of the 226 passengers survived. One of these was Spafford's wife, Anna. Their four young daughters—Maggie, Tanetta, Annie, and Bessie—drowned and perished in the harsh, icy waters. I can hardly imagine what Spafford must have felt when he received a telegram from his bereaved wife saying, "Saved alone."

Spafford immediately dropped all business and boarded the next ship so he could be with his wife. Upon reuniting, they met with Moody. Spafford said to him, "It is well. The will of God be done."

We do not know exactly when, but some time after this overwhelming personal tragedy, Spafford penned the lyrics to one of the most beloved hymns in Christian history, "It Is Well with My Soul." His words stir the soul:

> When peace, like a river, attendeth my way,
>> When sorrows like sea billows roll;
> Whatever my lot, Thou hast taught me to say,
>> It is well, it is well with my soul.
>
> *It is well with my soul;*
>> *It is well, it is well, with my soul.*
>
> Though Satan should buffet, though trials should come,
>> Let this blest assurance control,
> That Christ hath regarded my helpless estate,
>> And hath shed His own blood for my soul.
>
> *It is well with my soul;*
>> *It is well, it is well, with my soul.*
>
> My sin—oh, the bliss of this glorious thought:
>> My sin, not in part, but the whole
> Is nailed to the cross, and I bear it no more.
>> Praise the Lord, praise the Lord, O my soul.
>
> *It is well with my soul;*
>> *It is well, it is well, with my soul.*

And, Lord, haste the day when our faith shall be sight,
The clouds be rolled back as a scroll,
The trump shall resound, and the Lord shall descend;
"Even so," it is well with my soul...

It is well with my soul;
It is well, it is well, with my soul.

Horatio Gates Spafford experienced the reality that though God does not exempt us from suffering, He is always with us in and through our times of suffering. Spafford experienced a supernatural peace and comfort that only God can give.

It may be that you are facing deep waters and bitter trials in your own life. Dear friend, know that God is walking with you, side by side. Regardless of what you are facing, a supernatural tranquility and peace is available to you. It is yours for the taking. Cast yourself on God and His promises; truly trust in Him, and this peace will be yours. The apostle Paul tells us, "Do not be anxious about anything, but in everything, by prayer and petition, with thanksgiving, present your requests to God. And the peace of God, which transcends all understanding, will guard your hearts and your minds in Christ Jesus" (Philippians 4:6-7).

Do not forget that Jesus Himself was "a man of sorrows, and acquainted with grief" (Isaiah 53:3). Jesus knows the kind of pain that you are going through. He is our sympathetic high priest (Hebrews 4:15). And He will always be there right by your side through every trial you encounter. Trust Him. He will help you.

PART OF THE PROBLEM: MISGUIDED BELIEFS

Having read many books and articles on the problem of evil, I am surprised that so few scholars and writers have addressed the fact that faulty beliefs can bring about a significant amount of suffering in our lives. After all, theologians have long emphasized that what a person believes doctrinally will invariably impact the way that person lives and relates to others. In what follows, I offer five widely divergent case studies that show the wide range of damage that faulty beliefs can cause.

Case Study 1: Darwinism

Evolution is a naturalistic theory that proposes that simple life-forms evolved into complex life-forms by chance and random variation, with species giving rise to new species over billions of years.[1] Ultimately, this means that all living things—including human beings and apes—are related to each other through a common ancestor.[2] As evolutionists Dylan Evans and Howard Selina put it, "Ultimately, every species on Earth is descended from a single common ancestor, just as the branches on a tree all spring from a single trunk."[3]

In evolutionary theory, natural selection, mutations, and long periods of time play significant roles. J. William Scropf defines natural selection as "preferential survival of individuals having advantageous variations relative to other members of their population or species."[4] Let me simplify this for you. Evolutionists believe that each species produces far more offspring than can possibly survive. Because of limited resources, these offspring must compete with each other to survive. There will be winners and there will be losers in this competition. The winners are those who are best fit to survive in that environment; the losers are the least fit. The winners pass on their superior survival traits to their offspring so that they too can survive. As this process continues over many generations, the losers are continually weeded out, the superior traits of the winners are passed down to their offspring through positive mutations, and evolution occurs. "Over the course of many generations the advantageous gene (and its corresponding trait) will be found in a higher proportion of individuals."[5]

What does all this have to do with evil and suffering? The answer may surprise you. Did you know there is a connection between evolutionary theory and the philosophy of Adolf Hitler? Hitler was himself a Darwinian evolutionist, and he sought to implement a "survival of the fittest" philosophy in Germany.[6] How ironic that in the struggle for the survival of the fittest, Hitler and his Nazi thugs were apparently proven the weaker.[7]

Evolutionists are quick to point out that we cannot criticize Darwin's theory of natural selection simply because some people have perverted it.[8] This may be true, but the fact remains that evolutionary theory provides a philosophical platform for such abuses.

Evolutionary theory has fostered racism in America as well. The United States Congress once passed a bill that authorized the Census Bureau to count each slave as three-fifths of a person. This Congressional compromise resulted in what one African American writer of the 1890s called "the 'Inferior Race Theory,' the placing of the Negro somewhere between the barnyard animals and human beings."[9] This racist outrage took place just two decades after Darwin published *The Origin of Species*.

Some white people in those days tried to argue that blacks were less than human. Buckner H. Payne, in his book *The Negro: What Is His Ethnological Status?* (published in the decade following *The Origin of Species*), argued that "since blacks are present with us today, they must have been in the ark. There were only eight souls saved in the ark, however, and they are fully accounted for by Noah's family. As one of the beasts in the ark, the black has no soul to be saved."[10]

This racist attitude is clearly evident in the writings of numerous evolutionists, including the well-known Thomas Huxley. Even Charles Darwin believed a time was coming in the not-too-distant future when the lower races of man would be eliminated by the higher civilized races.[11]

Darwin's evolutionary views were also sexist. Darwin argued that men have substantially greater mental powers than do women, so men are likely to attain a higher eminence in whatever undertaking they attempt.[12]

Nazism, racism, and sexism have obviously caused untold suffering among millions of people in the world. Darwinism is not solely responsible for the emergence of these warped attitudes, but it has unquestionably played a notable role. Therefore, we can legitimately say that Darwinism has itself been a source of suffering for people.

Case Study 2: The Jonestown Cult

Who can forget the hundreds of people who died in the Jonestown tragedy? This cult was led by Jim Jones, who forced all members of the cult to subscribe to the beliefs he espoused. One father and mother who tried to get their five-year-old son, John Victor, out of Jonestown can tell you firsthand how faulty beliefs—such as those associated with destructive cults—can be damaging. In a letter to *Newsweek* magazine, the father lamented:

> When I tried to get him out, Jones refused. Grace and I spent months filing lawsuits and traveling to Guyana to free our boy. In November 1978, we accompanied Rep. Leo Ryan on his mission to Guyana to investigate alleged human-rights abuses. When Jones heard we were with Ryan, he specifically forbade us to travel to the compound. That's why I'm alive today. While waiting in our hotel, we heard that Ryan and his four companions had been killed on the Jonestown airstrip. We realized immediately there would be a collective suicide. We knew our son, along with the other 918 people in the compound, would die. We couldn't do a d**n thing. It was the most horrible night of my life.[13]

These individuals at Jonestown paid the ultimate price (their lives). I should note, however, that countless other people affiliated with various other cultic groups suffer spiritual, emotional, and psychological damage. Dr. Paul Martin, who is the director of the Wellspring Retreat and Resource Center (which provides counseling and help for ex-cultists), reports of countless tales of woe related by thousands of former cult members.[14] Martin tells us that "the most conservative estimates based on a number of surveys are that 185,000 Americans alone join a destructive cult each year. Of those 185,000 at least 25% will suffer enduring irreversible harm that will effect their ability to function adequately in the emotional, social, family, and occupational domains."[15] *Faulty beliefs can cause great suffering.*

Case Study 3: The Korean Rapture

In the 1990s, a full-page *USA Today* ad proclaimed that the Rapture would soon be happening, that event when all true Christians will be snatched off the earth by Jesus Christ.[16] This advertisement was run by the Hyoo-go ("Rapture") or Jong Mal Ron ("end-time theory") movement—a "loose connection of Korean sects mixing fanaticism, mysticism, and apocalyptic zeal."[17]

A special report on this movement in the *Christian Research Journal* noted that "as the predicted doomsday drew near, the Hyoo-go adherents provoked social upheaval in Korea." The report documents that

> at least four suicides and several abortions were linked with the movement—the latter because some women were afraid of being "too heavy" to be caught up to heaven. Numerous secondary and elementary school students abandoned classes. Parents and families of the movement's followers feared that if the Rapture did not take place as predicted there would be a mass suicide.[18]

Finally, the anticipated day arrived. Faithful believers gathered in the church in Seoul, Korea to await the Rapture. Over a thousand police officers were posted outside and inside the church in case sect members became violent or attempted suicide. When the appointed hour passed uneventfully, many sect members simply wept. One devastated member lamented: "God lied to us."[19]

After reading this account, can anyone doubt that faulty beliefs can cause great suffering? In this case, apocalyptic zeal—divorced from a proper understanding of Holy Scripture—caused inestimable suffering.

Case Study 4: The Jehovah's Witnesses

Jehovah's Witnesses have suffered in various ways as a result of the faulty doctrinal beliefs espoused by the sect. For example, the November 15, 1967, issue of the Jehovah's Witnesses' *Watchtower* magazine said that organ transplants amounted to cannibalism and are not appropriate for Christians.[20] The next year, an issue of *Awake!* magazine agreed that all organ transplants are cannibalism.[21] Organ transplants were forbidden by the Watchtower Society for some 13 years—during which time some Jehovah's Witnesses died or suffered terribly as a result. Obviously, in this case faulty beliefs caused not only suffering but even death.

Amazingly, the Watchtower Society changed its position when the medical benefits of such transplants became a proven fact. The March 15, 1980, issue of the *Watchtower* magazine said that organ transplants are *not necessarily* cannibalistic and began allowing them.[22]

We can make the same point with vaccinations. The Jehovah's Witnesses' *Golden Age* magazine said that a "vaccination is a direct violation of the everlasting covenant that God made with Noah after the flood."[23] Vaccinations were forbidden by the Watchtower Society for 20 years. However, the Watchtower Society dropped this prohibition in the 1950s, and since this time children in the sect have been openly vaccinated.[24] *Awake!* magazine even acknowledged that vaccinations seem to have caused a decrease in diseases.[25] One must wonder how parents of children who had died as a result of not being vaccinated felt when the Watchtower Society suddenly reversed its position.

The Watchtower Society continues to teach that a Jehovah's Witness must refuse blood transfusions in all circumstances—even when doctors say death is inevitable without one.[26] The

Watchtower Society also requires that parents do not let their children receive blood transfusions. Jehovah's Witnesses fallaciously believe that biblical references to the pagan practice of eating blood prohibit receiving a blood transfusion (Leviticus 7:26-27; 17:11-12). For this reason, many Jehovah's Witnesses carry a signed card with them stating that they are not to receive a blood transfusion in the event that they are found unconscious.[27]

Former Jehovah's Witnesses Leonard and Marjorie Chretien comment:

> [One man told of] the heartrending decision he was forced to make between his religion and the life of his child. His baby boy was born with a serious hernia. An immediate operation was required to save the child's life, but that would require a blood transfusion. Jehovah's Witnesses are taught that this is against God's law, and the penalty for not obeying this rule is removal from the organization and isolation from all friends and family members who are Witnesses. The heartbroken father chose to obey "God's law," and two days later his baby died.[28]

Many Jehovah's Witnesses and their children have died because they have put their confidence in this horribly erroneous Watchtower interpretation of "blood" passages in the Bible. The Watchtower's disallowal of a transfusion for the baby mentioned above reminds one of how the harsh-minded and heartless Pharisees condemned and chastised Jesus for healing someone on the Sabbath (Luke 6:6-11).[29]

One final example of how the Jehovah's Witnesses' Watchtower Society can cause suffering relates to the false prophecies set forth by the organization. For example, Charles Taze Russell, the founder of the Jehovah's Witnesses, prophesied that 1914 would be the year when God would overthrow all human governments and set up His government on earth.[30] Realizing that 1914 was rapidly approaching, Russell put out a call from his headquarters and garnered the help of hundreds of evangelists who went door-to-door distributing the magazines, books, and tracts that Russell and his associates published. This work was done with great religious fervor. When 1914 came and went, many Jehovah's Witnesses were heartbroken because God's Kingdom had not been set up as promised. They had worked hard spreading the word all over the world, and they were bitterly disillusioned when nothing happened.

Judge Rutherford, who led the Watchtower Society after Russell died, also tried his hand at Bible prophecy, focusing attention on the year 1925.[31] Not only was the "old order of things" to pass away that year, but the Old Testament patriarchs—Abraham, Isaac, and Jacob—were also to be resurrected and usher in the righteous government of Jehovah. In expectation of this event, a magnificent residence called Beth Sarim was constructed in San Diego, California.[32] Of course, the Old Testament patriarchs never showed up in 1925, and this led to bitter disappointment for many Jehovah's Witnesses. Judge Rutherford ended up moving into Beth Sarim during the winter months.

Unfortunately, the Society still had not learned any lessons from its past prophetic failures and now turned prophetic speculation to the year 1975. The Society told its followers that 6000 years of human history (from the time of Adam and Eve) would come to an end in 1975.[33] Armageddon was to occur that year, and Christ was to set up an earthly paradise. This prophecy led many Jehovah's Witnesses to sell their homes and quit their jobs in order to devote all their energy to witnessing to others. As was true with the earlier false predictions by the Watchtower, many Jehovah's Witnesses were heartbroken when 1975 came and went without anything happening. From 1976 to 1978, 390,000 Witnesses left the Watchtower organization.[34] These 390,000 would surely tell you that faulty beliefs can cause suffering.

Case Study 5: The Health and Wealth Gospel

"Name it and claim it" has become a household phrase in millions of homes across America. Word-Faith teachers teach this doctrine on national television. Just about every night one can tune in and learn how to gain health or wealth by following the prosperity formulas of Word-Faith teachers. These formulas, however, are unbiblical and even have connections to cultic metaphysics.

In reality, the Word-Faith teachers set forth a gospel of greed and avarice. The primary "miracle" in this gospel is the miracle of a fat wallet. This is not the gospel of the Bible (see 1 Corinthians 15:1-4). Their gospel is commonly known as the "prosperity gospel," teaching that God's will is that all Christians be wealthy. These are some of the key elements of this deviant theology:

God desires His children to be wealthy. We are told that God not only wants to deliver believers from poverty but also wants His children to eat the best food, wear the best clothing, drive the best cars, and have the best of everything.[35]

Being poor is a sin. Word-Faith teachers often teach that being poor is sinful.[36] One wonders whether such Word-Faith teachers have read their Bibles recently! Did not Jesus say, "Blessed are the poor" (Luke 6:20)?

Jesus is our example, and He was not poor. Jesus' alleged wealth is a favorite theme among Word-Faith teachers.[37] We are told that Jesus wore designer clothes[38] and had a very big house.[39] Of course, Scripture does not teach any of this.

God sets forth laws of prosperity in the Bible. Word-Faith teachers say there are certain laws governing prosperity in God's Word. Faith causes these laws to function. The success formulas in the Word of God are alleged to produce miraculous financial results when used as directed.[40]

Positive confession is a key to gaining wealth. If we want wealth, all we have to do is speak it into existence. That is the key to a financial miracle. We are told that confession brings possession.[41]

Giving money to God's work can yield a hundredfold increase. Based on a complete distortion of Mark 10:30, we are told that we will receive a miraculous hundredfold return when we give money to ministries.[42] We are assured that if we invest heavily in God, the financial returns will be staggering.[43] (One wonders why Word-Faith teachers do not give all *their* money to ministries in order to attain a hundredfold return. Instead, they constantly appeal for money on television.)

Healing is guaranteed in the atonement. Word-Faith teachers set forth the idea that physical healing is guaranteed in the atonement, and if you remain sick, you don't have enough faith to be healed, or perhaps there is sin in your life, or perhaps you have made a "negative confession." (Many Word-Faith teachers suggest that Job brought his suffering on himself by uttering a "negative confession."[44]) They often support the idea that health is guaranteed in the atonement by appealing to Isaiah 53:3-5, a prophetic passage about Jesus:

> He was despised and rejected by men, a man of sorrows, and familiar with suffering. Like from whom men hide their faces he was despised, and we esteemed him not. Surely he took up our infirmities and carried our sorrows, yet we considered him stricken by God, smitten by him, and afflicted. But

he was pierced for our transgressions, he was crushed for our iniquities; the punishment that brought us peace was upon him, and by his wounds we are healed.

Tragically, millions of Christians are being enticed by this false health-and-wealth gospel. I am even personally aware of elderly Christians who have given their life savings to television ministries in hopes of bringing financial blessing on themselves in their final retirement years. Instead, they end in bankruptcy. They end up with *nothing*. It is impossible to calculate just how many lives have been shattered as a result of this deviant, cruel theology that promises "miracle money."

God never promised such miracle money. Mark 10:30, which speaks of the so-called "hundredfold return," has nothing to do with money or riches. It is speaking specifically of those who forsake home and loved ones for the sake of Jesus and the gospel. These individuals will receive a "hundredfold return" in the sense that they become a part of a larger community of believers. In this new community they find a multiplication of relationships, many of which are ultimately closer and more spiritually meaningful than blood relationships (Mark 3:31-35; Acts 2:41-47; 1 Timothy 5:1-2).

As for the Word-Faith teaching that health is guaranteed in the atonement, this too is a woefully misguided idea. Some years ago, Larry Parker wrote a book titled *We Let Our Son Die*. In this book, Parker documented how he and his wife had been influenced by a faith healer, and they decided to withhold insulin from their 11-year-old diabetic son, Wesley. Over the next three days, Wesley's health deteriorated rapidly. He went into a diabetic coma, and no one called a doctor. They continued to make positive confessions, as advised by a faith healer. To call a doctor would amount to a negative confession. Wesley died. After his death, positive confessions *continued*—confessions engineered to raise Wesley from the dead. The Parkers were tried and convicted of manslaughter. They learned in a heartrending way that faulty beliefs can lead to great suffering.

The truth of the matter is that God never guaranteed health in the atonement. While *ultimate* physical healing is guaranteed in the atonement (a healing we will enjoy in our future resurrection bodies), the healing of our bodies while in the mortal state (prior to our death and resurrection) is not guaranteed in the atonement.

It is important to understand that the Hebrew word for healing *(napha)* can refer not only to physical healing but also to spiritual healing. The context of Isaiah 53 indicates that spiritual healing is in view. In verse 5 we are explicitly told, "He was pierced for our *transgressions*, he was crushed for our *iniquities*....By his wounds we are healed" (emphasis added). Because "transgressions" and "iniquities" set the context, spiritual healing from the misery of man's sin is in view.

Further, numerous verses in Scripture substantiate that physical healing in mortal life is not guaranteed in the atonement and that it is not always God's will to heal. For example, the great apostle Paul could not heal Timothy's stomach problem (1 Timothy 5:23), nor could he heal Trophimus at Miletus (2 Timothy 4:20) or Epaphroditus (Philippians 3:25-27). Paul spoke of "a bodily illness" he had (Galatians 4:13-15). He also suffered a "thorn in the flesh," which God allowed him to retain (2 Corinthians 12:7-9). God certainly allowed Job to go through a time of physical suffering (Job 1–2).

Finally, numerous verses in Scripture reveal that our physical bodies are continuously running down and suffering various ailments. Our present bodies are said to be perishable and weak (1 Corinthians 15:42-44). Paul said "our outer man is decaying" (2 Corinthians 4:16 NASB). Death and disease will be a part of the human condition until we receive resurrection bodies, which will be immune to such frailties (1 Corinthians 15:51-55). What a tragedy that the twisted interpretation of Scripture offered by Word-Faith teachers has caused so much suffering for so many people. Some people mail in their money to Word-Faith television shows, hoping for some miracle money in return, only to go bankrupt. Some people remain unhealed of their cancer and feel depression, guilt, and disillusionment for their apparent lack of skill in positive confession. Some people, when a loved one dies, wonder whether things might have been different if only they had properly applied the principles of the health gospel. Meanwhile, Word-Faith teachers enjoy the cash that has been sent in to their ministries.

Healing Hearts

If we can draw a positive application from this chapter, it is that we should all seek to be biblically and theologically literate. Biblical doctrine enables us to develop a realistic worldview, without which we are doomed to ineffectual living (see, for example, Matthew 22:23-33; Romans 12:3; 2 Timothy 4:3-4). Moreover, biblical doctrine can protect us from false beliefs that can lead to destructive behavior (see, for example, 1 Timothy 4:1-6; 2 Timothy 2:18; Titus 1:11). *Learn from your Bible and save yourself some grief!*

What is the best way to learn the truth of the Bible? I am not sure if there is a "best way," but one very good way is to use *The*

New Inductive Study Bible, published by Harvest House Publishers. This Bible does not have explanatory notes at the bottom of each page. Rather, this Bible teaches you how to interpret the Bible rightly for yourself, providing you with key words and concepts to watch for as you go through each biblical book. This Bible teaches you how to mark your Bible with colored markers, and it provides extra-wide margins so you can take plenty of notes. If you are unfamiliar with inductive Bible study, the introduction in this Bible tells you everything you need to know. Why not give it a try? This Bible will help you become biblically literate.

I have one more recommendation. To become theologically literate, I recommend *Approaching God: Daily Reflections for Growing Christians,* by Dr. Paul Enns.[45] This book contains a full year's worth of daily devotional readings that teach you all the basics of Christian doctrine. This is not one of those devotionals full of fluffy anecdotes *(yawn)*. Rather, this devotional is theological in nature, but it is not dry theology (Enns has a flare for making it interesting). In just a year, you can have a solid grasp on theology by daily studying this book—one page per day! Trust me— it is quite good.

The combination of *The New Inductive Study Bible* and *Approaching God: Daily Reflections for Growing Christians* will go a long way toward immunizing you from destructive faulty beliefs.

IS EVIL AN ILLUSION?

Okay, I admit it. I used to watch the original *Star Trek* series with Captain Kirk, Spock, and all the others. Decades later, when *Star Trek: The Next Generation* came out, I watched it too. As a Christian, I disagreed with the humanistic philosophy sometimes evident in these series, but I nevertheless enjoyed the space adventures and the high-tech gadgetry.

One of the unique things about *Star Trek: The Next Generation* was the introduction of a holodeck (a holographic recreation room) in which any environment—the Grand Canyon, a warm and sunny beach in South Florida, a nightclub scene taken from a popular novel, or perhaps a sunset on an entirely different planet—could be reproduced with absolute realism. The holodeck could create an exact replica of any environment imaginable. Crew members visited this room for recreational purposes. But all of it was an illusion. Everything that the five senses perceived was not real. Indeed, at the end of the recreational time, the crew member would simply say, "Computer, end program," and everything would simply vanish. The fantasy world the crew member was enjoying simply dissolved.

This reminds me of some religious groups today who argue that the present world that we perceive with our five senses is an illusion. What we perceive is not real. And the way to recognize and overcome this illusion is to follow certain religious teachings. The groups I am talking about are Hinduism and Christian Science. In the present chapter, I will focus brief attention on these groups, paying special attention to their view that evil is just an illusion.

Hinduism and Our Illusory World

A detailed history of Hinduism is far beyond the scope of this chapter. I do want to note that Hinduism had no specific founder, and no specific date marks its emergence. Scholar Bruce J. Nicholls observes that

> of all the world's great religions, Hinduism is the most dif-ficult to define. It did not have any one founder....It has many Scriptures which are authoritative but none that is exclusively so. Hinduism is more like a tree that has grown gradually than like a building that has been erected by some great architect at some definite point in time.[1]

Hinduism is a monistic ("all is one") and pantheistic ("all is God") religion, so Hindus believe that distinctions between things are ultimately unreal. They are nothing more than a mental illu-sion *(maya)*. So contrary to what may seem to be the case in day-to-day living, you and I are not individuals who are distinct from the impersonal god that underlies all reality, which Hindus call Brahman. As scholar Mark Albrecht put it, "Hinduism holds that the world is really 'Brahman in disguise'—all matter, especially biological and human life, is merely a temporary, illusory man-ifestation of this universal spirit."[2] In other words, "all is God."

The big problem for human beings, according to Hinduism, is that they are ignorant of their divine nature. People have forgotten that they are extended from Brahman. "Humans have a false knowledge *(maya)* when they believe that this life and our separation from Brahman are real."[3] They have mistakenly attached themselves to the desires of their separate selves (or egos). For this reason, people have become subject to the law of karma, which is basically a cosmic law of cause and effect. You reap in the next life (via reincarnation) what you sow in the present life. In other words, if you do good things in the present life, you will be born in a better state in the next life (via reincarnation). Likewise, if you do bad things in the present life, you will be born in a worse state in the next life.

Liberation from this continual cycle of rebirths *(samsara)* is called *moksha.* This liberation comes through the enlightened realization that the very idea of an individual self is *maya* (an illusion), and that only undifferentiated oneness with Brahman is real. When we grasp true knowledge of the illusion of life, we are freed from the bondage of life (and from the continual cycle of rebirths) and achieve ultimate unity with the Brahman.

Hindus choose from three paths to enlightenment. They are (1) *karma marga* (the way of action and ritual—prescribed ceremonies, duties, and religious rites), (2) *jnana marga* (the way of knowledge and meditation—dispelling ignorance and coming to experientially know that the only reality is Brahman), and (3) *bhakti marga* (the way of devotion—private and public acts of worship). Whichever way one attains enlightenment, the goal is for one's separate self or ego to lose its separate identity in Brahman or the Universal Soul.

This may sound complicated, and I have probably used some words you have not heard before. The main thing I want to emphasize is that what we perceive with our physical senses is considered an illusion or a dream. Further, because "all is one" and "all is God," there is no real difference between good and bad. And if there is no real difference between good and bad, then we should not even be concerned about the existence of evil.

Christian Science and the Illusion of Sin, Death, and Evil

The Christian Science church was founded by Mary Baker Eddy. Eddy was born on a farm in New Hampshire in 1821. She was raised by her parents as a Congregationalist, and she joined the Congregational church as a teenager. However, she was quite open about the fact that she did not like their teachings on predestination and hell.

Eddy had delicate features as a young girl, with extremely small hands and feet. During her childhood, she endured substantial illness, including spasmodic seizures. "She was subject from infancy to convulsive attacks of a hysterical nature," and had many nervous fits.[4] These illnesses made her highly neurotic. The attacks continued until late in life for Eddy.

Occultism would soon become a big part of Eddy's life. As an adult, she developed clairvoyant powers and dabbled in spiritualism. Sometimes she would fall into trances, and people sought advice from her while she was in such states. She would sometimes hear mysterious rappings at night and claim "she saw 'spirits' of the departed standing by her bedside, and she received messages in writing from the dead."[5]

Eddy later became interested in metaphysical theology. (Metaphysics is that branch of philosophy that inquires into the ultimate nature of reality.) She derived most of her theology from Phineas P. Quimby, a metaphysical writer whose views eventually gave rise to the New Thought movement. Eddy had become interested in Quimby because of his growing fame as a healer. Quimby believed that sin, sickness, and disease exist only in the mind. He believed that by following his New Thought techniques, people could correct their wrong thinking and eradicate these things from their lives. Quimby referred to his metaphysical belief system by various terms, including Science of Health and even Christian Science.[6] Eddy was not an original thinker but took what Quimby developed and popularized it in a new movement she called Christian Science.

Eddy first came into contact with Quimby in 1862 to seek treatment for a spinal inflammation. She claims that as a result of Quimby's care, she was healed. This subsequently motivated her to study and even begin teaching Quimby's metaphysical system of thought. However, her "cure" was short-lived as the pain soon returned—but she remained convinced that the answer to her suffering was the metaphysical teachings of Quimby.

In 1875, some nine years after Quimby died, Eddy published her book *Science and Health with Key to the Scriptures*, only mentioning Quimby in passing. In this book, Eddy set forth the metaphysical principles she learned from him but did not give him credit. She spoke of her ideas as new revelation, even though it was derived.[7] This plagiarism later became public. Eddy denied stealing her ideas from Quimby, but a *New York Times* article published in 1904 thoroughly documented it.[8]

Eddy rebutted that she herself had discovered miraculous metaphysical healing techniques three days after a fall on icy pavement. She claims she had only been given three days to live by medical authorities, but through metaphysical healing techniques she discovered, she was restored to health. The doctor who treated her, Dr. Alvin M. Cushing, contradicted her claim, stating in an affidavit that she had not been in critical condition or near death, and he knew of no such miracle.[9]

One of the main teachings of Eddy's *Science and Health with Key to the Scriptures* is that sin, evil, sickness, and death are mere illusions that can be conquered by denying them. Evil, sickness, and death are said to be "states of false belief."[10] The only reality that truly exists is God or "Divine Mind." Nothing "nonspiritual" can exist except in one's mind or thoughts. Matter does not truly exist, so neither can sickness, pain, death, or evil. "The cause of all so-called disease is mental, a mortal fear, a mistaken belief or conviction of the necessity and power of ill-health."[11] By following Christian Science techniques, Eddy says, these mental errors (and sickness and death) can be conquered.

This is allegedly why Jesus came. Indeed, Eddy tells us that Jesus came to rescue human beings "from the illusion which calls sin real, and man a sinner, needing a Savior; the illusion which calls sickness real, and man an invalid, needing a physician; the illusion that death is as real as life. From such thoughts—mortal inventions one and all—Christ Jesus came to save men."[12]

Debunking the Illusion Myth

Contrary to both Hinduism and Christian Science, evil is real. To suggest that sin and evil are not real is itself evil because it misleads people. Below, I offer summaries of six problems with the Hindu and Christian Science views of evil.

Where Did the Illusion Come From?

Where did the illusion of sin, sickness, death, and evil come from? If all is God, and if matter is unreal, then when and where did this widespread, universal delusion emerge? What is the source of this "mental error"?[13] If all is God, as Christian Scientists claim, then logically this error must be part of God himself. But how can that be? And if it is *not* of God, then clearly all reality is not of God. Such inconsistency severely undermines the illusion theory.

Sickness and Death Are Real

Even though Mary Baker Eddy said the evils of bodily sickness and death are illusions, in her declining years she was under a doctor's care, received morphine injections to ease her pain, wore eyeglasses, had teeth extractions, and eventually died, thus showing that all she professed to believe and teach was untrue.[14] And if Mary Baker Eddy died, what hope do for all lesser Christian Scientists have? After all, if anyone should have mastered the teaching that sin, death, and evil are an illusion, she should have. But her heart stopped pumping, her lungs stopped breathing, and her body remains dead to this day. Sickness and death are real!

Though Christian Science teaches that sin, death, and disease are caused by mental errors or false beliefs, the reality is that Christian Science itself is a false belief that can cause the very suffering Christian Scientists seek to deny. One example of this made national headlines across the country more than a decade ago. The case involved Christian Science parents David and Ginger Twitchell, who failed to give their dying boy, Robin (age two), medical treatment. Robin had a congenital bowel obstruction, and he died after suffering for five days. These parents chose to put their faith in Christian Science instead of medical doctors, who could have easily corrected this bowel obstruction by surgery. Mr. and Mrs. Twitchell were charged with manslaughter. Mr. Mitchell lamented that he had "failed" in his Christian Science belief.[15]

The Illusion Myth Is Not Livable

When one faces genuine pain in life—whether physical (like cancer eating away at the body), emotional (such as the grief one feels when a spouse dies), or mental (negative thoughts)—simply saying that all is rooted in errors of the mortal mind is no comfort. As one theologian put it, "While Christian Scientists assert that disease does not exist but is only an illusion, the illusion of disease is *still present*, and it produces the illusion of pain very genuinely."[16] Christian Science as a philosophy of life does not have the ring of truth.

Further, when people claim that evil is an illusion, we might ask whether they lock their front door at night. (If they do, why?) Do they leave their key in the ignition when their car is parked downtown on Main Street? Do they buckle their seat belts in the car? Do they go to the dentist? Do they put life vests on their little children when they swim in the ocean? Do they warn their little children not to get too close to the fire at the cookout? Do they support laws against pedophiles? If evil is an illusion, then such things are completely unnecessary and should be of no concern to anyone.

Pantheism and Monism Do Not Adequately Explain the Problem of Evil

When Francis Schaeffer spoke to a group of students at Cambridge University, a Hindu began criticizing Christianity. Schaeffer said, "Am I not correct in saying that on the basis of your system, cruelty and noncruelty are ultimately equal, that there is no intrinsic difference between them?"

The Hindu agreed.

One of the students immediately caught on to what Schaeffer was driving at. He picked up a kettle of boiling water that he was going to use to make tea and held the steaming pot over the Indian's head. This young Hindu looked up and asked the student what he was doing. The student said with a cold yet gentle finality, "There is no difference between cruelty and noncruelty." Thereupon the Hindu walked out into the night.[17] Despite the claims of the young Hindu, his worldview does not adequately deal with the problem of genuine evil in real life.

I had the opportunity to converse with former Hindu guru Rabi Maharaj. He spoke at length of the ethical dissatisfaction he had felt as a Hindu regarding a monistic ("all is one") and pantheistic ("all is God") worldview, especially pertaining to the problem of evil:

> My growing awareness of God as the Creator, separate and distinct from the universe he had made, contradicted the Hindu concept that God was everything, that the Creator and the Creation were one and the same. If there was only One Reality, then [God] was evil as well as good, death as well as life, hatred as well as love. That made everything meaningless, life an absurdity. It was not easy to maintain both one's sanity and the view that good and evil, love and hate, life and death were One Reality.[18]

Rabi made the only logical choice and became a Christian!

The Illusion Myth Contradicts Human Experience

The "illusion" explanation for evil flies in the face of all human experience and reason. Simply denying that evil exists does not negate its reality. The "illusion" explanation of evil is in itself delusional thinking at its worst. Jesus certainly believed in the reality of evil. In the Lord's Prayer, He did not teach us to pray, "Deliver us from the illusion of evil" but rather, "Deliver us from evil" (Matthew 6:13 NASB).

For us to accept the view of Christian Science that evil is an illusion, we would have to deny our own senses and personal experiences. It is worth noting that Scripture often exhorts us to pay attention to empirical evidence using our five senses. Jesus told doubting Thomas to stick his fingers into His crucifixion wounds as a way of proving to Thomas that indeed He had risen from the dead (John 20:27). In Luke 24:39 the resurrected Jesus told His followers, "Look at my hands and my feet. It is I myself! Touch me and see; a ghost does not have flesh and bones, as you see I have." We read in 1 John 1:1, "That which was from the beginning, which we have heard, which we have seen with our eyes, which we have looked at and our hands have touched—this we proclaim concerning the Word of life." The same senses that so convincingly testify to the resurrected Christ testify to the reality of evil in our world—not just to a few people, but universally and throughout all ages.

I came across the following amusing story that illustrates how the "evil is an illusion" myth contradicts human experience:

> There was once a little boy who was a Christian Scientist....This little boy went up to his Christian Science preacher and asked him to please pray for his father, who was very sick.
>
> The preacher replied, "Boy, you don't understand. Your father only thinks he's sick. Go tell him that. Tell him to have faith."
>
> The boy obeyed and met the preacher the next day. The preacher asked, "How's your father, boy?"
>
> "Oh, he thinks he's dead."[19]

Mary Baker Eddy Backs Down

In the *New York Sun* of December 19, 1898, Mary Baker Eddy "challenged the world to disprove" that she had healed a variety of serious illnesses, including cancer. Dr. Charles A. Reed, who would later become the president of the American Medical Association, offered to present Ms. Eddy similar cases for her to heal. He affirmed: "If she, by her Christian Science, shall cure any one of them, I shall proclaim her omnipotence from the housetops; and, if she shall cure all, or even half of them, I shall cheerfully crawl upon my hands and knees that I may but touch the hem of her walking-dress."[20] Eddy refused Dr. Reed's offer.

Healing Hearts

Please humor me for a moment. For the sake of illustration, let's say you go to a doctor regarding some severe headaches, hearing loss, partial blindness, and dizziness that you have been experiencing. The doctor smiles and pats you on the back and says, "I'm sure it's just your imagination. Go home. Think positive. Fill your mind with happy thoughts. You'll be fine." You'd conclude this guy was a nut case, right?

I offer this silly scenario only to make the point that *an accurate cure requires an accurate diagnosis.* If you receive an inaccurate diagnosis of your problem, the suggested cure will be wrong and will not help you a bit. But if the diagnosis is dead-on accurate, then you may quickly find the correct cure.

My friend, the only way for you to experience any semblance of a "healing heart" is to come to a correct diagnosis about human suffering. The correct diagnosis can only be found within the pages of the Bible, written by the Great Physician Himself (God). And it is from the Bible that I have sought in this book to provide an accurate diagnosis. We have seen, biblically, that evil first emerged among human beings following Adam and Eve's misuse of free will. Since then, each of us—infected with a sin nature passed onto us from Adam—has continued to suffer by making wrong choices. As well, we often suffer from the wrong choices others around us make. (Remember the ripples?) We even suffer from the choices evil spirits make as they seek to harm us in any way they can. Still further, we have seen that faulty beliefs can contribute to suffering. All these factors (and more) are parts of the biblical diagnosis regarding why our lives hurt.

The ultimate and final cure awaits us in heaven. There we will have perfect bodies (resurrection bodies no longer subject to pain and death), a perfect environment (no more sin and Satan), and perfect fellowship (that is, fellowship with a holy God and with His redeemed, fully sanctified children). Meanwhile, we can certainly minimize the painful symptoms of our present malady by following the wisdom of Scripture (much of which is contained in this book—especially the "Healing Hearts" sections at the end of each chapter).

One thing has especially helped me through times of suffering. I have said it many times in this book, but it bears repeating: It is the recognition that Jesus Christ is at our side through every trial we encounter. We are never alone in our trials. Jesus is always with us, just as a good shepherd is always with his sheep.

One of my favorite Bible passages about the good shepherd is Psalm 23:2-3: "He makes me lie down in green pastures, he leads me beside quiet waters, he restores my soul. He guides me in paths of righteousness for his name's sake."

Just as a shepherd leads his sheep to green pastures and quiet waters, so those who follow the Lord Jesus do not lack any spiritual nourishment or refreshment. Because of this, contentment should be the hallmark of one who has put his or her affairs in the hands of the Lord.

The phrase "quiet waters" can be translated "stilled waters." As in most of this Psalm, David is thinking of an incident that occurs in the shepherd life of Palestine. You see, sheep are deeply afraid of running water. By instinct they seem to realize that if water should get on their wool coats, they would become waterlogged and sink into the water. Because of this, a flock that is tired and thirsty will come to a running stream and then stand beside it and look. Fear of the water keeps them from partaking of the refreshing waters.

Aware of the fear of his sheep, the shepherd—perhaps taking his rod and staff—might pry loose a few large stones to dam up a quiet place where the sheep may drink. In the midst of a rushing stream, he provides refreshment for the flock with water that he has stilled.

A good Eastern shepherd will go to no end of trouble to supply his sheep with the finest grazing and the cleanest water. He does all in his power to ensure the highest possible quality of life for them. Likewise, our Shepherd Jesus makes it His personal business to make sure that those who follow Him stay spiritually nourished and refreshed.

Throughout Scripture, water often points to spiritual refreshment. For example, Jesus told the woman at the well in Samaria that He could give her "living water" (John 4:10). Jesus informed her that "whoever drinks the water I give him will never thirst. Indeed, the water I give him will become in him a spring of water welling up to eternal life" (verse 14). Later in John's Gospel we read that "on the last and greatest day of the Feast, Jesus stood and said in a loud voice, 'If anyone is thirsty, let him come to me and drink.

Whoever believes in me, as the Scripture has said, streams of living water will flow from within him'" (John 7:37-38).

The goal of Jesus our Shepherd is that we might be spiritually nourished and have life more abundantly. But there is a catch. Christ does not insist on imposing Himself upon us, forcing us to follow His lead. He does not override our wills. He does not rush into our daily experiences by gate-crashing His way into our lives. Having made us in His own likeness—as freewill agents able to choose to do as we wish—it is ultimately up to us as to whether or not we will follow His lead. This decision faces each of us.

If we choose to follow Christ's lead, we will find our souls refreshed and guided in paths of righteousness for His name's sake (Psalm 23:3). Christ our Shepherd will never lead us astray or on the wrong path. His paths lead to spiritual nourishment and refreshment.

If we find ourselves in a barren wasteland spiritually, He has not led us there, but we have chosen to stop following His lead. Without a conscientious effort to stay close to our divine Shepherd, we will likely end up somewhere out in the desert of life, torn and bleeding—like the unfortunate Israelites in their wilderness experience.

Perhaps even now you may feel that your spiritual life has been stagnating in a dry and barren wasteland. If so, take heart, for your Shepherd seeks your full restoration. His hands are opened wide, waiting to embrace you in unconditional love. His affection is as measureless as the sea. Turn to Him without delay, and you will be able to exult with David, "The LORD is my shepherd; I shall not be in want" (Psalm 23:1).

IS EVIL ALL IN OUR HEADS?

While in Southern California, I had the opportunity to visit The Boddhi Tree, an extremely large New Age mega-bookstore located in Hollywood, the city of the stars. I asked the manager of the store to show me his bestselling books. One was *Empowerment: The Art of Creating Your Life as You Want It* by David Gershon and Gail Straub. He said they could barely keep enough copies of this book in stock. They were "flying off the shelves."

Being a researcher of cultic phenomena, I bought a copy of the book and read it during the next three days. The book asks, "How would you like to have the power to attain everything you ever wished for in life? How would you like to be able to create your own miracles?"[1] The book promises that you can do this very thing by following the principles laid down in the book. Gershon and Straub tell us that "empowerment" is the key, for this will give you the miraculous ability to create your own reality by the power of your mind. What "manifests" in your life will be a direct result of the thoughts you affirm—either on a conscious or unconscious level.

Gershon and Straub's central idea is that empowerment "will free you from boundaries that have limited you in the past and show you your power to shape your own destiny. On this journey you will learn the art of creating your life as you want it."[2] They explain their theory this way:

Of all the knowledge pertaining to the evolution of the human condition that has come to light in this extraordinary time in which we live, none is more promising than this idea: We make and shape our character and the conditions of our life by what we think. What you think and believe will manifest in your life. By becoming adept at intelligently directing your thought, you can become adept at creating the life that you want. You can take charge of your destiny.[3]

Gershon and Straub note that "we can't avoid creating our reality; each time we think a thought we are creating it. Every belief we hold is shaping what we experience in our life."[4] In view of this, "if we accept the basic premise that our thoughts create our reality, it means that we need to take responsibility for creating *all* of our reality—the parts we like and the parts we don't like."[5] Ultimately, this means that bad things happen to us only because our minds have created that bad reality.

Affirmations and Visualizations

Gershon and Straub offer us a game plan for achieving empowerment that focuses on making effective use of *affirmations* (positive self-talk) and *visualizations* (mental pictures of what you want to create). This is the way to bring about miraculous changes in our lives. By using these affirmations and visualizations, Gershon and Straub assure us that we will attract the worldly "nutrients" needed to have our "mental seed" grow to "fruition."[6]

This New Age team also provides a list of "limiting beliefs" and accompanying "turnarounds." By affirming the turnarounds, we are told, we can dispose of unhealthy beliefs that limit us. Here are a few examples:

Limiting belief: God is a male figure with a lot of power who will punish me if I don't do the right thing.

Turnaround: I create God as a loving, kind, playful, wise, powerful friend. We play together co-creating the universe.[7]

Limiting belief: Spirituality means giving over control of my life to some higher power that's outside of me.

Turnaround: God's will is my own highest consciousness in this moment.[8]

Limiting belief: To be spiritual I must follow a code of conduct laid out by a religion/guru/writer of a spiritual book.

Turnaround: My spirituality grows out of my own self-knowledge. I trust it and found my actions upon it.[9]

Limiting belief: The world is full of corrupt, evil people who are leading it down a road of destruction.

Turnaround: I take responsibility to create the world as a beautiful and sacred place filled with beings committed to their own and the planet's evolution.[10]

By using positive affirmations such as these—combined with visualization—our thoughts can allegedly begin to change the reality around us. By using our minds, we have "true power." By using our minds, we can make "miraculous changes" in our lives.

New Age Seminars

Similar to the teachings of Gershon and Straub are some of the New Age human-potential seminars that have been so popular over the past few decades among Fortune 500 companies. These seminars typically teach attendees (1) you are your own god, (2) you can create your own reality, and (3) you have unlimited potential. Such seminars are heavily influenced by Eastern mysticism and promise enlightenment regarding one's true potential.

I have found that these seminars typically attempt to shred one's former worldview and replace it with an Eastern, mystical worldview. Sometimes these seminars seek to induce in the attendee an altered state of consciousness—a mental state other than normal waking consciousness that ranges from a mild sense of the transcendent to a deep trance, induced by spiritual exercises such as meditation or guided imagery. This mystical experience leads the attendee to question his or her former understanding of reality. Often such an experience causes the attendee to seek a new understanding of reality—such as the New Age worldview—that can explain the experience.

One reason so many Fortune 500 companies have been eager to use New Age seminars is that they promise increased productivity, better employee relations, more creativity among workers, and—bottom line—more sales. After all, if it is true that you are your own god and can create your own reality, then each employee ought to be able to create lots of sales.

The Alleged Omnipotence of Man

New Age celebrity Shirley MacLaine once said, "You are unlimited. You just don't realize it."[11] British New Ager George Trevelyan said that each human being is "an eternal droplet of the Divine Ocean, and that potentially it can evolve into a being who can be a co-creator with God."[12]

The New Age gospel by Levi Dowling—*The Aquarian Gospel of Jesus the Christ*—affirms that Jesus Himself taught that human beings have unlimited potential and can create their own miracles. Indeed, the Jesus of this gospel tells us, "Because I have the power to do these things is nothing strange. All men may gain the power to do these things…So man is God on earth, and he who honors God must honor man."[13] Dowling also cites this Jesus as saying: "I came to show the possibilities of man; what I have done all men may do, and what I am all men shall be."[14] And again, "What I can do all men can do. Go preach the gospel of the omnipotence of man."[15] Ultimately, this means that man has the power to create the perfect life he desires.

The Power of the Mind over Sickness

Many New Agers today believe that a key to overcoming disease and maintaining health is the proper use of the mind. Popular bestselling New Age authors who subscribe to this view include Andrew Weil, Bernie Siegel, and Deepak Chopra.

Let's briefly consider the teachings of Deepak Chopra. Chopra believes that our bodies are simply a manifestation of a universal field of energy and that the mind has the capability of controlling this energy in a way that yields health.[16] Ultimately, we are "one" with this universal energy. Chopra also believes our bodies are a projection of our consciousness. In view of this, an "unhealthy" or "unenlightened" consciousness will necessarily cause disease in the body. Therefore consciousness, which supposedly regulates this invisible process, is the true healer in Chopra's system of thought.[17] He views meditation as the most important tool.[18]

We must not forget, Chopra tells us, that "the mind and body are inseparably one,"[19] and that "the mind exerts the deepest influence on the body."[20] He says "our cells are constantly eavesdropping on our thoughts and being changed by them."[21] Indeed, "the mind can go deep enough to change the very patterns that design the body.

It can wipe mistakes off the blueprint, so to speak, and destroy any disease—cancer, diabetes, coronary heart disease—that has disturbed the design."[22] In fact, "because the mind influences every cell in the body, human aging is fluid and changeable. It can speed up, slow down, stop for a time and even reverse itself."[23]

The human body, Chopra says, "is a product of awareness."[24] "The world you live in, including the experience of your body, is completely dictated by how you learned to perceive it. If you change your perception, you change the experience of your body and your world."[25] He asserts, "Impulses of intelligence create your body in new forms every second. What you are is the sum total of these impulses, and by changing their patterns, you will change."[26] What all this boils down to is that by learning to use your mind rightly through meditation, you can bring perfect health to your body.

What About the Problem of Evil?

I think you can probably see where I'm going with all this. Many in our world today attribute evil strictly to human beings who create their own realities. New Age teaching makes humans responsible for *all* the things that "manifest" in their lives—both good and bad. If we find ourselves living in poverty, then we must take responsibility because we have created this reality by the power of our mind. If we find ourselves with cancer, then we must take responsibility because we created it as well by the power of our mind. Anything bad that exists in our world is rooted, in some way or another, in the faulty thought processes of human beings. Closer to home, my brother Paul as well as his son Greg must take ultimate responsibility for Greg's premature death, for that "negative reality" was somehow created by the power of their minds. Further, the grief *I myself* suffered through this ordeal was somehow created by my faulty thought processes.

Debunking the New Age Lie

The idea that we create our respective realities by the power of our minds has significant problems. I will briefly critique this idea, showing its weakness as a worldview and as an explanation for the problem of evil.

No Ethical Accountability

A critical problem with the create-your-own-reality view is that if man (as a god) creates his own reality, as New Agers argue, then one cannot condemn individuals who inflict evil upon others. For example, one must conclude that the millions of Jews who were executed under Hitler's Nazi thugs created their own reality. Hitler's actions were not ethically wrong because Hitler was only part of a reality that the Jews themselves created. Similarly, one cannot condemn terrorists who blow up passenger jets because the people on those jets created their own reality. One cannot condemn the terrorists who flew airplanes into the Twin Towers in New York City, for the people in those towers simply created their own reality.

In this viewpoint, then, we should really not be concerned when we see bad things happen to good people because they themselves created that reality. Further, when we see evil people doing bad things to people, we really should not be morally outraged at those evil people, because they are simply a part of the reality created by the so-called victims.

I think you'll agree that this worldview does not offer a satisfactory explanation for the problem of evil in the world. When I read about an infant boy accidentally run over by his father backing out of the garage, I hardly think this reality was created by their minds.

Man Is Not an Omnipotent God

Here is some new "enlightenment" for New Agers: Humans *are not* omnipotent gods who can create their own realities. Such an assertion is ridiculous and comical. If human beings were omnipotent gods, then one would expect them to display qualities similar to God's. However, when one compares the attributes of humankind with those of God, we find ample testimony for the truth of Paul's statement in Romans 3:23 that human beings "fall short of the glory of God." Consider that God is...

- *all-knowing* (Isaiah 40:13-14), but man is limited in knowledge (Job 38:4)

- *all-powerful* (Revelation 19:6), but man is weak (Hebrews 4:15)

- *everywhere-present* (Psalm 139:7-12), but man is confined to a single space at a time (John 1:50)

- *holy* (1 John 1:5), but even man's "righteous" deeds are as filthy garments before God (Isaiah 64:6)

- *eternal* (Psalm 90:2), but man was created at a point in time (Genesis 1:1, 26-27)

- *truth* (John 14:6), but man's heart is deceitful above all else (Jeremiah 17:9)

  ✍ *just* (Acts 17:31), but man is lawless (1 John 3:4; see also Romans 3:23)

  ✍ *love* (Ephesians 2:4-5), but man is plagued with numerous vices such as jealousy and strife (1 Corinthians 3:3)

If man is a god, one could never tell it by his attributes!

Man's ignorance of his alleged divinity also proves that he is not God. If human beings are essentially God, and if God is an infinite and changeless being, then how is it possible for man (if he is a manifestation of divinity) to go through a changing process of enlightenment by which he discovers his divinity? "The fact that a man 'comes to realize' he is God proves that he is not God. If he were God he would never have passed from a state of unenlightenment to a state of enlightenment as to who he is."[27] To put it another way, "God cannot bud. He cannot blossom. God has always been in full bloom. That is, God is and always has been God."[28]

The Incoherence of the New Age Worldview

If we are really a part of the divine, as New Agers typically argue, then why buy books from New Agers in order to find out about it? As noted above, if we were God, would we not already know it? And if all is truly "one" in the universe, as New Agers typically argue, then how can sickness and health coexist in the first place? How can good and evil coexist? Wouldn't all be *good* (as well as *God*) if all were truly one? Further, if we are already a part of the divine, then how can we ever get sick? Can any part of God get sick? What the worldview New Agers are trying to sell us seems to include numerous logical inconsistencies. These facts alone ought to make one highly suspicious about New Age explanations regarding evil in the world.

The Connection to the Occult

Those who think they can do away with evil circumstances by the power of the mind should reconsider their position, for participation in such mental exercises can lead them straight into the world of the occult and expose them to a truckload of even worse evil (demonic spirits). An undeniable and very strong connection exists between occultism and the New Age idea that the mind can control universal energy to bring health to the body. New Age critic Elliot Miller points out:

> Wherever it [belief in a universal energy] has appeared—in ancient paganism, modern occultism, or parapsychological research—this "life force" has been accompanied by altered states of consciousness, psychic phenomena, and contact with spirits. Additionally, those who are capable of perceiving, and adept at manipulating, this force invariably are shamans (e.g., witch doctors), "sensitives," or psychics, thoroughly immersed in the pagan/occult world.[29]

This claim is verified in examining the writings of Chopra, Siegel, Weil, and other New Agers. For example, consider the following excerpt from *Love, Medicine & Miracles*, in which Siegel speaks of how he met his spirit guide:

> The Simontons [a New Age husband-wife team] taught us how to meditate. At one point they led us in a directed meditation to find and meet an inner guide. I approached this exercise with all the skepticism one expects from a mechanistic doctor. Still, I sat down, closed my eyes, and followed directions. I didn't believe it would work, but if it did I expected to see Jesus or Moses. Who else would dare appear inside a surgeon's head?

Instead I met George, a bearded, long-haired young man wearing an immaculate flowing white gown and a skullcap. It was an incredible awakening for me, because I hadn't expected anything to happen. As the Simontons taught us to communicate with whomever we'd called up from our unconscious minds, I found that talking to George was like playing chess with myself, but without knowing what my alter ego's next move would be.

George was spontaneous, aware of my feelings, and an excellent adviser....All I know is that he has been my invaluable companion ever since his first appearance. My life is much easier now, because he does the hard work.[30]

This is sheer occultism! Yet couched in such seemingly benign and innocuous language, it sounds like what Siegel encountered should be a part of all our experiences.

Andrew Weil, too, speaks in a very positive way of occultic practices. During his trip to South America, Asia, and India, Weil openly admits to having worked with shamans and faith healers.[31] In his book *Natural Health, Natural Medicine,* he expresses openness to Zen meditation and the use of mantras for deep meditation.[32] These are distinctly unchristian practices that can lead one straight into the occult.

Christian apologists John Weldon and John Ankerberg have rightly noted that "almost all meditation other than biblical meditation develops psychic powers, inculcates a nonbiblical, occult worldview, and can open the door to spirit contact."[33] This is what can happen to anyone who engages in the type of meditation espoused by Siegel, Weil, and Chopra.

Visualization can also lead one straight into the occult:

The number of well-meaning people who have embarked on a visualization program for physical health, psychological understanding, or spiritual advancement and ended up involved in the occult is not small. Books on visualization carry numerous anecdotes of how even the well-intentioned and seemingly nonoccult use of visualization catapulted people into the New Age movement, psychic development, and/or spirit contact.[34]

Scripture warns us of the pervasive influence of Satan in this present world system. Indeed, "the whole world is under the control of the evil one" (1 John 5:19). We should not be surprised that millions of Americans have participated in New Age occultic practices. Christians should beware!

Healing Hearts

We close this chapter by replacing Eastern meditation with biblical meditation, for biblical meditation is truly a key to healing hearts. Eastern forms of meditation generally involve "focusing" or "centering" on various objects drawn from Hinduism or Buddhism. This ultimately involves losing one's personhood and individuality by merging with the "One." Biblical meditation, by contrast, involves pondering God's Word and His faithfulness (Joshua 1:8; Psalm 119:148). Emptying one's mind to meditate on nothing and filling one's mind with the Word of God to meditate on the Living God are very different things (see Psalm 48:9; 77:12; 143:5).

Many words in the Hebrew language are rich with nuances of meaning that sometimes fail to come across in the English translation. The Hebrew term for meditation is such a word. In different contexts, *meditate* can mean to utter, imagine, speak, roar, mutter, meditate, or muse. For example, the word is used in Isaiah

31:4 to express the roar of a lion. Similarly, it is used in Isaiah 38:14 in reference to the sound of the mourning of doves. In both cases, the idea seems to be that outward expression is an outgrowth of strong inner emotions and thought.

The term seems to carry the idea of murmuring. It portrays a person who is very deep in thought, mumbling with his lips as though talking to himself. It is as if strong feelings build up in the innermost depths of his soul, and the pressure is finally released in verbal expression. When David meditated on God's Word, he concentrated so intensely that he no doubt murmured with his lips as he read.

You and I should engage in this kind of biblical meditation. I can tell you from personal experience that it can be a great source of strength and blessing. As Scripture puts it, "Blessed is the man...[whose] delight is in the law of the LORD, and on his law he meditates day and night" (Psalm 1:1-2). Notice the reference to "day and night." The real blessing comes when we *perpetually* meditate on God's Word on an ongoing basis.

I recommend that you begin by meditating through Psalms. In Psalms, we find human beings struggling honestly with life and communicating honestly with God without holding anything back. Because we struggle with the same kinds of problems and emotions that the ancients did, the book of Psalms is one of the most relevant and loved books to modern Christians in the entire Bible. So dive into Psalms and prepare for blessing!

REINCARNATION AND THE PROBLEM OF EVIL

The word *reincarnation* literally means to "come again in the flesh." It represents the belief that the soul passes after death into another body.[1] You are born again and again and again, life after life after life.

Many Christians who claim to believe in the Bible strangely say they also believe in reincarnation. Currently 21 percent of Protestants and 25 percent of professing Catholics say they believe in reincarnation.[2]

Why do so many people opt for reincarnation today? One reason is that an increasingly large segment of the population is concerned about the prospect of death. Current estimates are that at least 50 million people die every year throughout the world. At any one time, approximately one million people are in the process of dying in the United States alone.[3] With the aging of America—with a larger and larger percentage of the American public entering old age—the issue of death has understandably become extremely relevant.

One report I came across tells us that "nearly 80 million baby boomers—one-third of the U.S. population—have reached an age in which they are confronting mortality, through the passing of a parent, the loss of a sibling or friend, or pains beneath their own breastbones." The report goes on to note: "Spurred by this mass experience, as well as by medical advances that enable doctors to prolong dying—if not living—the once-verboten subject of death has become a national topic of conversation."[4] This prospect of death has made reincarnation an appealing belief for many.

As well, many people find reincarnation much more appealing than the Christian belief that unbelievers will suffer eternally in hell. Pastor Douglas Connelly summarizes this viewpoint: "It is easier to think that you will return to human life again than that you will have to give an account of this [one] life to God, who has the power to cast people into eternal separation from him."[5]

Still further, reincarnation has grown in popularity as a result of the Eastern tidal wave that swept into this country beginning in the 1960s. As Os Guinness put it, "The East is still the East, but the West is no longer the West. Western answers no longer seem to fit the questions. With Christian culture disintegrating and humanism failing to provide an alternative, many are searching the ancient East."[6]

James Sire, author of *The Universe Next Door*, believes that the openness to Eastern ideas among the Western youth of the 1960s was largely a reaction against traditional Western values. These values include high technology, reason and rationalism, materialism, economics, and the like.[7] Sire observes that "with its antirationalism, its syncretism, its quietism, its lack of technology, its uncomplicated lifestyle, and its radically different religious framework, the East is extremely attractive." Many Americans have concluded that the East "has the answer to our longing for meaning and significance."

As a result of the Eastern explosion in the 1960s, American soil remains saturated with Eastern ideas. Though Americans in the new millennium may no longer be fascinated with the world of Eastern gurus, many of the *teachings* of these gurus remain with us.[8] The teachings of reincarnation and karma have certainly struck a nerve among Americans. Go into any mainstream bookstore like Barnes and Noble or Borders, and you will find plenty of volumes on this topic. Why? Because the market for such books today is *enormous!*

Born Again and Again and Again...

The process of reincarnation (continual rebirths) supposedly continues until the soul has reached a state of perfection and merges back with its source (God or the Universal Soul). Karma refers to the "debt" a soul accumulates because of good or bad actions committed during one's life (or past lives). The word *karma* comes from a root meaning "to do or act"; karma thus involves the idea that every action yields a consequence.[9] If one accumulates good karma, he or she will allegedly be reincarnated in a desirable state in the next life. If one accumulates bad karma, he or she will be reincarnated in a less desirable state in the next life. Eventually, over many lifetimes, karma can allegedly rid a person of all selfish desires.

In Shirley MacLaine's *Out on a Limb,* we read, "reincarnation is like show business. You just keep doing it until you get it right."[10] MacLaine affirms, "I know that I must have been many different people in many different times."[11] In various past lives MacLaine says she has been a prostitute, a male court jester who was beheaded by Louis XV of France, and a great male teacher very much in love with his wife. She is apparently still working to "get it right"! But she should not be in a rush, because reincarnationists say it could take billions of years to finally and definitively get it right. It takes a very long time for the gold to be sifted out from the dross through the process of reincarnation!

Reincarnation is rooted in Hinduism, and Hindu history reveals some interesting facts related to the emergence of reincarnation. As Indian society evolved, it began to be segregated into classes, and the system of classification was known as *Varian* (which means color). These classes included the Brahmins (priests), Ksatriyas (warriors or rulers), Vaisyas (merchants), and Sudra (laborers/servants). "Untouchables" were people who were forbidden contact with the other groups because they were regarded as impure. Eventually this evolved into the present caste system that is predominant in India. The breaking down of society into various classes or castes is based on Hinduism's belief in reincarnation. One's social status in life is dictated by the law of karma.[12] Build up good karma, and you increase your status in the next life. Build up bad karma, and you will find yourself born in a lower caste.

In Hinduism, the continual cycle of death and rebirth is known as *samsara* (transmigration).[13] *Samsara* literally means "to wander across." Scholar Lewis M. Hopfe tells us that "Indian religions believe that the life force of an individual does not die with the death of the body. Instead it 'wanders across.' The life force moves on to another time and body where it continues to live."[14] Scholar John H. Hick explains that "at death, this physical body dies and the soul survives as a mental entity called the 'subtle body' *(lingua sharira)*....This subtle body is the continuous element throughout the reincarnation process until salvation occurs. The soul, as the subtle body, bears the karma of its past lives."[15] The idea is that one's thoughts, words, and deeds have definite ethical consequences and determine one's lot in the next life. One's state in the present life hinges entirely on the karma built up in a previous life.[16]

In this view, when a person dies, his so-called "subtle body" makes "karmic calculations" and then attaches itself to a developing embryo. If the person was virtuous, the subtle body enters a "pleasant womb," and is born in a better socioreligious class. If the person lived a corrupt life, the subtle body enters a "foul and stinking womb" and is born in a lower class or perhaps as a vegetable or mineral.[17] I once spoke with a New Ager who, because of his less-than-virtuous lifestyle, was concerned that he might come back in the next life as a mere piece of ash.

Salvation, however, will eventually come, according to Hindus. Every person is on the wheel of life, and salvation involves breaking away from this wheel of life via reincarnation. The goal is to break the cycle of karma and samsara and be free from the burden of life. This salvation comes when one realizes that his individual soul *(atman)* is identical with the Universal soul (Brahman). Through seemingly endless deaths and rebirths, one finally comes to realize that atman is Brahman.

Reincarnation and the Problem of Evil

Reincarnationists believe their view is especially plausible because they think it effectively deals with the problem of evil. One advocate put it this way: "The strongest support of reincarnation is its happy solution of the problem of moral inequality and injustice and evil which otherwise overwhelms us as we survey the world."[18] Reincarnation supposedly presents a more rational and satisfying answer to the problem of evil than Christianity's view that we all get just one life, followed by either heaven or hell. The law of karma, we are told, guarantees that eventually—given enough time (it could take billions of years)—*all* inequities will be rectified and everybody will get what is coming to them. For the reincarnationist, "the law of karma entirely absolves God of the responsibility for human suffering, and man takes total responsibility for his life."[19] So, for example, if a young child suffers and then dies from leukemia, he or she is apparently suffering the consequences of bad karma accumulated in a former life, and therefore the child's suffering is perfectly fair and deserved and will contribute to the long-range (over many lives) good of the child.

In keeping with this, popular New Age writer Gary Zukav, who received a big boost from Oprah Winfrey's television show, says we must not presume to judge when people suffer cruelly, for "we do not know what is being healed [via karma] in these sufferings."[20] What Zukav calls "nonjudgmental justice" relieves us of having to be judge and jury regarding apparent evil; the law of karma will bring about justice in the end. So, what may appear to be horrible suffering in a person is actually good because it is bringing healing in some way to this suffering soul.[21]

Is Reincarnation in the Bible?

Hindus and New Agers typically argue that the early Christian church—and even the Christian Bible—taught reincarnation and the law of karma.[22] (Oprah Winfrey dedicated an entire show to this claim.) For example, in John 3:3 Jesus said, "no one can see the kingdom of God unless one is born again" (New Agers interpret "born again" to mean "born in another body"). In Matthew 11:14, we are told that John the Baptist is "Elijah who was to come" (that is, John must be a reincarnation of Elijah). And Jeremiah 1:5 seems to teach that the soul preexists birth and therefore supports reincarnation. Reincarnationists believe their solution to the problem of evil is biblical.

The Problem with Reincarnation

The Hindu and New Age hope in salvation through reincarnation is problematic on a number of levels and is ultimately unsatisfactory as an explanation for the problem of evil. Following is a brief summary of the more critical problems.

Reincarnation Is Not Fair

One must ask, Why is one punished, via karma, for something he or she cannot remember having done in a previous life? And how does a person become *better* by being punished for a sin he or she does not remember? More pointedly, if a young child develops cancer and dies, what possible healing can be brought to that baby's soul? The child has no recollection of sins committed in a previous life, and even if the child did have some such memory, he or she would not have the mental acumen to make sense of the hardship before he or she died. Where is the divine justice in this?

Reincarnation Does Not Work

If the purpose of karma is to rid humanity of its selfish desires, then why don't we see a noticeable improvement in human nature after all the millennia of reincarnations? Further, if reincarnation and the law of karma are so beneficial on a practical level, as Hindus claim, then how do they explain the immense and ever-worsening social and economic problems—including widespread poverty, starvation, disease, and horrible suffering—in India, where reincarnation has been systematically taught throughout its history?

Still further, as noted by scholar William L. de Arteaga, "perhaps the most important and often noted Christian objection to the concept of karma is that karmic theologies tend to make persons passive towards social or personal evil and injustice."[23] I think Arteaga is right. In reality, belief in reincarnation serves as a strong motivation *not* to be a "good neighbor" and lend a helping hand. After all, a person suffers precisely because he or she has not yet paid off the prescribed karmic debt for the sins committed in a previous life. If one should help such a suffering person, he or she will only serve to guarantee that the person will be born in a worse state in the next life to pay off the karmic debt that was supposed to be paid off in the present life. Further, the "good neighbor" would also accumulate more bad karmic debt for interfering with the law of karma in the suffering person's life. It is a no-win scenario.

Reincarnation Is Morally Repulsive

Gary Zukav's view that we must not presume to judge when people suffer cruelly because "we do not know what is being healed [via karma] in these sufferings" is morally repulsive. Would Zukav really have us believe that when soldiers in Ceylon shot a nursing mother and then shot off the toes of her baby for target practice, this was somehow bringing "healing" to her and her child's souls? When Shiites in the Soviet Union ripped open the womb of a pregnant Armenian woman and tore the limbs from the fetus (real events reported in the newspaper), does Zukav really expect us to place our faith in "nonjudgmental justice" instead of being morally outraged? Where is the divine and the sacred in this?

Reincarnation Is Fatalistic

The law of karma guarantees that whatever we sow in the present life, we will invariably reap in the next life. If we sow good seeds in the present life, we will reap a nice harvest (have a better situation) in the next life—guaranteed! But if we sow bad seeds in the present life, we will reap a bad harvest (have a worse situation) in the next life—guaranteed! We can do nothing to alter this chain of events. It works infallibly and inexorably. One cannot avoid the fate set in motion by one's action in the present life. This also means that whatever sufferings one may face in the present life are guaranteed to be part of your life because of what you did in your past life. Such a fatalistic philosophy can lead to despair.

Reincarnation Is Inconsistent with the Hindu/New Age Worldview

Reincarnation is inconsistent with the monistic ("all is one") worldview that both Hindus and New Agers subscribe to. After all, if all in the universe is "one," then how can there be individual souls that go through the process of reincarnation, with each different soul going into a different body? The oneness teaching and the "individual souls" teaching cannot both be true at the same time. It is one or the other. The Hindu and New Age worldview lacks coherence.[24]

Reincarnation Offers Little to Look Forward To

One cannot help but observe that being absorbed into Brahman (the Universal Soul) and losing one's personal identity has little appeal when compared to the possibility of living eternally, side by side, with the living, personal God of the universe (Revelation 22:1-5). Instead of being absorbed into a Universal Soul, Scripture tells us that Christians will be given a resurrection body that will never again get sick, age, suffer pain, or die

(1 Corinthians 15:35-58). Is this not an infinitely better and more appealing prospect?

Christianity Never Espoused Reincarnation

Contrary to the claim of some Hindus and New Agers (and Oprah Winfrey), Christianity has *never* espoused a belief in reincarnation. Nor do the verses they typically cite from the Bible support reincarnation.

John 3:3 certainly does not teach reincarnation. In this verse Jesus said to Nicodemus, "I tell you the truth, no one can see the kingdom of God unless he is born again." While New Agers try to argue that Jesus was referring to "cyclical rebirth" (reincarnation) in this verse, the context clearly shows that Jesus was referring to a *spiritual* rebirth or regeneration. In fact, the phrase "born again" carries the idea of "born from above," and can even be translated that way. Nicodemus could not have understood Jesus' statement in any other way, for Jesus clarified His meaning by affirming that "flesh gives birth to flesh, but the Spirit gives birth to spirit" (verse 6).

Nor does Matthew 11:14 teach reincarnation. In this verse Jesus said, "And if you are willing to accept it, he [John the Baptist] is the Elijah who was to come." While some claim John the Baptist was a reincarnation of Elijah, Luke 1:17 clarifies any possible confusion on the proper interpretation of this verse by pointing out that the ministry of John the Baptist was carried out "in the spirit and power of Elijah." Nowhere does the Bible say that John the Baptist was a reincarnation of Elijah. Hindus and New Agers conveniently forget that John the Baptist, when asked if he was Elijah, flatly answered *no* (John 1:21). And besides, Elijah does not fit the reincarnation model because he did not die. He was taken directly to heaven like Enoch, who did not see death (2 Kings 2:11; see also Hebrews 11:5). According to traditional reincarnation, one must first die before he can be reincarnated into another body.

Still further, Jeremiah 1:5 does not teach reincarnation. In this verse God said to Jeremiah: "Before I formed you in the womb I knew you, before you were born I set you apart; I appointed you as a prophet to the nations." This verse simply speaks of God calling and setting apart Jeremiah for the ministry long before he was born. "I knew you" does not refer to a preexistent soul, but to the prenatal person. Jeremiah was known by God in the womb (Jeremiah 1:5; compare with Psalm 51:6; 139:13-16). The Hebrew word for *know (yada)* implies a special relationship of commitment (see Amos 3:2). It is supported by words like *sanctified* (set apart) and *ordained,* which reveal that God had a special assignment for Jeremiah even before birth. *Know* in this context indicates God's act of making Jeremiah the special object of His sovereign choice.

Reincarnation Is Flatly Unbiblical

Scripture indicates that each human being lives once as a mortal on earth, dies once, and then faces judgment (see Hebrews 9:27). He does not have a second chance by reincarnating into another body. Scripture indicates that at death believers in the Lord Jesus go to heaven (2 Corinthians 5:8), and unbelievers go to a place of punishment (Luke 16:19-31). Moreover, Jesus taught that people decide their eternal destiny in a single lifetime (Matthew 25:46). This is precisely why the apostle Paul emphasized that "now is the day of salvation" (2 Corinthians 6:2).

Further, reincarnationists underestimate the seriousness of the sin problem. Jesus taught that human beings have a grave sin problem that is altogether beyond their means to solve. He taught that human beings are by nature evil (Matthew 12:34; Luke 11:13) and that man is capable of great wickedness (Mark 7:20-23; Luke 11:42-52). Moreover, Jesus said that man is utterly lost (Luke 19:10), that he is a sinner (Luke 15:10), and that he is in need of repentance before a holy God (Mark 1:15; Luke 15:10).

Jesus often spoke of man's sin with metaphors that illustrate the havoc sin can wreak in one's life. He described human sin as a blindness (Matthew 15:14; 23:16-26), a sickness (Matthew 9:12), slavery (John 8:34), and living in darkness (John 3:19-21; 8:12; 12:35-46). Moreover, Jesus taught that this is a universal condition and that all people are guilty before God (Luke 7:37-48). Jesus also taught that it is not only external acts that render a person guilty of sin but inner thoughts as well (Matthew 5:28). He taught that from within the human heart come evil thoughts, sexual immorality, theft, murder, adultery, greed, malice, deceit, envy, slander, arrogance, and folly. "All these evils," Jesus said, "come from inside and make a man 'unclean'" (Mark 7:21-23). Moreover, Jesus affirmed that God is fully aware of every person's sins—both external acts and inner thoughts; nothing escapes His notice (Matthew 10:26; 22:18; Luke 6:8; John 4:17-19).

The reincarnational belief that man can solve his own sin problem with a little help from karma (throughout many lifetimes) is itself a manifestation of the blindness that is part and parcel of human sin. Our problem is so severe that we need outside help—the help of a divine Savior. We do not need a mere karmic tune-up; we need a brand-new engine (new life from Jesus—John 3:1-5).

Finally, though reincarnationists have claimed their view provides a plausible explanation for the problem of evil, I have shown that reincarnation as a belief system is entirely *im*plausible. The Christian explanation for evil makes infinitely more sense. God's plan for humankind had the potential for evil when He bestowed upon humans the freedom of choice, but the actual origin of evil came as a result of a man who directed his will away from God and toward his own selfish desires.[25] "Whereas God created the *fact* of freedom, humans perform the *acts* of freedom. God made evil *possible*; creatures make it *actual*."[26] Since Adam and Eve made evil actual on that first occasion in the Garden of Eden, a sin nature has been passed on to every man and woman (Romans 5:12; 1 Corinthians 15:22), and it is out of the sin nature that we today continue to use our free wills to make evil actual (Mark 7:20-23).

Healing Hearts

The Christian alternative to reincarnation, plain and simple, is resurrection. The future day of our resurrection is a day to look forward to! Meditating on the truth of our future resurrection is often just what we need when we are confronted by severe illness or prospects of death.

Scripture indicates that in our mortality—that is, in our earthly human bodies—we simply cannot exist in the unveiled presence of God in heaven. God lives in unapproachable light (1 Timothy 6:16), and our present bodies cannot exist in His presence. The apostle Paul tells us, "I declare to you, brothers, that flesh and blood cannot inherit the kingdom of God, nor does the perishable inherit the imperishable" (1 Corinthians 15:50).

But all this will one day change. When we receive our glorified resurrection bodies, they will be specially suited to dwelling in the unveiled presence of God. Just as the caterpillar has to be changed into the butterfly in order to inherit the air, so we have to be changed in order to inherit heaven. Paul affirmed that

> the trumpet will sound, the dead will be raised imperishable, and we will be changed. For the perishable must clothe itself with the imperishable, and the mortal with immortality. When the perishable has been clothed with the imperishable, and the mortal with immortality, then the saying that is written will come true: "Death has been swallowed up in victory" (1 Corinthians 15:52-54).

Once we are changed, we will be able to fellowship with God face-to-face. What a glorious day that will be!

I think you'll agree with me that the seeds of disease and death are ever upon our present bodies. Fighting off dangerous infections is a constant struggle. We often get sick. And all of us eventually die—it is just a question of time. Our new resurrection bodies, however, will be raised imperishable (1 Corinthians 15:42-43). All liability to disease and death will be forever gone. Never again will we have to worry about infections or passing away.

Our present bodies are characterized by weakness. From the moment we are born, the "outward man is decaying" (2 Corinthians 4:16). Vitality decreases, illness comes, and then old age follows with its wrinkles and decrepitude. Eventually, in old age, we may become utterly incapacitated, not able to move around and do the simplest of tasks.

By contrast, our resurrection bodies will have great power. Never again will we be tired, weak, or incapacitated. Words are inadequate to describe the incredible differences between our present bodies and our future resurrection bodies. But the apostle Paul gives us at least a hint of this difference by comparing our present earthly bodies to tents and our future resurrection bodies to buildings (2 Corinthians 5:1-9).

I close with an exhortation. Commit 1 Corinthians 15:50-54—all five verses—to memory. We need to keep the rich truths of this passage ever before our minds. In times of crisis, the words of this passage will be a powerful source of strength—guaranteed!

PARADISE RESTORED

The Bible begins with paradise lost, at which time pain, suffering, and death first entered the human race. The Bible ends with paradise regained, at which time pain, suffering, and death will be a thing of the past.

Once we are in heaven, the sufferings we experienced during our time on earth will have been a momentary bother. As Mother Teresa put it, "In light of heaven, the worst suffering on earth, a life full of the most atrocious tortures on earth, will be seen to be no more serious than one night in an inconvenient hotel."[1] Theologian John Wenham commented, "Not only is it certain that this life will end, but it is certain that from the perspective of eternity it will be seen to have passed in a flash. The toils which seem so endless will be seen to have been quite transitory and abundantly worthwhile."[2] It is with this in mind that Christian writer Philip Yancey commented: "In the Christian scheme of things, this world and the time spent here are not all there is. Earth is a proving ground, a dot in eternity."[3]

In this chapter, I want to narrow our attention to an eternal perspective. I have briefly touched on this earlier in the book, but it is appropriate that I expand on this theme in this final chapter. My reason is simple: I believe that such a perspective gives us the strength we need to withstand the punches that life often throws at us during this "dot in eternity."

The writings of the apostle Paul help us immensely, for if ever
a man lived with an eternal perspective, he did. Contemplate his
words:

> We do not lose heart. Though outwardly we are wasting away,
> yet inwardly we are being renewed day by day. For our light
> and momentary troubles are achieving for us an eternal glory
> that far outweighs them all. So we fix our eyes not on what
> is seen, but on what is unseen. For what is seen is tempo-
> rary, but what is unseen is eternal (2 Corinthians 4:16-18).

This "dot in eternity" is quickly passing away. But our destiny
in heaven is an eternal destiny. We will live there forever in a pain-
free and death-free environment. *That's* something to look forward to.

Paul believed that our understanding of what awaits us in the
future encourages us in the present. This is no doubt one reason
he chose to contrast our flimsy mortal bodies on earth with the
rock-solid resurrection bodies that will be ours in heaven:

> Now we know that if the earthly tent we live in is destroyed,
> we have a building from God, an eternal house in heaven,
> not built by human hands. Meanwhile we groan, longing
> to be clothed with our heavenly dwelling, because when we
> are clothed, we will not be found naked. For while we are
> in this tent, we groan and are burdened, because we do not
> wish to be unclothed but to be clothed with our heavenly
> dwelling, so that what is mortal may be swallowed up by
> life. Now it is God who has made us for this very purpose
> and has given us the Spirit as a deposit, guaranteeing what
> is to come (2 Corinthians 5:1-5).

Let's face it. Our present bodies are wearing down. They've
been infected by the fatal disease of sin. One day, they will simply

cease functioning. By contrast, our resurrection bodies in heaven will never wear down, never get sick, and never die. Pastor Paul Powell tells us that "there will be no blind eyes in heaven. No withered arms or legs in heaven. No pain or agony there. Tears will be gone. Death will be gone. Separation will be gone. This will be the ultimate healing. Then and only then, we will be free at last."[4] Keeping this truth before our minds can really put wind in our sails when we seem to be languishing on the sea of suffering.

Notice that in 2 Corinthians 5:5 Paul said that God has given us the Holy Spirit as a deposit of what is yet to come. The word *deposit* was used among the Greeks to refer to a pledge that guaranteed final possession of an item. It was sometimes used of an engagement ring. The Holy Spirit is a "deposit" in the sense that His presence in our lives guarantees our eventual total transformation and glorification into the likeness of Christ's glorified resurrection body (see Philippians 3:21). The Holy Spirit in us is a guarantee of what is to come.

When you contemplate these wonderful words of Paul from 2 Corinthians, I recommend that you immediately turn your attention to Revelation 21 as a powerful cross-reference. Ponder these words of the apostle John:

> Then I saw a new heaven and a new earth, for the first heaven and the first earth had passed away, and there was no longer any sea. I saw the Holy City, the new Jerusalem, coming down out of heaven from God, prepared as a bride beautifully dressed for her husband. And I heard a loud voice from the throne saying, "Now the dwelling of God is with men, and he will live with them. They will be his people, and God himself will be with them and be their God. He will wipe every tear from their eyes. There will be no more death or mourning or crying or pain, for the old order of things has passed away."

He who was seated on the throne said, "I am making everything new!" Then he said, "Write this down, for these words
are trustworthy and true" (Revelation 21:1-10).

Anticipating Life in Heaven

One of the greatest evangelists to have ever graced this planet
was Dwight Moody. He had an eternal perspective and did not
fear what lay beyond death's door. He was excited about his heavenly destiny. He looked forward to living in the eternal city in the
very presence of God.

The day Moody entered into glory is a day to remember. Here
is the way it happened:

> "Some day you will read in the papers that Dwight
> Moody is dead," the great evangelist exclaimed one hot
> Sunday in August 1899 to a New York City crowd. "Don't
> you believe a word of it! At that moment I shall be more
> alive than I am now…I was born of the flesh in 1837; I was
> born of the Spirit in 1855. That which is born of the flesh
> may die. That which is born of the Spirit shall live forever."
>
> Four months later, exhausted from years of preaching
> and labor, Dwight Moody was dying. Early in the morning
> of December 22, Moody's son Will was startled by his father's
> voice from the bed across the room: "Earth recedes, heaven
> opens before me!"
>
> Will hurried to his father's side. "This is no dream, Will.
> It is beautiful…If this is death, it is sweet. God is calling me
> and I must go. Don't call me back!"
>
> A few hours later Moody revived to find his wife and
> family gathered around him. He said to his wife, "I went to
> the gate of heaven. Why, it is so wonderful, and I saw the
> children [Irene and Dwight, who had died in childhood]."
> Within hours the man who had stirred two nations for Christ
> took a few final breaths and then entered the gate of heaven.[5]

What a perfect illustration Moody's entry into glory is of the fact that Christ has taken the sting out of death for the Christian (1 Corinthians 15:55). The anticipation of entering heaven is altogether sweet for those who hold Christ dear to their hearts. So, dear saint, fear not that you will die. Your Savior has you in His hands in both life and death.

Putting Heaven in Perspective

Is not the stellar universe indescribably amazing? If you go outside on a clear night, you can see about 3000 stars—a glorious sight. What is astounding to realize is that Christ—the One who constructed this starry universe (Colossians 1:16; John 1:3; Hebrews 1:2)—is the same One who is building the heavenly city in which we will dwell for all eternity (John 14:1-3).

We have to stretch our minds to consider that the glorious stellar universe is dim in comparison to the glory of the divine abode. Indeed, as theologian Eric Sauer put it,

> The light in which He dwells is superior to all things visible; it is something other than the radiance of all suns and stars. It is not to be beheld by earthly eyes; it is "unapproachable" (1 Timothy 6:16), far removed from all things this side (2 Corinthians 12:4). Only the angels in heaven can behold it (Matthew 18:10); only the spirits of the perfected in the eternal light (Matthew 5:8; 1 John 3:2; Revelation 22:4); only the pure and holy, even as He Himself is pure (1 John 3:2, 3).[6]

The eternal city is an abode of resplendent glory. God Himself dwells there. And though in our mortal bodies we cannot exist in this divine abode in the presence of God—though we cannot behold the unapproachable light with earthly eyes—our future resurrection bodies will be specially suited for living in God's direct presence. And until that day of resurrection, if we should die, our disembodied spirits will go directly into the presence of God and enjoy His fellowship as we await that glorious resurrection day.

Our Heavenly Destiny

The better you understand what heaven is really like, the more you will look forward to going there. And the more you look forward to going there, the stronger your eternal perspective will be, even when life throws you a punch. Let us briefly consider how the Bible describes heaven.

The City of Glory

In Revelation 21 we find a description of the eternal city of God. This is a city of great glory that Jesus referred to during His earthly ministry when He told the disciples: "In my Father's house are many rooms; if it were not so, I would have told you. I am going there to prepare a place for you. And if I go and prepare a place for you, I will come back and take you to be with me that you also may be where I am" (John 14:2-3). This glorious abode has been personally prepared by Christ for His followers.

Revelation 21 presents us with a scene of such transcendent splendor that the human mind can scarcely take it in. This is a scene of ecstatic joy and fellowship of sinless angels and redeemed glorified human beings. The voice of the Alpha and the Omega, the Beginning and the End, utters a climactic declaration: "I am making everything new" (Revelation 21:5).

Theologian Millard Erickson comments on the glorious splendor of this city: "Images suggesting immense size or brilliant light depict heaven as a place of unimaginable splendor, greatness, excellence, and beauty....It is likely that while John's vision employs as metaphors those items which we think of as being most valuable and beautiful, the actual splendor of heaven far exceeds anything that we have yet experienced."[7] Truly, as the apostle Paul said, "No eye has seen, no ear has heard, no mind has conceived what God has prepared for those who love him" (1 Corinthians 2:9).

Revelation 21:23 tells us "the city does not need the sun or the moon to shine on it, for the glory of God gives it light, and the Lamb is its lamp." This is in keeping with the prophecy in Isaiah 60:19: "The sun will no more be your light by day, nor will the brightness of the moon shine on you, for the LORD will be your everlasting light, and your God will be your glory."

Dr. Lehman Strauss's comments on the Lamb's glory are worthy of meditation:

> In that city which Christ has prepared for His own there will be no created light, simply because Christ Himself, who is the uncreated light (John 8:12), will be there....The created lights of God and of men are as darkness when compared with our Blessed Lord. The light He defuses throughout eternity is the unclouded, undimmed glory of His own Holy presence. In consequence of the fullness of that light, there shall be no night.[8]

The Heavenly Country

Hebrews 11 is the Faith Hall of Fame in the Bible. In this pivotal chapter we read of the eternal perspective of many of the great faith warriors in biblical times:

> All these people were still living by faith when they died. They did not receive the things promised; they only saw them

and welcomed them from a distance. And they admitted that they were aliens and strangers on earth. People who say such things show that they are looking for a country of their own. If they had been thinking of the country they had left, they would have had opportunity to return. Instead, they were longing for a better country—a heavenly one (Hebrews 11:13-15).

This passage tells us that the great warriors of the faith in biblical times were not satisfied with earthly things. They looked forward to "a better country." And what a glorious "country" it is. Eighteenth-century Bible expositor John Gill contemplates how the heavenly country

> is full of light and glory; having the delightful breezes of divine love, and the comfortable gales of the blessed Spirit; here is no heat of persecution, nor coldness, nor chills of affection; here is plenty of most delicious fruits, no hunger nor thirst; and here are riches, which are solid, satisfying, durable, safe and sure: many are the liberties and privileges here enjoyed; here is a freedom from a body subject to diseases and death, from a body of sin and death, from Satan's temptations, from all doubts, fears, and unbelief, and from all sorrows and afflictions.[9]

The Holy City

In Revelation 21:1-2 we find heaven described as "the holy city." This is a fitting description. Indeed, in this city there will be no sin or unrighteousness of any kind. Only the pure of heart will dwell there.

This doesn't mean you and I must personally attain moral perfection in order to dwell there. Those of us who believe in Christ have been given the very righteousness of Christ. Because of what

Christ accomplished for us at the cross (taking our sins upon Himself), we have been made holy (Hebrews 10:14). He is the reason we will have the privilege of living for all eternity in the holy city.

The Home of Righteousness

Second Peter 3:13 tells us that "in keeping with his promise we are looking forward to a new heaven and a new earth, the home of righteousness." What a perfect environment this will be to live in. During our earthly lives, we have to lock up our houses and we fear the possibility of intruders breaking in. Unrighteousness is everywhere. But heaven will be the home of righteousness. It will therefore be a perfect living environment for those who have been made righteous by Christ.

The Kingdom of Light

Colossians 1:12 refers to heaven as "the kingdom of light." Christ, of course, is the light of the world (John 8:12). The eternal kingdom thus takes on the character of the King. Christ, the "Light of the world," rules over the "kingdom of light." Moreover, Christ's own divine light illumines the holy city of light (Revelation 21:23). How glorious it will be!

The Paradise of God

The word *paradise* literally means "garden of pleasure" or "garden of delight." Revelation 2:7 makes reference to heaven as the "paradise of God." The apostle Paul in 2 Corinthians 12:4 said he "was caught up to paradise" and "heard inexpressible things, things that man is not permitted to tell" (2 Corinthians 12:4).

Apparently this paradise of God is so resplendently glorious, so ineffable, so wondrous, that Paul was forbidden to say anything about it to those still in the earthly realm. But what Paul saw instilled in him an eternal perspective that enabled him to face the trials that lay ahead of him.

The New Jerusalem

Perhaps the most elaborate description of the heavenly city contained in the Bible is in Revelation 21 where we read of the New Jerusalem. The city measures approximately 1500 miles by 1500 miles by 1500 miles. The eternal city is so huge that it would measure approximately the distance between the Mississippi River and the Atlantic Ocean.

The eternal city could either be cube-shaped or pyramid-shaped. It may be preferable to consider it shaped as a pyramid, for this would explain how the river of the water of life can flow down its sides as pictured in Revelation 22:1-2. As we read of John's description of the New Jerusalem, we find a whole series of contrasts with the earth. Bruce Shelley offers a summary:

> In contrast to the darkness of most ancient cities, John says heaven is always lighted. In contrast to rampant disease in the ancient world, he says heaven has trees whose leaves heal all sorts of sicknesses. In contrast to the parched deserts of the Near East, he pictures heaven with an endless river of crystal-clear water. In contrast to a meager existence in an arid climate, John says twelve kinds of fruit grow on the trees of heaven. In a word, heaven is a wonderful destiny, free of the shortages and discomforts of this life.[10]

Revelation 21:12 tells us that the New Jerusalem has "a great, high wall with twelve gates, and with twelve angels at the gates. On the gates were written the names of the twelve tribes of Israel." Moreover, we are told, "the wall of the city had twelve foundations, and on them were the names of the twelve apostles of the Lamb" (Revelation 21:14).

Perhaps the angels are at each of the twelve gates not only as guardians but also in view of their role as ministering spirits to the heirs of salvation (Hebrews 1:14). Perhaps the names of the twelve tribes of Israel are written on the gates to remind us that "salvation is of the Jews" (John 4:22). And perhaps the names of the apostles appear on the foundations to remind us that the church was built upon these men of God (Ephesians 2:20).

The "river of the water of life" has intrigued Bible interpreters since the first century. In Revelation 22:1 we read, "Then the angel showed me the river of the water of life, as clear as crystal, flowing from the throne of God and of the Lamb down the middle of the great street of the city." Perhaps one of the best explanations is that this pure river of life, though it may be a real and material river, is nevertheless symbolic of the abundance of spiritual life that will characterize those who are living in the eternal city.[11] The stream seems to symbolize the perpetual outflow of spiritual blessing to all the redeemed of all ages, now basking in the full glow of eternal life. What spiritual blessedness we will enjoy in the eternal state.

The Blessing of Heaven

As we explore what the Scriptures say about the blessing of heaven for believers, let us ever keep before our minds what this information means to each of us personally. Heaven is not just a doctrine. Our forward gaze of heaven will help us live as Christians in the present. And our forward gaze of heaven will help put the problem of evil during our short sojourns on earth in proper perspective.

The Absence of Death

The Old Testament promises that the Lord Almighty will swallow up death forever (Isaiah 25:8). Paul ties this same reality to the future resurrection: "When the perishable has been clothed with the imperishable, and the mortal with immortality, then the saying that is written will come true: 'Death has been swallowed up in victory'" (1 Corinthians 15:54). Revelation 21:4 tells us that God "will wipe every tear from their eyes. There will be no more death or mourning or crying or pain, for the old order of things has passed away."

What an awesome blessing this is: There will be no more death—no more fatal accidents, incurable diseases, funeral services, or final farewells. Death will be gone and done with, never again to sting those who dwell in heaven. Life in the eternal city will be painless, tearless, and deathless.

Intimate Fellowship with God and Christ

Can anything be more sublime and more utterly satisfying for the Christian than to enjoy the sheer delight of unbroken fellowship with God and have immediate and completely unobstructed access to the divine glory (John 14:3, 2 Corinthians 5:6-8, Philippians 1:23, 1 Thessalonians 4:17)? We shall see him "face to face" in all His splendor and glory. We will gaze upon His countenance and behold His resplendent beauty forever.

Surely our greatest joy and most exhilarating thrill will be to look upon the face of the divine Creator and fellowship with Him forever. He "who alone possesses immortality and dwells in unapproachable light" (1 Timothy 6:16) shall reside intimately among His own, and "they will be His people, and God Himself will be with them" (Revelation 21:3).

In the afterlife, our fellowship with the Lord will not be intermittent or blighted by sin and defeat. Instead, we will enjoy continuous fellowship. Spiritual death shall never again cause human beings to lose fellowship with God, because believers will have no more sin problem. When we enter into glory we will no longer have the sin nature within us. Sin will be banished from our being.

To fellowship with God is the essence of heavenly life, the fount and source of all blessing: "You will fill me with joy in your presence, with eternal pleasures at your right hand" (Psalm 16:11). We may be confident that the crowning wonder of our experience in the eternal city will be the perpetual and endless exploration of the unutterable beauty, majesty, love, holiness, power, joy, and grace of God Himself.[12]

Revelation 21:3 assures us, "Now the dwelling of God is with men, and he will live with them. They will be his people, and God himself will be with them and be their God." God in His infinite holiness will dwell among redeemed human beings because Adam's curse will be removed, Satan and the fallen angels will be judged, the wicked will be punished and separated from God, and the universe will be made sinless (except for the "Lake of Fire") (Revelation 20:15; 21:8; 22:15).

Reunion with Christian Loved Ones

One of the most glorious aspects of our lives in heaven will be our reunion with Christian loved ones. The Thessalonian Christians were apparently very concerned about their Christian loved ones who had died. They expressed their concern to the apostle Paul. So in 1 Thessalonians 4:13-17, Paul deals with the "dead in Christ" and assures the Thessalonian Christians that there will indeed be a reunion. And yes, believers will recognize their loved ones in the eternal state.

How do we know believers will recognize their loved ones? Besides the clear teaching of 1 Thessalonians 4, we are told in 2 Samuel 12:23 that David knew he would be reunited with his deceased son in heaven. He had no doubt about recognizing him. As well, when Moses and Elijah (who had long passed from earthly life) appeared to Jesus on the Mount of Transfiguration (Matthew 17:1-8), all who were present recognized them. Furthermore, in Jesus' story of the rich man and Lazarus in Luke 16:19-31, the rich man, Lazarus, and Abraham all recognized each other in the intermediate state.

Not only that, but 1 Corinthians 13:12 tells us that "now we see but a poor reflection as in a mirror; then we shall see face to face. Now I know in part; then I shall know fully, even as I am fully known." The mirrors of the ancients were made of polished metal and were far inferior to the mirrors we have today. The images were dark and indistinct. Similarly, our present knowledge is but a faint reflection of the fullness of knowledge we will have in the afterlife. This being so, we shall surely recognize our Christian loved ones in the eternal state.

Satisfaction of All Needs

In our present life on earth, we sometimes go hungry and thirsty. Our needs are not always met. But in the eternal state, God will abundantly meet each and every need.

As we read in Revelation 7:16-17, "Never again will they hunger; never again will they thirst. The sun will not beat upon them, nor any scorching heat. For the Lamb at the center of the throne will be their shepherd; he will lead them to springs of living water. And God will wipe away every tear from their eyes."

Serene Rest

The Scriptures indicate that a key feature of heavenly life is rest (Revelation 14:13). No more deadlines to work toward. No more overtime work in order to make ends meet. No more breaking one's back. Just rest—sweet serene rest. And our rest will be especially sweet because it is ultimately a rest in the very presence of God, who meets our every need.

Sharing in Christ's Glory

As difficult as this may be to fully understand, the Scriptures indicate that in the heavenly state believers will actually share in the glory of Christ. Romans 8:17 tells us, "Now if we are children, then we are heirs—heirs of God and coheirs with Christ, if indeed we share in his sufferings in order that we may also share in his glory." Likewise, Colossians 3:4 informs us that "when Christ, who is your life, appears, then you also will appear with him in glory."

This, of course, does not mean that we become deity. But it does mean that you and I as Christians will be in a state of glory, sharing in Christ's glory, wholly because of what Christ has accomplished for us. We will have glorious resurrection bodies and be clothed with shining robes of immortality, incorruption, and splendor.

The Old Heaven and Earth

As we think back to the scene in the Garden of Eden in which Adam and Eve sinned against God (the entrance of evil among humans), we remember that God cursed the earth (Genesis 3:17-18). Before the eternal kingdom can appear, God must deal with this cursed earth. Indeed, the earth—along with the first and second heavens (the earth's atmosphere and the stellar universe)—must be renewed. The old must make room for the new.

The Scriptures often speak of the passing of the old heaven and earth. Psalm 102:25-26, for example, says of the earth and the stellar universe: "They will perish, but you [O God] remain; they will all wear out like a garment. Like clothing you will change them and they will be discarded." In Isaiah 51:6 we read, "Lift up your eyes to the heavens, look at the earth beneath; the heavens will vanish like smoke, the earth will wear out like a garment....But my salvation will last for ever, my righteousness will never fail." This reminds us of Jesus' words in Matthew 24:35: "Heaven and earth will pass away, but my words will never pass away."

Perhaps the most extended section of Scripture dealing with the passing of the old heaven and earth is 2 Peter 3:7-13:

> The present heavens and earth are reserved for fire, being kept for the day of judgment and destruction of ungodly men...The heavens will disappear with a roar; the elements will be destroyed by fire, and the earth and everything in it will be laid bare. Since everything will be destroyed in this way, what kind of people ought you to be? You ought to live holy and godly lives as you look forward to the day of God and speed its coming. That day will bring about the destruction of the heavens by fire, and the elements will melt in the heat. But in keeping with his promise we are looking forward to a new heaven and a new earth, the home of righteousness.

The New Heaven and the New Earth

In Isaiah 65:17 God spoke prophetically, "Behold, I will create new heavens and a new earth. The former things will not be remembered, nor will they come to mind." In the Book of Revelation we read, "Then I saw a new heaven and a new earth, for the first heaven and the first earth had passed away, and there was no longer any sea....He who was seated on the throne said, 'I am making everything new!'" (Revelation 21:1-5). You and I are destined for a new heaven and a new earth!

Bible scholars tell us that the Greek word used to designate the newness of the cosmos is not *neos* but *kainos*. *Neos* means new in time or new in origin. But *kainos* means new in nature or new in quality. The phrase "new heavens and a new earth" refers not to a cosmos that is totally other than the present cosmos. Rather, the new cosmos will stand in continuity with the present cosmos, but it will be utterly renewed and renovated.[13] In keeping with this, Matthew 19:28 speaks of "the renewal of all things." Acts 3:21 speaks of the "restoration of all things." Our planet will be altered, changed, and made new, to abide forever.

The new earth, being a renewed and an eternal earth, will be adapted to the vast moral and physical changes that the eternal state necessitates. Everything is new in the eternal state. Everything will be according to God's own glorious nature. The new heavens and the new earth will be brought into blessed conformity with all that God is—in a state of fixed bliss and absolute perfection.

The new earth will surely undergo geological changes, for it will have no more sea (Revelation 21:1). At present about three-quarters of the earth's surface is covered with water and is therefore uninhabitable. In the new earth, an immensely increased land surface will result from the disappearance of the oceans. Glorified humanity will inhabit a glorified earth recreated and adapted to eternal conditions.

Incredibly, heaven and earth will no longer be separate realms in the next life. Believers will be in heaven even while they are on the new earth.[14] The new earth will be utterly sinless, bathed and suffused in the light and splendor of God, unobscured by evil of any kind or tarnished by evildoers of any description. "Heaven" will thus encompass the new heaven and the new earth. And the New Jerusalem—the eternal city, which measures 1500 by 1500 by 1500 miles—will apparently "come down" and rest upon the newly renovated earth (see Revelation 21:2). This city, as noted earlier, will be the eternal dwelling place of the saints of all ages.

How glorious the new heaven and the new earth will be! Even on our present earth we find dazzling untouched areas and an occasional glorious sunrise. When the weather is virtually perfect and we enjoy the world of nature around us, we might wonder, How could anyone improve on such a day?

And yet the finest earth day shall be as nothing, for "no eye has seen, no ear has heard, no mind has conceived what God has prepared for those who love him" (1 Corinthians 2:9).

A Top-Down Perspective

The incredible glory of the afterlife should motivate each of us to live faithfully during our relatively short time on earth. Especially when difficult times come, we must remember that we are but pilgrims on our way to another land—to the undiscovered country, the final frontier of heaven, where God Himself dwells.

J.I. Packer once said that the "lack of long, strong thinking about our promised hope of glory is a major cause of our plodding, lackluster lifestyle."[15] Packer points to the Puritans as a much-needed example for us, for they believed that "it is the heavenly Christian that is the lively Christian" and that we "run so slowly, and strive so lazily, because we so little mind the prize....So let Christians animate themselves daily to run the race set before them by practicing heavenly meditation."[16]

I have come to appreciate the Puritans, and I seek to imitate their example! The Puritans "saw themselves as God's pilgrims, traveling home through rough country; God's warriors, battling the world, the flesh, and the devil; and God's servants, under orders to worship, fellowship, and do all the good they could as they went along."[17] We should all have this attitude.

I am particularly impressed with the writings of Puritan Richard Baxter. Truly he had some habits worthy of imitation. His first habit was to "estimate everything—values, priorities, possessions, relationships, claims, tasks—as these things will appear when one actually comes to die."[18] In other words, he weighed everything in terms of eternal benefit. After all, our life on earth is short; our life in heaven is forever. If we work only for the things of this earth, what eternal benefit will all of it have?

Baxter's second habit was to "dwell on the glory of the heavenly life to which one was going" and to practice "holding heaven at the forefront of his thoughts and desires."[19] The hope of heaven brought him joy, and joy brought him strength. Baxter once said, "A heavenly mind is a joyful mind; this is the nearest and truest way to live a life of comfort....A heart in heaven will be a most excellent preservative against temptations, a powerful means to kill thy corruptions."[20]

Christian apologists Gary R. Habermas and J. P. Moreland have come up with a term I like a lot: a "top-down" perspective. That's precisely what we need during our earthly pilgrimage as we sojourn toward our heavenly destiny:

> The God of the universe invites us to view life and death from his eternal vantage point. And if we do, we will see how readily it can revolutionize our lives: daily anxieties, emotional hurts, tragedies, our responses and responsibilities to

others, possessions, wealth, and even physical pain and death. All of this and much more can be informed and influenced by the truths of heaven. The repeated witness of the New Testament is that believers should view all problems, indeed, their entire existence, from what we call the "top-down" perspective: God and his kingdom first, followed by various aspects of our earthly existence.[21]

A key passage on the "top-down" perspective is Matthew 6:19-34. Here Jesus informs us that anxiety will not change anything. Certainly it will not increase the length of our lives (see verse 27). Our goal therefore should be to store up treasures in heaven. This will help rid our lives of anxiety. Make note of this principle: *Our hearts will coincide with the placement of our treasures.*

If we are usually anxious over temporal problems, our hearts are not centered on what should properly be our first love. If we have perpetual anxiety, we are more occupied with transient realities than Jesus intended. So here we have a ready-made test by which we can assess the depth of our beliefs.[22]

Our goal, then, should be to maintain a "top-down" perspective. This perspective is a radical love of God that places Him first and foremost in every aspect of our lives. "Set your minds on things above, not on earthly things" (Colossians 3:2). And when we do this, God has promised to meet all our earthly needs as part of the package (Matthew 6:33)!

EPILOGUE

Several years have passed since Greg died. My brother Paul has also passed into eternity. Father and son have reunited in heaven. Indeed, there has been a father-son-grandfather reunion in heaven, for exactly one year after my brother Paul died, my father also passed away. It was a precious thing to be with him, holding his hand, the moment he passed over from this life into the next.

I opened the introduction of this book with the words, "Life can be cruel sometimes." I think that statement is true. But I can tell you, based on my experience over the past few years, that God's grace is greater than *any* cruelty this life can throw at me.

I may not have all the answers. But I do have a personal, intimate relationship with the One who does have all the answers. He is the One who sustains me daily. He is the One who gives me peace in the midst of the storm. He is the One who informs me, through His Word, about my glorious future with Him.

It is well with my soul. It is well, it is well with my soul.

The LORD bless you and keep you;
the LORD make his face to shine upon you and be gracious to you;
the LORD turn his face toward you and give you peace.

Numbers 6:24-26

JUSTICE IN THE END

I have pointed out that too often people fall into the trap of thinking that because God has not dealt with evil yet, He is not dealing with evil at all. Scripture indicates that God will one day do away with evil. Just because He has not destroyed evil at this very moment does not mean He never will.

One day in the future, Christ will return, strip power away from the wicked, and hold all men and women accountable for the things they did during their time on earth (Matthew 25:31-46; Revelation 20:11-15). Justice will ultimately prevail. Those who enter eternity without having trusted in Christ for salvation will understand just how effectively God has dealt with the problem of evil.

I must also note, however, that Christians too will understand just how effectively God has dealt with the problem of evil. I am referring to the fact that the wicked aren't the only ones who will face the judgment. Scripture indicates that Christians will also face judgment—not to determine whether or not they are saved, but to reward or withhold reward from them according to their level of faithfulness to Christ during their sojourn on earth. In this brief appendix, I will summarize what Scripture says about the judgment of Christians, the judgment of the wicked, and the final destiny of the wicked in hell. I discussed the final destiny of Christians (heaven) in chapter 15.

The Judgment of Christians

All believers will one day stand before the Judgment Seat of Christ (Romans 14:8-10). At that time God will examine the deeds each believer has done while in the body. Personal motives and intents of the heart will also be weighed.

The idea of a "judgment seat" comes from the athletic games of Paul's day. When the races and games were over, a dignitary or perhaps the emperor himself would take a seat on an elevated throne in the arena. Then one by one the winning athletes approached the throne to receive a reward—usually a wreath of leaves or a victor's crown.[1] Each Christian will stand before Christ the Judge and receive (or lose) rewards.

Christ's judgment of us will not be in a corporate setting, like a big class being praised or scolded by a teacher. Rather it will be individual and personal. "We will all stand before God's judgment seat" (Romans 14:10). Each of us will be judged on an individual basis.

This judgment has nothing to do with whether or not the Christian will remain saved. Those who have placed faith in Christ *are* saved, and nothing threatens that. Believers are eternally secure in their salvation (Romans 8:30; Ephesians 4:30). Rather, this judgment has to do with receiving or losing rewards.

Scripture indicates that some believers at the Judgment may have a sense of deprivation and suffer some degree of forfeiture and shame. Indeed, certain rewards may be forfeited that otherwise might have been received, and this will involve a sense of loss. The fact is, Christians differ radically in holiness of conduct and faithfulness in service. God in His justice and holiness takes all this into account. For this reason, 2 John 8 warns us, "Watch out that you do not lose what you have worked for, but that you may be rewarded fully." In 1 John 2:28 John wrote about the possibility of a believer actually being ashamed at Christ's coming. We must keep all this in perspective, however. The prospect of living eternally with Christ in heaven is something that should give each of us joy. And our joy will last for all eternity. How can we reconcile this eternal joy with the possible loss of reward and perhaps even some level of shame at the Judgment Seat of Christ? I think Herman Hoyt's explanation is the best I have seen:

> The Judgment Seat of Christ might be compared to a commencement ceremony. At graduation there is some measure of disappointment and remorse that one did not do better and work harder. However, at such an event the overwhelming emotion is joy, not remorse. The graduates do not leave the auditorium weeping because they did not earn better grades. Rather, they are thankful that they have been graduated, and they are grateful for what they did achieve. To overdo the sorrow aspect of the Judgment Seat of Christ is to make heaven hell. To underdo the sorrow aspect is to make faithfulness inconsequential.[2]

First Corinthians 3:11-15 describes the believer's future judgment in terms of the "building materials" he has used throughout life:

> No one can lay any foundation other than the one already laid, which is Jesus Christ. If any man builds on this foundation using gold, silver, costly stones, wood, hay or straw, his work will be shown for what it is, because the Day will bring it to light. It will be revealed with fire, and the fire will test the quality of each man's work. If what he has built survives, he will receive his reward. If it is burned up, he will

suffer loss; he himself will be saved, but only as one escaping
through the flames.

Notice that the materials Paul mentions in this passage are
increasingly combustible. Obviously the hay and straw are the
most combustible. Then comes wood. Precious metals and stones
are not combustible.

Some of these materials are useful for building, while others
are not. If you construct a house made of hay or straw, it surely
will not stand long. But a house constructed with solid materials
such as stones and metals will stand and last a long time.

What do these building materials represent? Pastor Douglas
Connelly insightfully suggests that "gold, silver, and costly stones
refer to the fruit of the Spirit in our lives; they refer to Christ-
honoring motives and godly obedience and transparent integrity.
Wood, hay, and straw are perishable things—carnal attitudes, sinful
motives, pride-filled actions, selfish ambition."[3]

Fire in Scripture often symbolizes the holiness of God (Leviticus 1:8; Hebrews 12:29). And the Bible clearly uses fire to portray God's judgment upon that which His holiness has condemned
(Genesis 19:24; Mark 9:43-48). God will examine our works and
test them against the fire of His holiness. If we build with good
materials—like precious metals and stones—our works will stand.
But if we build with less valuable materials—wood, hay, or straw—
they will burn up.

The Scope of the Judgment Includes Actions

The Christian's judgment will focus on his personal steward-
ship of the gifts, talents, opportunities, and responsibilities given
to him in this life. The very character of each Christian's life and

service will be utterly laid bare under the unerring and omniscient vision of Christ, whose "eyes were like blazing fire" (Revelation 1:14).

Numerous Scripture verses reveal that each of our actions will be judged before the Lord. The psalmist said to the Lord, "Surely you will reward each person according to what he has done" (Psalm 62:12; compare with Matthew 16:27). In Ephesians 6:7-8 we read that the Lord "will reward everyone for whatever good he does, whether he is slave or free."

Christ's judgment of our actions will be infallible. There will be no confusion on His part. He fully understands the circumstances we live and labor in. As John Wesley once put it, "God will then bring to light every circumstance that accompanied each word and action. He will judge whether they lessened or increased the goodness or badness of them."[4]

The Scope of the Judgment Includes Thoughts

At the Judgment Seat of Christ, our thoughts as well as our actions will come under scrutiny. In Jeremiah 17:10 God said, "I the LORD search the heart and examine the mind, to reward a man according to his conduct, according to what his deeds deserve." The Lord "will bring to light what is hidden in darkness and will expose the motives of men's hearts" (1 Corinthians 4:5). The Lord is the One "who searches hearts and minds" (Revelation 2:23).

The Scope of the Judgment Includes Words

Christ once said that "men will have to give account on the day of judgment for every careless word they have spoken" (Matthew 12:35-37). This is an important aspect of judgment, for tremendous damage can be done through the human tongue (see James 3:1-12).

John Blanchard reminds us that "if even our careless words are carefully recorded, how can we bear the thought that our calculated boastful claims, the cutting criticisms, the off-color jokes, and the unkind comments will also be taken into account? Even our whispered asides and words spoken in confidence or when we thought we were 'safe' will be heard again."[5]

Rewards and Crowns

What kinds of rewards will believers receive at the Judgment Seat of Christ? Scripture often speaks of crowns. In fact, a number of different crowns symbolize the various achievements and awards in the Christian life.

The crown of life is given to those who persevere under trial, and especially to those who suffer to the point of death (James 1:12; Revelation 2:10). The crown of glory is given to those who faithfully and sacrificially minister God's Word to the flock (1 Peter 5:4). The crown incorruptible is given to those who win the race of temperance and self-control (1 Corinthians 9:25). The crown of righteousness is given to those who long for the second coming of Christ (2 Timothy 4:8).

Revelation 4:10 shows believers casting their crowns before the throne of God in an act of worship and adoration. This teaches us something very important. Clearly God rewards us with crowns not for our own glory but ultimately for His own glory. Scripture tells us that believers are redeemed in order to bring glory to God (1 Corinthians 6:20). Placing our crowns before the throne of God seems to be an illustration of this.

Here is something else to think about. The greater the reward or crown one has received, the greater his capacity to bring glory to the Creator. The lesser the reward or crown one has received, the lesser his capacity to bring glory to the Creator. Because of the different rewards handed out at the Judgment Seat of Christ, believers will have differing capacities to bring glory to God.

Still, we should not take this to mean that certain believers will have a sense of lack throughout eternity. After all, each believer will be glorifying God to the fullness of his capacity in the next life. Each one of us, then, will be able to "declare the praises of him who called [us] out of darkness into his wonderful light" (1 Peter 2:9).[6]

The Judgment of Nonbelievers

Unlike believers, whose judgment deals only with rewards and loss of rewards, nonbelievers face a horrific judgment that leads to their being cast into the Lake of Fire. The judgment that nonbelievers face is called the Great White Throne judgment (Revelation 20:11-15). Christ is the divine Judge, and those who are judged are the unsaved dead of all time. The judgment takes place at the end of the Millennial Kingdom, Christ's 1000-year reign on planet earth.

Those who face Christ at this judgment will be judged on the basis of their works (Revelation 20:12-13). It is critical to understand that they actually get to this judgment because they are *already* unsaved. This judgment will not separate believers from unbelievers, for all who will experience it will have already made the choice during their lifetimes to reject salvation in Jesus Christ. Once they are before the divine Judge, they are judged according to their works not only to justify their condemnation but to determine the degree to which each person should be punished throughout eternity.

Resurrected to Judgment

Those who participate in the Great White Throne judgment are resurrected to judgment. Jesus Himself affirmed that "a time is coming when all who are in their graves will hear his voice and come out—those who have done good will rise to live, and those who have done evil will rise to be condemned" (John 5:28-29).

We need to emphasize, though, that Jesus is not teaching that there is just one general resurrection that will take place at the end of time. Contrary to this idea, the Scriptures indicate that there are two types of resurrection, respectively referred to as the "first resurrection" and the "second resurrection" (Revelation 20:5-6,11-15). The first resurrection is the resurrection of Christians; the second resurrection is the resurrection of the wicked.

The second resurrection is an awful spectacle. All the unsaved of all time will be resurrected at the end of Christ's Millennial Kingdom, judged at the Great White Throne judgment, and then cast alive into the Lake of Fire (Revelation 20:11-15). Unsaved human beings will be given bodies that will last forever, which means they will be subject to pain and suffering forever.

Degrees of Punishment

The Scriptures indicate that all those who are judged at the Great White Throne judgment have a horrible destiny ahead. Indeed, their destiny will include weeping and gnashing of teeth (Matthew 13:41-42), condemnation (Matthew 12:36-37), destruction (Philippians 1:28), eternal punishment (Matthew 25:46), separation from God's presence (2 Thessalonians 1:8-9), and trouble and distress (Romans 2:9). Nevertheless, the Scriptures also refer to degrees of punishment in hell. And these degrees of punishment will be determined at the Great White Throne judgment when Christ examines each person with His penetrating eyes.

Common observation shows that unsaved people vary as much in their quality of life as saved people do. Some saved people are spiritual and charitable (for example), and other saved people are carnal and unloving. Some unbelievers are terribly evil (like Hitler), while others, such as unbelieving moralists, are much less evil. Just as believers differ in how they respond to God's law, and therefore in their reward in heaven, so unbelievers differ in their response to God's law, and therefore in their punishment in hell. Just as there are degrees of reward in heaven, so there are degrees of punishment in hell (see Matthew 10:15; 16:27; Luke 12:47-48; Revelation 20:12-13; 22:12).

Hell: The Destiny of the Wicked

Hell is as awful as heaven is wonderful. The Scriptures assure us that hell is a real place. But hell was not part of God's original creation, which He called "good" (Genesis 1). Hell was created later to accommodate the banishment of Satan and his fallen angels, who rebelled against God (Matthew 25:41). Human beings who reject Christ will join Satan and his fallen angels in this infernal place of suffering.

One of the more important New Testament words for hell is Gehenna (Matthew 10:28; 2 Kings 23:10). This word has an interesting history. For several generations in ancient Israel, atrocities were committed in the Valley of Ben Hinnom—atrocities that included human sacrifices, even the sacrifice of children (2 Chronicles 28:3; 33:6; Jeremiah 32:35). These unfortunate victims were sacrificed to the false Moabite god Molech. Jeremiah appropriately called this valley a "valley of slaughter" (Jeremiah 7:31-34).

Eventually the valley came to be used as a public rubbish dump into which all the filth in Jerusalem was poured. Not only garbage but also the bodies of dead animals and the corpses of criminals were throne on the heap where they would burn with everything else in the dump. The fires never stopped burning, and hungry worms could always find a good meal.

This place was originally called (in the Hebrew) *Ge[gen]hinnom* (the valley of the sons of Hinnom). It was eventually shortened to the name *Ge-Hinnom*. The Greek translation of this Hebrew phrase is *Gehenna*. It became an appropriate and graphic term for the reality of hell. Jesus Himself used the word metaphorically 11 times to describe the eternal place of suffering of unredeemed humanity.

The Scriptures use a variety of words to describe the horrors of hell:

The Lake of Burning Sulfur/The Lake of Fire. One day the wicked dead will be resurrected, face the Great White Throne judgment, and then be tossed into the Lake of Fire. Those who end up there will be tormented day and night forever (Revelation 19:20; 20:14-15).

Eternal Fire. Jesus often referred to the eternal destiny of the wicked as "eternal fire." Following His second coming, when He separates the sheep (believers) from the goats (unbelievers), Jesus will say to the goats, "Depart from me, you who are cursed, into the eternal fire prepared for the devil and his angels" (Matthew 25:41).

What precisely is the "fire" of hell? Some believe it is literal. And, indeed, that may very well be the case. Others believe "fire" is a metaphorical way of expressing the great wrath of God. Scripture tells us, "The LORD your God is a consuming fire, a jealous God" (Deuteronomy 4:24). "God is a consuming fire" (Hebrews 12:29). "His wrath is poured out like fire" (Nahum 1:6).

"Who can stand when he appears? For he will be like a refiner's fire" (Malachi 3:2). God said, "My wrath will break out and burn like fire because of the evil you have done—burn with no one to quench it" (Jeremiah 4:4). How awful is the fiery wrath of God!

Fiery Furnace. Scripture sometimes refers to the destiny of the wicked as the "fiery furnace." Jesus said that at the end of the age the holy angels will gather all evildoers and "throw them into the fiery furnace, where there will be weeping and gnashing of teeth" (Matthew 13:42). "Weeping" carries the idea of wailing as an outward expression of deep grief. This weeping will be caused by the environment, the company, the remorse and guilt, and the shame that is part and parcel of hell.

Destruction. Second Thessalonians 1:8-9 tells us that unbelievers "will be punished with everlasting destruction and shut out from the presence of the Lord and from the majesty of his power." The Greek word translated "destruction" in this verse carries the meaning "sudden ruin" or "loss of all that gives worth to existence." The word refers not to annihilation but rather indicates separation from God and a loss of everything worthwhile in life.

Eternal Punishment. Jesus affirmed that the wicked "will go away to eternal punishment, but the righteous to eternal life" (Matthew 25:46). Notice that the eternality of the punishment of the wicked equals the eternality of the eternal life of the righteous. One is just as long as the other.

Exclusion from God's Presence. The greatest pain suffered by those in hell is that they are forever excluded from the presence of God. If ecstatic joy is found in the presence of God (Psalm 16:11), then utter dismay is found in the eternal absence of His presence.

The Final Justice of God

Clearly, *justice delayed* is not *justice denied*, as so many wrongly conclude today. A day is coming when God Almighty will settle accounts with every human being, and what a sobering day that will be. They will be held responsible for every evil they have ever committed. And every day that passes brings us that much closer to the final justice of God.

BIBLIOGRAPHY

Adams, Marilyn McCord, and Robert Merrihew Adams. *The Problem of Evil*. Oxford, London: Oxford University Press, 1990.

Berkhof, Louis. *Manual of Christian Doctrine*. Grand Rapids, MI: William B. Eerdmans Publishing Company, 1983.

————. *Systematic Theology*. Grand Rapids, MI: William B. Eerdmans Publishing Company, 1982.

Boice, James M. *The Sovereign God*. Downers Grove, IL: InterVarsity Press, 1978.

Bridges, Jerry. *Trusting God Even When Life Hurts*. Colorado Springs, CO: NavPress, 1988.

Bruce, F.F. *The Hard Sayings of Jesus*. Downers Grove, IL: InterVarsity Press, 1983.

Buswell, James O. *A Systematic Theology of the Christian Religion*. Grand Rapids, MI: Zondervan, 1979.

Calvin, John. *Institutes of the Christian Religion*. Edited by John T. McNeill. Translated by Ford Lewis Battles. Philadelphia, PA: The Westminster Press, 1960.

Campbell, Donald K., ed. *Walvoord: A Tribute*. Chicago, IL: Moody Press, 1982.

Carson, D.A. *How Long, O Lord? Reflections on Suffering and Evil*. Grand Rapids, MI: Baker Book House, 1990.

Chafer, Lewis Sperry. *Systematic Theology*. Wheaton, IL: Victor Books, 1988.

Charnock, Stephen. *The Existence and Attributes of God*. Grand Rapids, MI: Baker Book House, 1996.

Clouse, Robert G., ed. *War: Four Christian Views*. Downers Grove, IL: InterVarsity Press, 1991.

Cobb, John B. and David Ray Griffin. *Process Theology: An Introductory Exposition*. Philadelphia, PA: The Westminster Press, 1976.

Craig, William Lane. *No Easy Answers: Finding Hope in Doubt, Failure, and Unanswered Prayer*. Chicago, IL: Moody Press, 1990.

Davids, Peter. *More Hard Sayings of the New Testament*. Downers Grove, IL: InterVarsity Press, 1991.

Eareckson, Joni. *Joni*. Grand Rapids, MI: Zondervan, 1976.

Elwell, Walter A., ed. *Evangelical Dictionary of Theology*. Grand Rapids, MI: Baker Book House, 1984.

———, ed. *The Concise Evangelical Dictionary of Theology*. Grand Rapids, MI: Baker Book House, 1991.

Enns, Paul. *The Moody Handbook of Theology*. Chicago, IL: Moody Press, 1989.

Erickson, Millard J. *Christian Theology*, Unabridged, one-volume edition. Grand Rapids, MI: Baker Book House, 1987.

Erickson, Millard J. *Introducing Christian Doctrine*. Grand Rapids, MI: Baker Book House, 1996.

Feinberg, John S. *The Many Faces of Evil: Theological Systems and the Problem of Evil*. Grand Rapids, MI: Zondervan, 1994.

Geisler, Norman. *Baker Encyclopedia of Christian Apologetics*. Grand Rapids, MI: Baker Book House, 1999.

———. *Christian Apologetics*. Grand Rapids, MI: Baker Book House, 1976.

———. *Philosophy of Religion*. Grand Rapids, MI: Zondervan, 1974.

———. *The Roots of Evil*. Grand Rapids, MI: Zondervan, 1978.

Geisler, Norman, and Ronald Brooks. *When Skeptics Ask*. Wheaton, IL: Victor Books, 1990.

Geisler, Norman, and Thomas Howe. *When Critics Ask: A Popular Handbook on Bible Difficulties.* Wheaton, IL: Victor Books, 1992.

Geivett, R. Douglas. *Evil and the Evidence for God: The Challenge of John Hick's Theodicy.* Philadelphia, PA: Temple University Press, 1993.

Grudem, Wayne. *Systematic Theology: An Introduction to Biblical Doctrine.* Grand Rapids, MI: Zondervan, 1994.

Gundry, Stanley, and Alan F. Johnson, eds. *Tensions in Contemporary Theology.* Chicago, IL: Moody Press, 1976.

Henry, Carl F.H., ed. *Baker's Dictionary of Christian Ethics.* Grand Rapids, MI: Baker Book House, 1978.

———, ed. *Basic Christian Doctrines.* Grand Rapids, MI: Baker Book House, 1983.

Hick, John. *Evil and the God of Love.* New York, NY: Harper & Row Publishers, 1966.

Hodge, Charles. *Systematic Theology,* Abridged Edition. Edited by Edward N. Gross. Grand Rapids, MI: Baker Book House, 1988.

Howard-Snyder, Daniel, ed. *The Evidential Argument from Evil.* Indianapolis, IN: Indiana University Press, 1996.

Kaiser, Walter. *Hard Sayings of the Old Testament.* Downers Grove, IL: InterVarsity Press, 1988.

———. *More Hard Sayings of the Old Testament.* Downers Grove, IL: InterVarsity Press, 1992.

Kreeft, Peter, and Ronald Tacelli. *Handbook of Christian Apologetics.* Downers Grove, IL: InterVarsity Press, 1994.

Kreeft, Peter. *Making Sense Out of Suffering.* Ann Arbor, MI: Servant Books, 1986.

Leibniz, G.W. *Theodicy.* Chicago, IL: Open Court, 1990.

Lewis, C.S. *The Screwtape Letters.* London, England: Fontana Books, 1973.

Lewis, Gordon, and Bruce Demarest. *Integrative Theology.* Grand Rapids, MI: Zondervan, 1996.

Lightner, Robert. *Evangelical Theology: A Survey and Review.* Grand Rapids, MI: Baker Book House, 1986.

———. *The God of the Bible: An Introduction to the Doctrine of God.* Grand Rapids, MI: Baker Book House, 1973.

McDowell, Josh, and Don Stewart. *Answers to Tough Questions Skeptics Ask About the Christian Faith.* Wheaton, IL: Tyndale House Publishers, 1988.

———. *Reasons Skeptics Should Consider Christianity.* Wheaton, IL: Tyndale House Publishers, 1988.

McGill, Arthur C. *Suffering: A Test of Theological Method.* Philadelphia, PA: The Westminster Press, 1982.

Milne, Bruce. *Know the Truth: A Handbook of Christian Belief.* Downers Grove, IL: InterVarsity Press, 1982.

Moreland, J.P. and Kai Nielsen. *Does God Exist?* Nashville, TN: Thomas Nelson Publishers, 1990.

Morey, Robert. *The New Atheism and the Erosion of Freedom.* Minneapolis, MN: Bethany House Publishers, 1986.

O'Brien, David. *Today's Handbook for Solving Bible Difficulties.* Minneapolis, MN: Bethany House Publishers, 1990.

Packer, J.I. *Knowing God.* Downers Grove, IL: InterVarsity Press, 1979.

Pentecost, J.D. *God's Answers to Man's Problems.* Chicago, IL: Moody Press, 1985.

Pink, A.W. *The Attributes of God.* Alexandria, LA: Lamplighter Publications, n.d.

———. *The Sovereignty of God.* London, England: The Banner of Truth Trust, 1972.

Plantinga, Alvin C. *God, Freedom, and Evil.* Grand Rapids, MI: William B. Eerdmans Publishing Company, 1974.

Plantinga, Cornelius Jr. *Not the Way It's Supposed to Be: A Breviary of Sin.* Grand Rapids, MI: William B. Eerdmans Publishing Company, 1995.

Ramm, Bernard. *Protestant Biblical Interpretation*. Grand Rapids, MI: Baker Book House, 1978.

Rhodes, Ron. *Angels Among Us: Separating Truth from Fiction*. Eugene, OR: Harvest House Publishers, 1994.

————. *Christ Before the Manger: The Life and Times of the Preincarnate Christ*. Grand Rapids, MI: Baker Book House, 1992.

————. *Heaven: The Undiscovered Country—Exploring the Wonder of the Afterlife*. Eugene, OR: Harvest House Publishers, 1996.

————. *Quick-Reference Guide to Angels*. Eugene, OR: Harvest House Publishers, 1997.

————. *The Heart of Christianity: What It Means to Believe in Jesus*. Eugene, OR: Harvest House Publishers, 1996.

————. *When Servants Suffer: Finding Purpose in Pain*. Wheaton, IL: Harold Shaw Publishers, 1989.

Ryrie, Charles C. *Basic Theology*. Wheaton, IL: Victor Books, 1986.

Salisbury, Judy. *A Christian Woman's Guide to Reasons for Faith*. Eugene, OR: Harvest House Publishers, 2003.

Sauer, Erich. *From Eternity to Eternity*. Grand Rapids, MI: William B. Eerdmans Publishing Company, 1979.

————. *The Dawn of World Redemption*. Grand Rapids, MI: William B. Eerdmans Publishing Company, 1977.

————. *The Triumph of the Crucified*. Grand Rapids, MI: William B. Eerdmans Publishing Company, 1977.

Smith, David. L. *A Handbook of Contemporary Theology*. Grand Rapids, MI: Baker Book House, 1992.

Story, Dan. *Defending Your Faith: How to Answer the Tough Questions*. Nashville, TN: Thomas Nelson Publishers, 1992.

Stowell, Joseph M. *Eternity: Reclaiming a Passion for What Endures*. Chicago, IL: Moody Press, 1995.

Strobel, Lee. *The Case for Faith*. Grand Rapids, MI: Zondervan, 2000.

Swinburne, Richard. *Providence and the Problem of Evil.* Oxford, England: Clarendon Press, 1998.

Swindoll, Charles R. *The Mystery of God's Will.* Nashville, TN: Word Publishing, 1999.

———. *The Tale of the Tardy Oxcart.* Nashville, TN: Word Publishing, 1998.

Thiessen, Henry Clarence. *Lectures in Systematic Theology.* Grand Rapids, MI: William B. Eerdmans Publishing Company, 1981.

Tozer, A.W. *The Knowledge of the Holy.* New York, NY: Harper & Row Publishers, 1961.

Walvoord, John F., and Roy B. Zuck, eds. *The Bible Knowledge Commentary: New Testament.* Wheaton, IL: Victor Books, 1983.

———, eds. *The Bible Knowledge Commentary: Old Testament.* Wheaton, IL: Victor Books, 1985.

Wenham, John W. *The Enigma of Evil: Can We Believe in the Goodness of God?* Grand Rapids, MI: Zondervan, 1985.

Yancey, Philip. *Pain: The Gift Nobody Wants.* Grand Rapids, MI: Zondervan, 1993.

NOTES

Introduction—A Hard Look at Reality

1. Cited by Lee Strobel, "Why Does God Allow Suffering?" Message delivered at Saddleback Valley Community Church, El Toro, California, February 26, 2000.

2. "Car Strikes Praying High School Runners, Killing 1," The Associated Press, October 12, 2003.

3. John W. Wenham, *The Enigma of Evil: Can We Believe in the Goodness of God?* (Grand Rapids, MI: Zondervan, 1985), p. 8.

4. William Lane Craig, *No Easy Answers* (Chicago, IL: Moody Press, 1990), pp. 73-74.

5. Tadeusz Borowski, *This Way for the Gas, Ladies and Gentlemen* (New York, NY: Penguin, 1992), pp. 15, 16, 20, 22, 24-25, 31, 32, 39, 40, 43, 54, 85, 93, 108, 118, 131, 144, 159.

6. Wenham, p. 8.

7. Cited in Ron Rhodes, *When Servants Suffer: Finding Purpose in Pain* (Wheaton, IL: Harold Shaw Publishers, 1989), p. 5.

8. Craig, pp. 77-78; see also Peter Kreeft, *Making Sense Out of Suffering* (Ann Arbor, MI: Servant Books, 1986), p. viii.

9. Kreeft, p. 5.

10. 2000 Uniform Crime Report (Federal Bureau of Investigation). Available online at www.fbi.gov/ucr/ucr.htm; cited in Gannon Murphy, "God and the Problem of Evil" (Minnesota Apologetics Project). Available online at www.geocities.com/mnapologetics/art12.htm.

11. Cornelius Plantinga, Jr. *Not the Way It's Supposed to Be: A Breviary of Sin* (Grand Rapids, MI: William B. Eerdmans Publishing Company, 1995), p. 1.

12. Paul W. Powell, *When the Hurt Won't Go Away* (Wheaton, IL: Victor Books, 1976), p. 41.

13. Cited in W. Gary Phillips, "The Problem of Evil: A Pastoral Approach," adapted from W. Gary Phillips and William E. Brown, *Making Sense of Your World* (Chicago, IL: Moody Press, June 1991), cited in *Michigan Theological Journal*, vol. 2, no. 1 (Spring 1991). Insert added.

14. Epicurus, cited in Lee Strobel, *The Case for Faith* (Grand Rapids, MI: Zondervan, 2000), p. 25.

15. Cited in Charles R. Swindoll, *The Mystery of God's Will* (Nashville, TN: Word Publishing, 1999), p. 6.

16. Cited in Swindoll, p. 7.

17. Ibid.

18. Cited in Rhodes, p. 5.

Chapter 1—Does Evil Prove God Doesn't Exist?

1. Alvin C. Plantinga, *God, Freedom, and Evil* (Grand Rapids, MI: William B. Eerdmans Publishing Company, 2002), p. 7.

2. Millard Erickson, *Introducing Christian Doctrine* (Grand Rapids, MI: Baker Book House, 1996), pp. 138-39.

3. Erickson, *Introducing Christian Doctrine*, p. 139.

4. Norman L. Geisler and Ronald M. Brooks, *When Skeptics Ask* (Wheaton, IL: Victor Books, 1990), pp. 59-60.

5. Ken Boa and Larry Moody, *I'm Glad You Asked* (Colorado Springs, CO: Victor Books, 1994), p. 122.

6. Erickson, *Introducing Christian Doctrine*, pp. 138-39.

7. Robert Morey, *The New Atheism and the Erosion of Freedom* (Minneapolis, MN: Bethany House Publishers, 1986), p. 153.

8. Morey, p. 153. Insert added.

9. Morey, p. 153.

10. Peter Kreeft, *Making Sense Out of Suffering* (Ann Arbor, MI: Servant Books, 1986), p. 30.

11. William Lane Craig, *No Easy Answers* (Chicago, IL: Moody Press, 1990), p. 86.

12. Craig, p. 86.

13. Boa and Moody, p. 129.

14. Norman L. Geisler, *Baker Encyclopedia of Christian Apologetics* (Grand Rapids, MI: Baker Book House, 1999), p. 220.

15. William A. Dembski, *Intelligent Design: The Bridge Between Science and Theology* (Downers Grove, IL: InterVarsity Press, 1999), p. 263.

16. Geisler, *Baker Encyclopedia of Christian Apologetics*, p. 220.

17. Jimmy H. Davis and Harry L. Poe, *Designer Universe: Intelligent Design and the Existence of God* (Nashville, TN: Broadman & Holman Publishers, 2002), p. 221. Emphasis added.

18. Gordon R. Lewis and Bruce A. Demarest, *Integrative Theology*, vol. 1 (Grand Rapids, MI: Zondervan, 1996), p. 243. Insert added.

19. R. T. France, *The Living God* (Downers Grove, IL: InterVarsity Press, 1972), p. 25.

20. Robert Lightner, *The God of the Bible* (Grand Rapids, MI: Baker Book House, 1973), p. 77.

21. James Montgomery Boice, *The Sovereign God* (Downers Grove, IL: InterVarsity Press, 1978), p. 151.

22. Jerry Bridges, *Trusting God Even When Life Hurts* (Colorado Springs, CO: NavPress, 1988), p. 39.

23. Bridges, p. 48.

24. Judy Salisbury, *A Christian Woman's Guide to Reasons for Faith: Understanding Why You Believe* (Eugene, OR: Harvest House Publishers, 2003), p. 125.

25. Charles R. Swindoll, *The Mystery of God's Will* (Nashville, TN: Word Publishing, 1999), p. 91.

26. Swindoll, p. 91.

Chapter 2—Does Evil Prove God Isn't Good?

1. Cited in Ron Rhodes, *When Servants Suffer: Finding Purpose in Pain* (Wheaton, IL: Harold Shaw Publishers, 1989), p. 5.

2. James Montgomery Boice, *The Sovereign God* (Downers Grove, IL: InterVarsity Press, 1978), pp. 229-30.

3. Millard Erickson, *Introducing Christian Doctrine* (Grand Rapids, MI: Baker Book House, 1992), p. 139.

4. Most Calvinists subscribe to five key tenets: total depravity, unconditional election, limited atonement, irresistible grace, and perseverance of the saints. See Ron Rhodes, *The Complete Book of Bible Answers* (Eugene, OR: Harvest House Publishers, 1997), p. 197.

5. Gordon Clark, *Religion, Reason, and Revelation* (Philadelphia, PA: Presbyterian and Reformed, 1961), p. 206.

6. Clark, p. 206.

7. See Millard Erickson, *Christian Theology* (Grand Rapids, MI: Baker Book House, 1987), p. 417.

8. Erickson, *Christian Theology*, p. 418.

9. Clark, p. 222.

10. Clark, pp. 237-38.

11. Erickson, *Christian Theology*, p. 418.

12. Clark, pp. 239-40.

13. Erickson, *Christian Theology*, p. 418.

14. Clark, p. 241.

15. Abdiyah Akbar Abdul-Haqq, *Sharing Your Faith with a Muslim* (Minneapolis, MN: Bethany, 1980), p. 159.

16. Kenneth Cragg, *The Call of the Minaret* (New York, NY: Oxford University Press, 1964), pp. 42-43.

17. Quoted in Haqq, p. 152.

18. Quoted in Gerhard Nehls, *Christians Ask Muslims* (Bellville: SIM International Life Challenge, 1987), p. 21.

19. Lewis M. Hopfe, *Religions of the World* (New York, NY: Prentice Hall, 2000), p. 410.

20. Bruce A. McDowell and Anees Zaka, *Muslims and Christians at the Table* (Phillipsburg, NY: Presbyterian and Reformed Press, 1999), p. 124.

21. John Gilchrist, *Quran: The Scripture of Islam* (Muslim Evangelicalism Resource Center, 1995), in *The World of Islam* CD-ROM (Global Mapping International, 2000). Insert added.

22. Norman Geisler and Abdul Saleeb, *Answering Islam: The Crescent in the Light of the Cross* (Grand Rapids, MI: Baker Book House, 1993), pp. 141-42.

23. Geisler and Saleeb, pp. 137-38.

24. Norman Geisler, *Thomas Aquinas: An Evangelical Appraisal* (Grand Rapids, MI: Baker Book House, 1991), chapter 10.

25. A.W. Tozer, *The Knowledge of the Holy*; cited in Charles R. Swindoll, *The Tale of the Tardy Oxcart* (Nashville, TN: Word, 1998), p. 240.

26. See Norman Geisler, "God, Evil, and Dispensations," *Walvoord: A Tribute*, ed. Donald K. Campbell (Chicago, IL: Moody Press, 1982), p. 98.

27. Norman Geisler and Thomas Howe, *When Critics Ask: A Popular Handbook on Bible Difficulties* (Wheaton, IL: Victor Books, 1992), p. 271.

28. Frank E. Gaebelein, ed., *The Expositor's Bible Commentary*, ed. (Grand Rapids, MI: Zondervan). Available on Accordance Bible Software CD-ROM (Oak-Tree Software, Inc., 2003).

29. C.F. Keil and F. Delitzsch, *Commentary on the Old Testament in Ten Volumes*, vol. 6 (Grand Rapids, MI: William B. Eerdmans Publishing Company, 1989), p. 337.

30. Joseph M. Stowell, *Eternity: Reclaiming a Passion for What Endures* (Chicago, IL: Moody Press, 1995), p. 27.

31. "Fear of Death," quoted by Ray C. Stedman in "The Death of Death," *The Ray C. Stedman Library* (Discovery Publishing, 2003). Available online at 216.239.41.104/search?q=cache:VHrojoUcHsQJ:www.pbc.org/dp/stedman/misc/pdf/0275.pdf.

Chapter 3—Does Evil Prove God Is Finite?

1. *Webster's Revised Unabridged Dictionary*, CD-ROM version, 1998 edition.

2. Cited in Peter Kreeft, *Making Sense Out of Suffering* (Ann Arbor, MI: Servant Books, 1986), p. 6. Insert added.

3. Millard Erickson, *Christian Theology*, unabridged one-volume edition (Grand Rapids, MI: Baker Book House, 1987), p. 415.

4. Cited in Jerry Bridges, *Trusting God Even When Life Hurts* (Colorado Springs, CO: NavPress, 1988), p. 23.

5. Rabbi Harold Kushner, *When Bad Things Happen to Good People* (New York, NY: Schocken Books, 1981), p. 134.

6. Kushner, p. 43.

7. Walter A. Elwell, ed., *Evangelical Dictionary of Theology* (Grand Rapids, MI: Baker Book House, 1984), p. 880. Emphasis added.

8. Millard Erickson, *The Word Became Flesh* (Grand Rapids, MI: Baker Book House, 1991), p. 244.

9. John B. Cobb, Jr., and David Ray Griffin, *Process Theology: an Introductory Exposition* (Philadelphia, PA: The Westminster Press, 1976), p. 56.

10. See Erickson, *The Word Became Flesh*, p. 248.

11. Cobb and Griffin, p. 69.

12. Cobb and Griffin, p. 57.

13. Cobb and Griffin, p. 69.

14. Clark Pinnock, et al. *The Openness of God: A Biblical Challenge to the Traditional Understanding of God* (Downers Grove, IL: InterVarsity Press, 1994), p. 156.

15. Norman L. Geisler, H. Wayne House, with Max Herrera, *The Battle for God: Responding to the Challenge of Neotheism* (Grand Rapids, MI: Kregel Publications, 2001), p. 56.

16. John Sanders, *The God Who Risks* (Downers Grove, IL: InterVarsity Press, 1998), p. 198.

17. Gregory Boyd, *God of the Possible: A Biblical Introduction to the Open View of God* (Grand Rapids, MI: Baker Book House, 2000), p. 156.

18. Geisler, House, and Herrera, p. 49.

19. Boyd, p. 31.

20. Geisler, House, and Herrera, p. 92.

21. Norman L. Geisler, "Neotheism: Orthodox or Unorthodox? A Theological Response to Greg Boyd," Available online at www.normgeisler.com/neothism.htm.

22. Norman L. Geisler, *The Baker Encyclopedia of Apologetics* (Grand Rapids, MI: Baker Book House, 2002). Available in *The Norman Geisler CD-ROM Library*.

23. John W. Wenham, *The Enigma of Evil: Can We Believe in the Goodness of God?* (Grand Rapids, MI: Zondervan, 1985), p. 44.

24. Ken Boa and Larry Moody, *I'm Glad You Asked* (Colorado Springs, CO: Victor Books, 1994), p. 127.

25. R.C. Sproul, *Doubt and Assurance*, cited in Charles R. Swindoll, *The Tale of the Tardy Oxcart* (Nashville, TN: Word Publishing, 1998), p. 578.

26. Erickson, *Christian Theology*, p. 280.

27. Isaac Asimov, "In the Game of Energy and Thermodynamics, You Can't Even Break Even," *Smithsonian* (June 1970), p. 10.

28. Norman Geisler, "Process Theology," *Tensions in Contemporary Theology*, ed. Stanley N. Gundry and Alan F. Johnson (Chicago, IL: Moody Press, 1976), p. 274.

29. Lewis Sperry Chafer, *Systematic Theology*, vol. 1 (Dallas, TX: Dallas Seminary Press, 1947), p. 196.

30. Geisler, House, and Herrera, p. 24.

31. Geisler, "Process Theology," in *Tensions in Contemporary Theology*, p. 273.

32. Geisler, House, and Herrera, p. 92.

33. Ontology focuses on the nature of being.

34. Robert G. Gromacki, *The Virgin Birth: Doctrine of Deity* (Grand Rapids, MI: Baker Book House, 1984), p. 107.

35. Gromacki, p. 106.

36. John F. Walvoord, *Jesus Christ Our Lord* (Chicago, IL: Moody Press, 1980), p. 115.

37. Robert P. Lightner, *Evangelical Theology* (Grand Rapids, MI: Baker Book House, 1986), p. 82.

38. Walvoord, p. 115.

39. Geisler, "Process Theology," p. 251.

Chapter 4—Why Doesn't God Abolish Evil Immediately?

1. Annie Besant, "Why I Do Not Believe in God," *The American Atheist*, vol. 35 no. 4 (1997). Available online at http://www.AmericanAtheist.org/. Insert added.

2. Billy Graham, *How to be Born Again* (Dallas, TX: Word Publishing, 1989), p. 118.

3. Paul E. Little, *Know Why You Believe* (Downers Grove, IL: InterVarsity Press, 1975), p. 81.

4. Christians rejoice that despite the fact that they are stained by sin, Christ has substitutionally died for them upon the cross so that they could be forgiven and live forever with God in heaven (see 2 Corinthians 5:21).

5. Judy Salisbury, *A Christian Woman's Guide to Reasons for Faith: Understanding Why You Believe* (Eugene, OR: Harvest House Publishers, 2003), p. 119.

6. Millard Erickson, *Christian Theology,* unabridged one-volume edition (Grand Rapids, MI: Baker Book House, 1987), p. 425.

7. Sid Litke, "Why Is There Suffering?" Available online at www.bible.org/docs/splife/misc/suff.htm.

8. Peter Kreeft, *Making Sense Out of Suffering* (Ann Arbor, MI: Servant Books, 1986), p. 123.

9. Ibid.

10. Robert A. Morey, *The New Atheism and the Erosion of Freedom* (Minneapolis, MN: Bethany House Publishers, 1987), pp. 154-55.

11. Dan Story, *Defending Your Faith* (Nashville, TN: Thomas Nelson Publishers, 1992), pp. 176-77.

Chapter 5—The Problem with Free Will

1. Cornelius Plantinga, Jr. *Not the Way It's Supposed to Be: A Breviary of Sin* (Grand Rapids, MI: William B. Eerdmans Publishing Company, 1995), p. 2.

2. Gregory Boyd, *Is God to Blame? Beyond Pat Answers to the Problem of Suffering* (Downers Grove, IL: InterVarsity Press, 2003), pp. 97-98.

3. Rick Rood, "The Problem of Evil: How Can a Good God Allow Evil?" (Richardson, TX: Probe Ministries, 1996).

4. Sid Litke, "Why Is There Suffering?" Available online at www.bible.org/ docs/splife/misc/suff.htm.

5. Ken Boa and Larry Moody, *I'm Glad You Asked* (Colorado Springs, CO: Victor Books, 1994), p. 428.

6. Paul E. Little, *Know Why You Believe* (Downers Grove, IL: InterVarsity Press, 1975), p. 81. See also Robert A. Morey, *The New Atheism and the Erosion of Freedom* (Minneapolis, MN: Bethany House Publishers, 1986), p. 155.

7. Little, p. 81.

8. Cited in Lee Strobel, *The Case for Faith* (Grand Rapids, MI: Zondervan, 2000), p. 37.

9. Boyd, p. 63.

10. Norman L. Geisler and Ronald M. Brooks, *When Skeptics Ask* (Wheaton, IL: Victor Books, 1990), p. 73.

11. Little, p. 87.

12. William Lane Craig, *No Easy Answers* (Chicago, IL: Moody Press, 1990), p. 80.

13. Norman L. Geisler, *The Baker Encyclopedia of Apologetics* (Grand Rapids, MI: Baker Book House, 2002). Available in *The Norman Geisler CD-ROM Library*.

14. Judy Salisbury, *A Christian Woman's Guide to Reasons for Faith: Understanding Why You Believe* (Eugene, OR: Harvest House Publishers, 2003), pp. 119-20.

15. Norman Geisler, "Why Does God Permit Evil to Exist?" Part Two, interview by Dr. John Ankerberg. Available from Ankerberg Theological Research Institute, 1-800-805-3030.

16. Boa and Moody, p. 131. Related to this, Bruce Milne writes: "Adam's open-eyed disobedience created the 'way in' for evil and suffering in human life (Genesis 3:14-19; Romans 5:12-21). As an act of rebellion against the creator, sin cannot but have the most serious and extensive implications in a

moral universe which reflects the holy character of its creator" (Bruce Milne, *Know the Truth* [Downers Grove, IL: InterVarsity Press, 1988], p. 83).

17. Norman L. Geisler and Jeff Amanu, "Evil," in *New Dictionary of Theology*, Sinclair B. Ferguson and David F. Wright, eds. (Downers Grove, IL: InterVarsity Press, 1988), p. 242.

18. Gordon R. Lewis and Bruce A. Demarest, *Integrative Theology*, vol. 1 (Grand Rapids, MI: Zondervan, 1996), p. 322.

19. Lewis and Demarest, p. 323.

20. Cited in Dan Story, *Defending Your Faith* (Nashville, TN: Thomas Nelson Publishers, 1992), pp. 171-72. Insert added.

21. Geisler and Brooks, p. 73. See also Alvin C. Plantinga, *God, Freedom, and Evil* (Grand Rapids, MI: William B. Eerdmans Publishing Company, 2002), p. 27.

Chapter 6—Satan and Suffering

1. Donald Grey Barnhouse, *The Invisible War* (Grand Rapids, MI: Zondervan, 1965), pp. 26-27.

2. C. Fred Dickason, *Angels, Elect and Evil* (Chicago, IL: Moody Press, 1978), p. 133.

3. Charles C. Ryrie, *Basic Theology* (Wheaton, IL: Victor Books, 1986), p. 145.

4. This is the view of Paul Enns, *The Moody Handbook of Theology* (Chicago, IL: Moody Press, 1989), p. 294.

5. Cited in Henry Clarence Thiessen, *Lectures in Systematic Theology* (Grand Rapids, MI: William B. Eerdmans Publishing Company, 1981), p. 141.

6. Merrill F. Unger, *Demons in the World Today* (Wheaton, IL: Tyndale House Publishers, 1972), p. 28.

7. Thomas Ice and Robert Dean, *A Holy Rebellion* (Eugene, OR: Harvest House Publishers, 1990), p. 46.

8. Dickason, p. 122.

9. Charles Hodge, *Systematic Theology*, ed. Edward N. Gross (Grand Rapids, MI: Baker Book House, 1988), p. 235.

10. Ray C. Stedman, *Spiritual Warfare* (Waco, TX: Word Books, 1976), p. 22.

11. Thiessen, p. 142.

12. Lewis Sperry Chafer; cited in Ice and Dean, p. 60.

13. Thiessen, p. 142.

14. Charles C. Ryrie, *A Survey of Bible Doctrine* (Chicago, IL: Moody Press, 1980), p. 94.

15. Ryrie, *Basic Theology*, p. 147.

16. Charles C. Ryrie, *Balancing the Christian Life* (Chicago, IL: Moody Press, 1978), p. 124.

17. Enns, p. 297.

18. Millard J. Erickson, *Christian Theology* (Grand Rapids, IL: Baker Book House, 1983), p. 450.

19. Bible Illustrations Hypercard stack.

20. J. Dwight Pentecost, *God's Answers to Man's Problems* (Chicago, IL: Moody Press, 1985), p. 9.

21. Warren W. Wiersbe, *Strategy of Satan* (Wheaton, IL: Tyndale House Publishers, 1980), p. 47.

22. Card deck file of illustrations, Dallas Theological Seminary, 3909 Swiss Avenue, Dallas, Texas, 75204.

23. See, for example, Ice and Dean, chapter 8.

24. Stedman, *Spiritual Warfare*, p. 114.

Chapter 7—Divine Discipline and Suffering

1. J. Dwight Pentecost, *God's Answers to Man's Problems* (Chicago, IL: Moody Press, 1985), pp. 26-27.

2. Warren Wiersbe, *The Strategy of Satan* (Wheaton, IL: Tyndale House Publishers, 1980), p. 45.

3. Martyn Lloyd-Jones, *Spiritual Depression: Its Causes and Cure* (Grand Rapids, IL: William B. Eerdmans Publishing Company, 1976), p. 235.

4. Norman Geisler, *The Roots of Evil* (Grand Rapids, IL: Zondervan, 1978), p. 12.

5. C.S. Lewis, *The Problem of Pain* (New York, NY: Macmillan, 1975), p. 40.

6. John W. Wenham, *The Eigma of Evil: Can We Believe in the Goodness of God?* Grand Rapids, MI: Zondervan, 1985), p. 56.

7. Millard Erickson, *Christian Theology* (Grand Rapids, MI: Baker Book House, 1983), p. 430.

Chapter 8—Can God Bring Good Out of Evil?

1. Millard Erickson writes: "We must consider the dimension of time or duration. Some of the evils which we experience are actually very disturbing on

a short-term basis, but in the long term work a much larger good. The pain of the dentists' drill and the suffering of postsurgical recovery may seem like quite severe evils, but they are in actuality rather small in light of the long-range effects that flow from them." (Millard Erickson, *Christian Theology* [Grand Rapids, MI: Baker Book House, 1985], p. 426.)

2. Joni Eareckson, *Joni* (Grand Rapids, MI: Zondervan, 1976), p. 27.

3. Eareckson, p. 50.

4. www.joniandfriends.org.

5. Eareckson, p. 152.

6. Peter Kreeft, cited in Lee Strobel, *The Case for Faith* (Grand Rapids, MI: Zondervan, 2000), p. 32.

7. Kreeft, cited in Strobel, p. 32.

8. William Lane Craig, *No Easy Answers* (Chicago, IL: Moody Press, 1990), pp. 96-97.

9. Theologian John Wenham notes: "In the circumstances of our present life, pain is not altogether an evil.... Normally physical pains in the early stages are a warning, and a valuable deterrent against the misuse of things which are in themselves good. It is a good thing that the child quickly withdraws its fingers at the touch of something hot." (John W. Wenham, *The Enigma of Evil: Can We Believe in the Goodness of God?* [Grand Rapids, MI: Zondervan, 1985], p. 54.)

10. Norman L. Geisler and Ronald Brooks, *When Skeptics Ask* (Wheaton, IL: Victor Books, 1990). Available on CD-ROM in *The Norman Geisler CD-ROM Library*.

11. Charles Durham, *Temptation: Help for Struggling Christians*, cited in *The Devotional Bible*, ed. Max Lucado (Nashville, TN: Thomas Nelson Publishers, 2003), pp. 15-16.

12. William Lane Craig writes: "The fact is that in many cases we allow pain and suffering to occur in a person's life in order to bring about some greater good or because we have some sufficient reason for allowing it. Every parent knows this fact. There comes a point at which a parent can no longer protect his child from every scrape, bruise, or mishap; and there are other times when discipline must be inflicted on the child in order to teach him to become a mature, responsible, adult. Similarly, God may permit suffering in our lives to build us or to test us, or to build and test others, or to achieve some other overriding end." (Craig, p. 81.)

Chapter 9—The School of Suffering

1. Judy Salisbury, *A Christian Woman's Guide to Reasons for Faith: Understanding Why You Believe* (Eugene, OR: Harvest House Publishers, 2003), p. 117.

2. Gordon R. Lewis and Bruce A. Demarest, *Integrative Theology*, vol. 1 (Grand Rapids, MI: Zondervan, 1996), p. 323.

3. It is not unexpected that there will be those who would rather "opt out" of any possible good that may derive from God's allowance of evil in their lives. Rabbi Kushner writes: "I am a more sensitive person, a more effective pastor, a more sympathetic counselor because of [my son] Aaron's life and death than I would ever have been without it. And I would give up all of those gains in a second if I could have my son back. If I could choose, I would forego all the spiritual growth and depth which has come my way because of our experiences, and be what I was fifteen years ago, an average rabbi, an indifferent counselor, helping some people and unable to help others, and the father of a bright, happy boy. But I cannot choose" (insert added). (Rabbi Kushner, cited in W. Gary Phillips, "The Problem Of Evil: A Pastoral Approach—Part Two: The Good News," adapted from *Making Sense of Your World* by W. Gary Phillips and William E. Brown [Chicago, IL: Moody Press, June 1991], *Michigan Theological Journal*, vol. 2 no. 1 [Spring 1991], p. 5).

4. William Lane Craig, *No Easy Answers* (Chicago, IL: Moody Press, 1990), p. 90.

5. Paul Powell, *When the Hurt Won't Go Away* (Wheaton, IL: Victor Books, 1986), p. 62.

6. Miles Stanford, *Principles of Spiritual Growth* (Lincoln, NE: Back to the Bible, 1976), p. 11.

7. M.R. Dehaan, "Broken Things," cited in Charles Swindoll, *The Tale of the Tardy Oxcart* (Nashville, TN: Word Publishing, 1998), p. 547.

8. Charles Swindoll, *The Mystery of God's Will* (Nashville, TN: Word Publishing, 1999), p. 22.

9. See Elisabeth Elliot, *Shadow of the Almighty: The Life and Testament of Jim Elliot* (San Francisco, CA: Harper SanFrancisco, 1989).

10. See John Sherrill and Corrie Ten Boom, *The Hiding Place* (New York, NY: Bantam Books, 1984).

11. Cited in Swindoll, *The Tale of the Tardy Oxcart*, p. 549.

12. William L. Lane, *The Gospel According to Mark* (Grand Rapids, MI: William B. Eerdmans Publishing Company, 1974), p. 307.

Chapter 10—When God Says No

1. Blaine Allen, *When God Says No* (Nashville, TN: Thomas Nelson Publishers, 1981), p. 35.

2. J. Dwight Pentecost, *God's Answers to Man's Problems* (Chicago, IL: Moody Press, 1985), p. 34.

3. Paul Powell, *When the Hurt Won't Go Away* (Wheaton, IL: Victor Books, 1986), p. 34.

4. See Ron Rhodes, *Christ Before the Manger: The Life and Times of the Preincarnate Christ* (Eugene, OR: Wipf and Stock Publishers, 2002).

5. Haddon W. Robinson, *Psalm Twenty-Three* (Chicago: Moody Press, 1979), p. 35.

6. Robinson, p. 43.

Chapter 11—Part of the Problem: Misguided Beliefs

1. *Evolution: A Handbook for Students by a Medical Scientist* (Toronto: International Christian Crusade, 1951), p. 7.

2. See Chris Colby, "Evolution," *The World and I*, vol. 11 (January 1, 1996), p. 294. Available online at www.worldandi.com.

3. Dylan Evans and Howard Selina, *Introducing Evolution* (Cambridge: Totem Books, 2001), p. 8.

4. J. William Schopf, *Evolution: Facts and Fallacies* (San Diego, CA: Academic Press, 1999), p. 146.

5. Jonathan Wells, "Issues in the Creation-Evolution Controversies," *The World and I*, vol. 11 (January 1, 1996), p. 294. Available online at www.worldandi.com.

6. Hank Hanegraaff, *The Face that Demonstrates the Farce of Evolution* (Nashville, TN: W Publishing Group, 1998), p. 28.

7. Peter Hoffman, *Hitler's Personal Security*, p. 264, cited in Ken Ham, *The Lie* (El Cajon, CA: Master Books, 1991), p. 85.

8. Stephen Jay Gould, *I Have Landed: The End of a Beginning in Natural History* (New York, NY: Harmony Books, 2002), p. 336.

9. James W. English, "Could Racism Be Hereditary?" *Eternity* (September 1970), p. 22.

10. Buckner H. Payne, *The Negro: What Is His Ethnological Status?* 2d ed. (Cincinnati, OH: 1867), pp. 45-46; summarized by Millard J. Erickson, *Christian Theology* (Grand Rapids, MI: Baker Book House, 1983), p. 543.

11. See Hanegraaff, pp. 24-25.

12. See Hanegraaff, p. 29.

13. Letter to the Editor, *Newsweek* (April 7, 1997).

14. Paul R. Martin, "The Psychological Consequences of Cultic Involvement," *Christian Research Journal* (Winter/Spring 1989). Available online at www.equip.org.

15. Paul R. Martin, "Cults and Health," *Wellspring Messenger* (Winter 1996), p. 3.

16. B.J. Oropeza, "One More End-Time Scare Ends with a Whimper," *Christian Research Journal* (Winter 1993), pp. 6, 43.

17. Oropeza, p. 43.

18. Ibid.

19. Ibid.

20. *The Watchtower* (November 15, 1967), pp. 702-04.

21. *Awake!* (June 8, 1968), p. 21.

22. *The Watchtower* (March 15, 1980), p. 31.

23. *The Golden Age* (February 4, 1931), p. 293.

24. David Reed, *How to Rescue Your Loved One from the Watch Tower* (Grand Rapids, MI: Baker Book House, 1989), p. 104.

25. *Awake!* (August 22, 1965), p. 20.

26. Reed, *How to Rescue Your Loved One from the Watch Tower*, p. 20.

27. David Reed, *Jehovah's Witnesses Answered Verse by Verse* (Grand Rapids, MI: Baker Book House, 1992), p. 22.

28. Leonard & Marjorie Chretien, *Witnesses of Jehovah* (Eugene, OR: Harvest House Publishers, 1988), p. 14.

29. See Reed, *Jehovah's Witnesses Answered Verse by Verse*, p. 89.

30. *The Truth Shall Make You Free* (Brooklyn, NY: Watchtower Bible and Tract Society, 1943), p. 300.

31. David Reed, *Blood on the Altar* (Amherst, MA: Prometheus Books, 1996), p. 79.

32. *The New World* (Brooklyn, NY: Watchtower Bible and Tract Society, 1942), p. 104.

33. *Our Kingdom Ministry* (March 1968), pp. 3-4.

34. See Chretien, p. 58.

35. Kenneth Hagin, quoted in D. R. McConnell, *A Different Gospel* (Peabody, MA: Hendrickson Publishers, 1988), p. 175.

36. Robert Tilton, *Success-N-Life* television program (December 27, 1990).

37. Frederick Price, *Ever Increasing Faith* television program (December 9, 1990).

38. John Avanzini, *Believer's Voice of Victory* television program (January 20, 1991).

39. Avanzini, *Believer's Voice of Victory.*

40. Kenneth Copeland, cited in McConnell, p. 171.

41. Marilyn Hickey; see Hank Hanegraaff, *Christianity in Crisis* (Eugene, OR: Harvest House Publishers, 1993), pp. 31, 36, 63, 79, 203, 207, 238, 249, 351-52, 417.

42. Kenneth Copeland, cited in McConnell, p. 172.

43. Kenneth Copeland, *Laws of Prosperity* (Fort Worth, TX: Kenneth Copeland Publications, 1974), p. 67.

44. Robert M. Bowman Jr., "The Book of Job: God's Answer to the Problem of Evil." Available online at http://www.apologetics.com/default.jsp?bodycontent=/articles/doctrinal_apologetics/bowman-job.html.

45. Paul Enns, *Approaching God: Daily Reflections for Growing Christians* (Grand Rapids, MI: Kregel Publications, 2003).

Chapter 12—Is Evil an Illusion?

1. Bruce J. Nicholls, "Hinduism," in *The World's Religions* (Grand Rapids, MI: William B. Eerdmans Publishing Company, 1974), p. 136.

2. Mark Albrecht, "Hinduism," in *Evangelizing the Cults*, ed. Ronald Enroth (Ann Arbor, MI: Servant Publications, 1990), p. 22.

3. Lewis M. Hopfe, *Religions of the World* (New York, NY: Macmillan, 1991), p. 98.

4. Willa Cather and Georgine Milmine, *The Life of Mary Baker G. Eddy and the History of Christian Science* (Lincoln, NE: University of Nebraska Press, 1993), p. 12.

5. Cather and Milmine, p. 30.

6. Quimby Manuscripts, 389, cited in Todd Ehrenborg, *Mind Sciences* (Grand Rapids, MI: Zondervan, 1996), p. 8.

7. Orville Swenson, *The Perilous Path of Cultism* (Briercrest, CN: Briercrest Books, 1987), p. 160.

8. See Walter Martin, *The Kingdom of the Cults* (Minneapolis, MN: Bethany House Publishers, 1985), pp. 128-33.

9. Todd Ehrenborg, *Speaking the Truth in Love to "The Mind Sciences"* (self-published), p. 50.

10. Mary Baker Eddy, *Unity of Good* (Boston, MA: Trustees under the Will of Mary Baker G. Eddy, 1908), p. 50.

11. Mary Baker Eddy, *Science and Health with Key to the Scriptures* (Boston, MA: Trustees under the Will of Mary Baker G. Eddy, 1934), p. 377.

12. Eddy, *Unity of Good*, p. 60.

13. Millard Erickson, *Christian Theology* (Grand Rapids, MI: Baker Book House, 1983), p. 421.

14. Martin, *The Kingdom of the Cults*, pp. 40-41.

15. See James Walker, "Christian Science: Couple Found Guilty of Manslaughter," *The Watchman Expositor*, vol. 7 no. 9 (1990).

16. Erickson, *Christian Theology*, p. 421.

17. Norman Geisler and Yutaka Amano, *Reincarnation Sensation* (Wheaton, IL: Tyndale House Publishers, 1986), p. 20.

18. Rabi Maharaj, "Death of a Guru," *Christian Research Newsletter*, vol. 3 no. 3, p. 2.

19. Peter Kreeft, *Making Sense Out of Suffering* (Ann Arbor, MI: Servant Books, 1986), p. 43.

20. Walter Martin, *Martin Speaks Out on the Cults* (Ventura, CA: Regal Books, 1983), p. 75.

Chapter 13—Is Evil All in Our Heads?

1. David Gershon and Gail Straub, *Empowerment: The Art of Creating Your Life as You Want It* (New York, NY: Delta, 1989), back cover.

2. Ibid., p. 5.

3. Ibid., p. 21.

4. Ibid., p. 35.

5. Ibid., p. 36.

6. Ibid., p. 36.

7. Ibid., p. 200.

8. Ibid., p. 199.

9. Ibid., p. 199.

10. Ibid., p. 200.

11. Shirley MacLaine, *Dancing in the Light* (New York, NY: Bantam, 1985), p. 133.

12. George Trevelyan, *Operation Redemption* (Walpole, NH: Stillpoint Publishing, 1981), p. 83.

13. Levi Dowling, *The Aquarian Gospel of Jesus the Christ* (London: L.N. Fowler & Co., 1947), p. 126.

14. Dowling, p. 15.

15. Dowling, p. 263.

16. David Van Biema, "Emperor of the Soul Combining Medical Advice with Indian Metaphysics," *Time* (June 24, 1996), p. 64.

17. John Weldon and Stephen C. Myers, "A Summary Critique," *Christian Research Journal*, Winter 1994, p. 43.

18. Chip Brown, "Deepak Chopra Has (Sniff) a Cold," *Esquire* (October 1, 1995), p. 118.

19. Deepak Chopra, *Ageless Body, Timeless Mind* (New York, NY: Harmony Books, 1993), p. 6.

20. Deepak Chopra, *Perfect Health: The Complete Mind/Body Guide* (New York, NY: Harmony Books, 1990), p. 6.

21. Chopra, *Ageless Body, Timeless Mind*, p. 5.

22. Deepak Chopra. *Quantum Healing: Exploring the Frontiers of Mind/Body Medicine* (New York, NY: Bantam Books, 1989), p. 2.

23. Doug Levy, "Deepak Chopra's Path Toward an 'Ageless Body,'" *USA Today* (July 1994), p. 1.

24. Chopra, *Ageless Body, Timeless Mind*, p. 6.

25. Ibid.

26. Ibid.

27. Norman L. Geisler and Ronald M. Brooks, *Christianity Under Attack* (Dallas, TX: Quest Publications, 1985), p. 43.

28. Norman L. Geisler and Jeff Amano, *The Infiltration of the New Age* (Wheaton, IL: Tyndale House, 1989), p. 20.

29. Elliot Miller, "The Christian, Energetic Medicine, and 'New Age Paranoia,'" *Christian Research Journal* (Winter 1992), p. 26. Insert added.

30. Bernie Siegel, *Love, Medicine & Miracles* (New York, NY: Harper and Row Publishers, 1986), pp. 19-20.

31. Cathy Hainer, "An Alternative Prescription for Health," *USA Today* (March 26, 1997).

32. Andrew Weil, *Natural Health, Natural Medicine: A Comprehensive Manual for Wellness and Self-Care* (Boston, MA: Houghton Mifflin Company, 1990), pp. 124-25.

33. John Weldon and John Ankerberg, "Visualization: God-given Power or New Age Danger?" Part 1, *Christian Research Journal* (Summer 1996), p. 27.

34. John Weldon and John Ankerberg, "Visualization: God-given Power or New Age Danger?" Part 2, *Christian Research Journal* (Fall 1996), p. 21.

Chapter 14—Reincarnation and the Problem of Evil

1. Geoffrey Parrinder, *Dictionary of Non-Christian Religions* (Philadelphia, PA: Westminster Press, 1971), p. 286.

2. See Norman L. Geisler and J. Yutaka Amano, *The Reincarnation Sensation* (Wheaton, IL: Tyndale House Publishers, 1987), p. 8.

3. "Death," in *The 1995 Grolier Multimedia Encyclopedia.* Available on CD-ROM (Grolier Electronic Publishing, Inc., 1994).

4. John Barry, "The Changing American Way of Death," *Orange County Register* (July 4, 1994).

5. Douglas Connelly, *Afterlife: What the Bible Really Says* (Downers Grove, IL: InterVarsity Press, 1995), p. 45. Insert added.

6. Os Guinness, *The Dust of Death* (Downers Grove, IL: InterVarsity Press, 1973), p. 195.

7. The quotes in this paragraph are from James Sire, *The Universe Next Door* (Downers Grove, IL: InterVarsity Press, 1992), pp. 138-39.

8. Douglas Groothuis, *Confronting the New Age* (Downers Grove, IL: InterVarsity Press, 1988), p. 19.

9. Walter Martin, *The New Cults* (Ventura: Regal Books, 1980), pp. 82-83.

10. Shirley MacLaine, *Out on a Limb* (New York, NY: Bantam, 1983), p. 233.

11. William Henry, "The Best Year of Her Lives," *Time* (May 14, 1984), p. 62.

12. Ken Boa, *Cults, World Religions, and You* (Wheaton, IL: Victor Books, 1979), p. 13.

13. John B. Noss, *Man's Religions* (New York, NY: Macmillan, 1974), p. 101.

14. Lewis M. Hopfe, *Religions of the World* (New York, NY: Macmillan, 1991), p. 100.

15. John H. Hick, *Death and Eternal Life* (New York, NY: Harper & Row, 1976), p. 315.

16. See Noss, p. 90.

17. Geisler and Amano, p. 30.

18. E.D. Walker; cited in Geisler and Amano, p. 92.

19. Geisler and Amano p. 93.

20. Gary Zukav, *The Seat of Soul* (New York, NY: Simon and Schuster, 1989), p. 45.

21. Zukav, *The Seat of Soul*, pp. 45ff.

22. Paramahansa Yogananda, *Autobiography of a Yogi* (Los Angeles, CA: Self-Realization Fellowship, 1972), p. 199.

23. William L. de Arteaga, *Past Life Visions: A Christian Exploration* (New York, NY: Seabury Press, 1983), p. 81.

24. Douglas Groothuis, "Evangelizing New Agers," *Christian Research Journal*, Winter/Spring 1987, p. 7.

25. Ken Boa and Larry Moody, *I'm Glad You Asked* (Colorado Springs, CO: Victor Books, 1994), p. 131.

26. Norman L. Geisler and Jeff Amanu, "Evil," in *New Dictionary of Theology*, eds. Sinclair B. Ferguson and David F. Wright (Downers Grove, IL: InterVarsity Press, 1988), p. 242.

Chapter 15—Paradise Restored

1. Lee Strobel, *The Case for Faith* (Grand Rapids, MI: Zondervan, 2000), p. 47.

2. John Wenham, *The Enigma of Evil: Can We Believe in the Goodness of God?* (Grand Rapids, MI: Zondervan, 1985), p. 55.

3. Philip Yancey, *Where Is God When It Hurts?* (Grand Rapids, MI: Zondervan, 1977), p. 176.

4. Paul Powell, *When the Hurt Won't Go Away* (Wheaton, IL: Victory Books, 1986), p. 119.

5. Douglas Connelly, *Afterlife: What the Bible Really Says* (Downers Grove, IL: InterVarsity Press, 1995), p. 92.

6. Eric Sauer, *From Eternity to Eternity* (Grand Rapids, MI: William B. Eerdmans Publishing Company, 1979), p. 30.

7. Millard Erickson, *Christian Theology* (Grand Rapids, MI: Baker Book House, 1987), p. 1229.

8. Cited in Tim LaHaye, *Revelation: Illustrated and Made Plain* (Grand Rapids, MI: Zondervan, 1975), p. 315.

9. John Gill, "Hebrews 11:13-15" in *The Online Bible* CD-ROM, version 2.5.2.

10. Bruce Shelley, *Theology for Ordinary People* (Downers Grove, IL: InterVarsity Press, 1994), p. 212.

11. John F. Walvoord, *The Church in Prophecy* (Grand Rapids, MI: Zondervan, 1964), p. 164.

12. Bruce Milne, *Know the Truth* (Downers Grove, IL: InterVarsity Press, 1982), p. 278.

13. Anthony A. Hoekema, *The Bible and the Future* (Grand Rapids, MI: William B. Eerdmans Publishing Company, 1984), p. 280.

14. Hoekema, p. 285.

15. J.I. Packer, ed. *Alive to God: Studies in Spirituality* (Downers Grove, IL: InterVarsity Press, 1992), p. 162.

16. Packer, p. 171.

17. Packer, p. 163.

18. Packer, p. 164.

19. Packer, p. 165.

20. Cited in Packer, p. 167.

21. Gary R. Habermas and J. P. Moreland, *Immortality: The Other Side of Death* (Nashville, TN: Thomas Nelson Publishers, 1992), p. 185.

22. Habermas and Moreland, p. 186.

Appendix: Justice in the End

1. Douglas Connelly, *Afterlife: What the Bible Really Says* (Downers Grove, IL: InterVarsity Press, 1995), p. 119.

2. Cited in Charles C. Ryrie, *Basic Theology* (Wheaton, IL: Victor Books, 1986), p. 513.

3. Connelly, p. 118.

4. John Wesley, *The Nature of Salvation* (Minneapolis, MN: Bethany House, 1987), p. 135.

5. John Blanchard, *Whatever Happened to Hell?* (Durham, NC: Evangelical Press, 1993), p. 116.

6. J. Dwight Pentecost, *Things to Come* (Grand Rapids, MI: Zondervan, 1974), p. 226.

About the Author

Dr. Ron Rhodes
Reasoning from the Scripture Ministries
P.O. Box 2526
Frisco, TX 75034

Web site: www.ronrhodes.org

E-mail: ronrhodes@earthlink.net

Free newsletter available upon request.

HARVEST HOUSE
PUBLISHERS

Other Harvest House Books
You Can Believe In by Ron Rhodes

THE COMPLETE BOOK OF BIBLE PROMISES

Bible promise books abound—but not like this one! Two hundred alphabetized categories of verses include explanatory headings, insights from the original languages, and deeply moving quotes from famous Christian authors and hymns.

THE COMPLETE BOOK OF BIBLE ANSWERS

This great resource addresses the difficult Bible questions that arise during Bible sudies and witnessing—covering topics that range fom the conflicts between science and the Bible to reconciling God's sovereignty with man's free will.

FIND IT FAST IN THE BIBLE

A quick reference that lives up to its name! With more than 400 topics and 800-plus references, this comprehensive, topical guide provides one-line summaries of each verse. Perfect for research, discussions, and Bible studies.

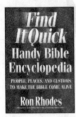

FIND IT QUICK HANDY BIBLE ENCYCLOPEDIA

Complete enough to be called an encyclopedia but compact enough to be quick and easy to use, this reference book includes approximately 1500 entries, each containing pronunciations, concise definitions, interesting information, and Scripture references.

HARVEST HOUSE
PUBLISHERS